Religion

Religion

MATERIAL DYNAMICS

David Chidester

UNIVERSITY OF CALIFORNIA PRESS

University of California Press, one of the most distinguished university presses in the United States, enriches lives around the world by advancing scholarship in the humanities, social sciences, and natural sciences. Its activities are supported by the UC Press Foundation and by philanthropic contributions from individuals and institutions. For more information, visit www.ucpress.edu.

University of California Press
Oakland, California

Library of Congress Cataloging-in-Publication Data

Names: Chidester, David, author.
Title: Religion : material dynamics / David Chidester.
Description: Oakland, California : University of California Press, [2018] | Includes bibliographical references and index. |
Identifiers: LCCN 2017049897 (print) | LCCN 2017053702 (ebook) | ISBN 9780520969933 (e-edition) | ISBN 9780520297654 (cloth) | ISBN 9780520297661 (pbk.)
Subjects: LCSH: Materialism—Religious aspects. | Religion—Philosophy.
Classification: LCC B825 (ebook) | LCC B825 .C45 2018 (print) | DDC 200—dc23
LC record available at https://lccn.loc.gov/2017049897

27 26 25 24 23 22 21 20 19 18
10 9 8 7 6 5 4 3 2 1

For Reinhard Schmecht

Contents

Preface

Religion, according to the great psychologist William James, does two things: it diagnoses the problem with the human condition and prescribes the cure.[1] All kinds of different problems and cures—sin and salvation, karma and liberation—have circulated in the history of religions. In a Russian television documentary broadcast in 2009, *Plesen* (Mold), the real problem of the human condition is identified as mold. This documentary argues, as one reviewer observes, "that mold is taking over the earth, that it has been doing so since the days of Moses. It is the devil's weapon, mentioned in ancient mystic texts, an invisible but omnipresent enemy whose evil spores have been invading our lives, causing death and disease." This diagnosis of the problem with the human condition, which references ancient mystics and apocalyptic disaster, leads in the film to a technological solution, "mold-cleaning machines." As the reviewer concludes, "When the film ends[,] large numbers of fearful people go out and buy the 'mold-cleaning machines' that were advertised in the film; its manufacturers were among the producers."[2] In this film, therefore, mold is the material basis for a drama of religious evil, the devil's weapon, being conquered by technology.

By contrast, an American documentary released in 2015, *Moldy*, dwells on the misery caused by technological failures in homes, workplaces, and public spaces to maintain healthy environments. *Moldy*, according to its promotional literature, "is a gripping documentary that explores toxic mold and how it has become a modern-day health problem of monumental proportions that affects us all." For most of the film, interviews with medical experts on mold and survivors of mold are interspersed to create a chronicle of human misery. However, the documentary has a happy ending in a celebration of New Age spirituality, suggesting that people can be free from the effects of mold by entering spiritual energy, spiritual freedom, and spiritual light, as the inspirational song, "Light," plays over the closing credits.[3] In *Moldy*, therefore, a technological problem, the breakdown in the material conditions of health and safety, is given a religious solution in the light of spirituality.

Mold is something. It is fungus growing over things all over the place. But is it a religious thing? *Religion: Material Dynamics* explores the making, ordering, and circulating of religious things. Nothing, we will see, is inherently religious. In fact, the very notion of religious things is problematic because the term *religion* is an artificial construction, an invention, with multiple histories, that nevertheless operates in the real world. Rejecting yet retaining the term, this book deconstructs and reconstructs religion as material categories, social formations, and mobile circulations.

First, we will examine basic categories, such as spiritual beings or the sacred, in their material productions, attending to the labors of discursive interpretation and ritualized mediation involved in producing spiritual ancestors like Moses, spiritual dangers like the devil, or spiritual liberation like the spiritual energy promised in *Moldy*. These religious labors entail productions of sacred space and time, which, in these films, is a space, extending from the entire earth to the vulnerable human body, which we know is sacred because it is being desecrated by mold, and a time, which we know is sacred because it is organized into compelling apocalyptic narratives of disaster for the many and redemption for the few who will be saved from mold. Since it is possible, perhaps even likely, that the "mold-cleaning machines" advocated in *Plesen* do not actually work, making this technology no match for the "devil's weapon," we must recognize incongruity, the mismatch between expectation and actuality, as an important category in material productions of religion.

Second, we will examine social formations, the configurations of cultural, economic, and political forces that are not external contexts but material conditions of religion. Culture and economy intersect in the religious formations of the two films about mold, perhaps most obviously in the Russian film, which is deploying religious fears and hopes to sell a product. But the American film, too, is promoting a value proposition, which Jeremy Carrette and Richard King have called "selling spirituality," through fears of environmental degradation and hopes for spiritual redemption.[4] Religious formations, as we will see, emerge under material conditions of asymmetrical power relations, evident in colonialism, imperialism, and apartheid, which constitute conditions of possibility for religious classifications and orientations. Formed within the power relations of neoliberal capitalism, *Plesen* and *Moldy* signal new cultural economies in which the source of value is a mystery, produced in ways that are unseen, even when portrayed on film, from new mergers of technology and spirituality, resulting in new formations of spiritual technology and technological spirituality.

Third, we will examine mobile circulations of religion in motion, from the visceral body to the expansive oceans, in which religious materiality flows through circuits of dispersion across political boundaries and circuits of diffusion through popular culture. While *Plesen* relies upon a Christian narrative of demonic evil and apocalyptic destruction, with a promise of redemption for the chosen few who have purchased mold-cleaning machines, *Moldy* evokes, in its conclusion, the spiritual energy and ecstasy associated with the shaman, a religious specialist, initially identified in Siberia, then colonized by Russia, and eventually transported all over the world. These circulations of religious thematics call our attention to religious change, the fluctuations and flows of religion, but they also point to the mobility of religion in religious diffusions through a variety of popular cultural formations revolving around communities of sacred allegiance, devotions to sacred objects, and rituals of collective effervescence in sacred exchange.

Religion: Material Dynamics, I hope, will be a lively resource for thinking about religious materiality and the material study of religion. Gaining momentum from the "material turn" in religious studies, anthropology, history, and other disciplines, the book develops the meaning and significance of key terms in the study of material religion through vivid illustrations drawn from a variety of religious formations. As an alternative to organizing religion into world religions, the book can be read as a kind of handbook, vocabulary, or keywords compendium providing multiple points of entry into the field of material religion. The introduction outlines the general rationale for the book; the beginning of each section—categories, formations, and circulations—gives an overview of chapters, showing how each chapter identifies an important feature of material religion. Although the book reflects my locations in North America and South Africa and consolidates what I have learned over forty years of studying religion, I trust that the chapters will be of wider interest in offering useful orientations and surprising possibilities for studying material religion. Exploring the material dynamics of religion from poetics to politics, the book participates in critical and creative thinking about religion.

.   .   .   .   .

I dedicate this book to Professor Reinhard Schmecht, who wrote a paper, "Comparison and Persecution," presented at the annual meeting of the American Academy of Religion in San Francisco in 1981, read in his absence by Ninian Smart and Richard Hecht, which had a great impact on the development of my thinking about religion and the study of religion. While his paper helped me think about the centrality of classifications and orientations in the dynamics of religion, it also helped me think about their consequences in the world. In all of my work, I have been profoundly indebted to Professor Reinhard Schmecht.

Besides acknowledging Professor Schmecht, I thank Duane Jethro for editorial assistance; the Board of Directors for existing; my friend Ed Linenthal for hunting mold; my wife, Careen, for our life; and the National Research Foundation for support. I thank all of the graduate students at the University of Cape Town who, when we tested this book in manuscript in the classroom, showed faith in me by referring to the manuscript as "forthcoming," and I thank the four manuscript reviewers mobilized by the University of California Press for their lively and constructive engagement with this project. Senior editor at the press Reed Malcolm once again brought my book home with style. Finally, I thank various publishers for allowing me to rework material that has previously appeared in print.

By permission of ABC-CLIO, material has been adapted from "Popular Culture," in *Religion and American Cultures: Traditions, Diversity, and Popular Expressions,* ed. Luis Léon and Gary Laderman, 4 vols., 2nd ed. (Santa Barbara, CA: ABC-CLIO, 2014), 2:495–506; and "Colonialism and Shamanism," in *Shamanism: An Encyclopedia of World Beliefs, Practices, and Culture,* ed. Mariko Namba Walter and Eva Jane Neumann Fridman, 2 vols. (Santa Barbara, CA: ABC-CLIO, 2004), 1:41–49.

Material has been adapted from "Animism," in *Encyclopedia of Religion and Nature,* ed. Bron Taylor and Jeffrey Kaplan (New York: Continuum, 2005), 78–81; and from "The American Touch: Tactile Imagery in American Religion and Politics," in *The Book of Touch,* ed. Constance Classen (Oxford: Berg, 2005), 49–65, with permission of Bloomsbury Publishing, PLC.

By permission of Oxford University Press, material has been adapted from "Space" and "Time," in *Oxford Handbook of the Study of Religion,* ed. Michael Stausberg and Steven Engler (Oxford: Oxford University Press, 2016), 329–39, 340–35.

By permission of University of Virginia Press, material has been adapted from *Savage Systems: Colonialism and Comparative Religion in Southern Africa* (Charlottesville: University of Virginia Press, 1996), 192, 195–99, 226–31.

Material has been adapted from "Apartheid Comparative Religion in South Africa," in *Theory/Religion/Critique: Classic and Contemporary Approaches,* ed. Richard King (New York: Columbia University Press, 2017). Copyright © 2017. Reprinted with permission of Columbia University Press.

Material has been adapted from "Colonialism" and "Material Culture," in *Vocabulary for the Study of Religion,* ed. Robert Segal and Kocku von Stuckrad (Leiden: Brill, 2015), 1:268–75, 2:373–79, with permission of Koninklijke Brill NV.

By permission of Taylor & Francis, material has been adapted from "Economy," in *Key Words for Religion, Media, and Culture,* ed. David Morgan (London: Routledge, 2008), 83–95, and "Sacred," *Material Religion* 7, no. 1 (2011): 84–91.

Material has been adapted from "Colonialism and Religion," *Critical Research on Religion* 1, no. 1 (2013): 87–94, with permission of SAGE Publications.

Material has been adapted from "Beyond Religious Studies? The Future of the Study of Religion in a Multidisciplinary Perspective," *NTT: Journal for Theology and the Study of Religion* 71, no. 1 (2017): 74–85, with permission of the journal.

Introduction

MATERIAL DYNAMICS

We study religion in the midst of compelling critiques of the concept. I have participated in those critiques.[1] The concept of religion bears indelible traces of imperial ambitions, colonial conflicts, and persistent ambiguity. Get rid of the term, some say. But there it is. We are stuck with it. For those of us interested in an academic study of religion, how do we make a disabling term, which bears this legacy of ambiguity, colonialism, and imperialism, an enabling vortex for thinking, especially for thinking about the human in the humanities and social sciences?

Now that we know that *religion* is a modern invention, a Western construction, a colonial imposition, or an imperial expansion, how do we study religion? How do we reject yet still retain the qualifier *religious* in our study of human discourses, practices, personal experiences, and social formations? How do we move beyond religious studies and stay within religious studies?

Religion: Material Dynamics identifies openings for multidisciplinary research and reflection in the study of religion, looking beyond religious studies, not in a temporal, but in a spatial sense, for points of entry, intersection, and connection in the academic study of religion. The book focuses on categories, formations, and circulations, highlighting the

1

historical contingency of basic categories of religion, the colonial and imperial forces in formations of religion, and the mobility of materiality in circulations of religion. The book participates in the revolution that has liberated materiality—embodiment and the senses, objects and their social lives, exchange and power relations, media and mediation, and all the forces and fluctuations in the production, circulation, and consumption of things—as the stuff of religion that demands the attention of the study of religion. Important programmatic overviews and orientations to the material study of religion have been provided.[2] Indicating a remarkably multidisciplinary and interdisciplinary enterprise, the authors of these introductions to the study of material religion are variously situated in religious studies, anthropology, history, sociology, and art history, while each dwells deeply in the repertoires and intersections of academic disciplines. As their profiles of the field demonstrate, this grounded and dynamic range of inquiry creates openings in religious studies through the study of religious materiality.

What holds this study of material religion together? What opens this area of inquiry to multidisciplinary engagements?

Clearly, no single center holds for the study of material religion, but a shared orientation is evident in the impetus to move beyond any restriction of the scope of religion to the authority of texts and the interiority of beliefs. Rejecting this Protestant construction of religion, the study of material religion has nevertheless retained the term *religion* by demonstrating how even the most dematerialized religion entails material senses, practices, and exchanges. Taking a cue from David Morgan, we can relate this theoretical orientation of rejecting and retaining to Hegel's logic of sublation *(Aufhebung)*, the simultaneous destruction and preservation—canceling and keeping, disposing and transposing—that results in a new synthesis.[3] However, instead of resulting in a synthesis, rejecting and retaining can produce an enjambment of disparity, a palimpsest of illegibility, or a mash-up of incongruity. In the study of material religion, theoretical resources are deployed to move through disparity, illegibility, and incongruity into surprise.

Rejecting the very term *religion* as an invention and construction, as an imposition and expansion, the study of material religion can retain the term to signal a terrain in which human beings engage in meaningful and powerful ways with the material constraints and animations of matter, the interplay of sacralizing and desecrating, the labor of producing space and time, and the myriad ways in which incongruity, the material effect of the collision of incommensurables, can be transposed into moments, perhaps fleeting moments, of congruence. Studying religion, in this sense, focuses attention, not on religion, but on the material conditions of possibility for negotiating the human.

In search of openings inside and beyond religious studies, I propose here that we can find multidisciplinary crossings of disciplinary boundaries in the study of three things: categories, formations, and circulations.

CATEGORIES

As an overarching category, *religion* is a relational term, emerging and shifting as it is deployed in relation to such terms as *superstition* and *magic, heresy* and *infidelity,* and *secularism* and *irreligion,* which have all acted at one time or another as defining oppositions for *religion.* Not merely the product of scholarly inquiry, "religion" has been produced in a diverse array of human engagements, including politics, legislation, public discourse, and popular culture, which have rendered the term as not only meaningful but also powerful in the world. Over the last few decades, thinking about the category of religion has moved away from any Aristotelian distinction between inherent substance and accidents, or any Kantian notion of a priori categories, or even Wittgenstein's logic of family resemblances, into the historical contingencies of religion's production and deployment as a category.

Demonstrating the relational productions of the religious and the secular, the sacred and the profane, in the contemporary United States, a recent book by Nicolas Howe, *Landscapes of the Secular: Law, Religion, and American Sacred Space,* illuminates how the U.S. legal system shapes American landscapes by staging crises of interpretation of profound emotional, religious, and political significance. Dwelling on detailed case studies of legal disputes over Christian displays, Native American traditions, and wilderness preservation, Howe enters the changing contours of the sacred in America at the intersection of the religious and the secular. In legal disputes, basic categories are defined, often with surprising results. For example, in the longest-running church-state case in the United States, a cross displayed on Mount Soledad in La Jolla, California, has been interpreted by secular opponents as an offending religious symbol and by religious defenders as a secular war memorial.[4] As these conflicting interpretations move through the courts, the cross becomes simultaneously more sacred and more profane. In this dispute over the meaning of a material object, basic categories for the study of religion are contested as the secular struggles to define the religious and the religious struggles to define the secular.

E. B. Tylor's minimum definition of *religion* as "belief in spiritual beings" was based on a fundamental dualism that separated the realms of spirit and matter.[5] By imagining animated materiality, religion was essentially a category mistake, a failure to distinguish spiritualism from materialism, a distinction that could be made only by a scientific materialist. Although Tylor drew on African evidence in developing his theory of religion, literary scholar Harry Garuba has identified the "animist realism" in contemporary African poetry and novels not as a category mistake but as a way of negotiating community through the "refusal to countenance unlocalized, unembodied, unphysicalized gods and spirits."[6] This recovery of animist realism resonates with recent research on dynamic objects, from the social lives of things, through assemblages, networks, and entanglements of humans and things, to vibrant materiality, which are at work and at play in producing the sacred.[7]

Shifting from the distinction between spirit and matter, Emile Durkheim regarded the basic categories of sacred and profane as separate and distinct, observing, "In the history of human thought, there is no other example of two categories of things as profoundly differentiated or as radically opposed to one another."[8] However, in tracking the sacred in the history of religions, we see that these categories are not so easily distinguished, because anything can be sacralized through the labor of intensive interpretation and formal ritualization; the transformation of scarce resources, especially material objects, space, and time, into sacred surplus; and the contestation over legitimate ownership of that sacred surplus.[9] In the political economy of the sacred, the categories of the sacred and profane are not separate and distinct, because they are mutually entangled within the social fields of meaning and power in which the sacred is produced, exchanged, circulated, owned, operated, and contested.

The political economy of the sacred is evident in the categories of religious space and time. Here multidisciplinary resources are needed to analyze the poetics, politics, and economics of sacred space and sacred time. With respect to space, structural oppositions—inside and outside, up and down—are deployed in producing spatial orientations of religious purity and power: religious purity through rituals of exclusion; and religious power through rituals of subordination, subjection, and extraction of human and material resources. While an embodied poetics is involved in these structural oppositions, a poetics perhaps derived from the left-right axis of the human body,[10] an oppositional politics is also integral to productions of sacred space. With respect to time, poetics and politics also merge, with embodied sensory rituals marking out temporal processes and authoritative mythic narratives marking out temporal origins. Long regarded as basic categories in the history of religions, space and time can be reopened through research at the multidisciplinary intersections of aesthetics, politics, and economics.

Although the study of religion can identify coherence and cohesion, the most promising openings in religious studies can be found in critical reflection on incongruity. Attention to incongruity was pioneered by Jonathan Z. Smith in rethinking such basic categories as myth and ritual. Confronting order with its violation, especially in the disorder of colonial situations, myth is a way of "working with this incongruity." In the disjuncture between ideal and actual conduct, "ritual gains force where incongruity is perceived and thought about."[11] Incongruity, in these instances, appears in the gaps, but it can also register in mixtures and mergers, in syncretisms and hybridities, in which disparate factors converge without synthesis. As both an unstable category and a destabilizing category, incongruity challenges all of the categories in the academic study of religion.

FORMATIONS

Multidisciplinary resources are necessary for studying religion in context. What are the relationships between religion and culture, politics, and economics? Perhaps that is the wrong way to formulate the question of context, because "relationships" assumes relations between discrete entities—religion, culture, politics, and economics—that are thoroughly entangled. Perhaps we need a wider sense of context. Broadening the scope of context, however, does not necessarily help. In his definition of *environment* in *A Dictionary of Ecology,* Michael Allaby expands the scope of context to such an extent that it includes absolutely everything: "The complete range of external conditions, physical and biological, in which an organism lives. Environment includes social, cultural, and (for humans) economic and political considerations, as well as the more usually understood features such as soil, climate, and food supply."[12] Following this definition, if we wanted to study religion in its environment, we would have to study everything. Although it seems like a reasonable proposal, studying religion in context, in these terms, is actually an impossible undertaking.

Situating religion at the intersection of different domains, such as culture and economics, might be a more feasible way of studying religion in context. However, the most challenging research in this regard has explored the entanglements of these apparently different domains, giving us insight into the economy of culture and the culture of economy. In the economy of culture, as Pierre Bourdieu proposed, if we "abandon the dichotomy of the economic and the non-economic," we can see cultural practices as "economic practices directed towards the maximization of material or symbolic profit."[13] Simultaneously material and symbolic, the economy of culture has consequences for analyzing religion. Attention to the "political economy of religion," Bourdieu promised, would advance "the full potential of the materialist analysis of religion without destroying the properly symbolic character of the phenomenon."[14] In the culture of economy, we find the production, circulation, and consumption of signs that are mediated through economic activity but which bear wide-ranging cultural significance. With respect to religion, analysis of the culture of economy has generated research on "capitalism as religion," the "religion of the market," and money as "a system of symbols that generates powerful moods and motivations, desire and agency, and clothes those human dispositions in an aura of factuality that makes them seem ultimately real."[15] As these examples can only suggest, exploring the intersections, mutual implications, and surprising reversals of culture and economics is not merely about context; it is about the dynamics of religious formations.

A recent, groundbreaking book on African American religion, Sylvester A. Johnson's *African American Religions, 1500–2000: Colonialism, Democracy, and Freedom,* illustrates what I mean by religious formations. This book is not a conventional survey of African American religion, which might trace religious origins and developments, placing African survivals, adaptations, and innovations in different historical contexts. Instead, the book is an exploration of the conditions of possibility for thinking about African American religion. Transatlantic empires, colonial enclosures, and political engagements, as Sylvester Johnson shows, are more than historical contexts; they are forces of religious formation. As Johnson explains, "The specific historical formations that have constituted African American religion have been derived through transnational networks and global linkages of trade, politics, and religious exchanges."[16] These constitutive forces enabled the emergence of specific religious subjectivities and mobilizations, not merely within changing contexts, but within the shifting pressures, power relations, limitations, and possibilities of colonialism and empire in the Atlantic world.

Although colonialism and imperialism bear specific histories and localizations, some generalizations are possible. For example, in the history of British colonization a significant transition occurred when a mercantile capitalist mode of colonialism shifted to a more expansive empire. Analyzing this shift in terms of power relations, Lisa Lowe has observed that an earlier "negative" power of occupation was overlaid with a new "positive" power of administration. "While colonial power had employed 'negative' powers to seize, enslave, occupy, and destroy," she notes, "a new mode of imperial sovereignty also expanded the 'productive' power to administer the life, health, labor, and mobility of colonized bodies."[17] Under these changing conditions, different religious formations emerged, not only among the colonized, but also among colonizers, whether situated on the front lines of contact or in the metropoles of empire. This mutual implication of colonizers and colonized in changing bodies, subjectivities, and cosmologies under colonial conditions, as Tony Ballantyne has argued, indicates the far-reaching "entanglements of empire."[18] Colonial and imperial forces shaped Black American religion; however, as

Sylvester Johnson insists, "the same holds true for White American religion."[19] Attention to these religious formations allows for studying multiple and entangled histories of meaning and power not only in modern but also in ancient empires.[20]

CIRCULATIONS

Increasingly, the study of religion has become the study of flows, the study of religion in motion through the circulations of people, objects, technology, money, images of human possibility, and ideals of human solidarity. Transnational circulations of people, as Nilüfer Göle has observed, have affected the very categories of the religious and the secular because the "configurations between the secular and the religious are shaped not only by nation-states but also by transnational dynamics and global migratory flows."[21] In *Crossing and Dwelling: A Theory of Religion*, Thomas A. Tweed defines religion as circulation and religions as flows, as "confluences of organic-cultural flows that intensify joy and confront suffering by drawing on human and suprahuman forces to make homes and cross boundaries."[22] While this definition focuses on religious space, a similar focus on flows could apply to religious time, attending to temporal rhythms (from the Greek *rhythmos*, "flowing") in religious practices and performances.[23] Although circulations are perhaps most evident in the transnational or global migratory flows of diaspora and dispersion, religion also flows through popular culture, social networks, political mobilizations, economic transactions, and other configurations.

A brilliant illustration of religious circulations appears in the recent book by Thomas Alberts, *Shamanism, Discourse, Modernity*.[24] Leaving behind Mircea Eliade's construction of shamanism as archaic (and timeless) "techniques of ecstasy," Alberts treats shamanism as a total social fact—religious, political, and economic—embedded in modern discourses of subjectivity and alterity. Against representations of shamanism as premodern or antimodern, he locates shamanism at the center of crucial mediations of modernity. Here the key is tracking circulations. Shamanism discourse, which bears traces of a particular history of colonial and imperial relations in Siberia, has circulated widely through networks of human-rights activism, environmentalism, and neoliberal commodification. The discourse of shamanism, becoming central to what Alberts calls *indigenism*, is deployed in political struggles over indigenous rights to land, sovereignty, and religious freedom. Emerging as an exemplar of natural wisdom, the shaman is mobilized in campaigns for ecological awareness and environmental sustainability. In a neoliberal economy, shamanism is bought and sold in a global market of shamanic tourism. All of these circulations show how shamanism is moving not only through global flows but also through specific political, social, and economic circuits of modernity.

These circulations require new ways of thinking about religious change and diffusion, religious mobility and plasticity, beyond the frameworks provided by religious institutions. With respect to religious change, research on tradition and innovation tends to assume an underlying continuity, a tradition handed down from the past that might be engaged in new ways. This assumption of continuity, however, cannot capture the kinetic dynamics in which tradition is not that which is handed down but that which is taken up in ongoing material negotiations over the production, surplus, and ownership of the sacred. Here religious mobility signifies more than simply moving from place to place: it signifies constantly shifting configurations of religion in motion. Challenging research that recognizes religious change only within the framework of continuous religious traditions, Walter H. Capps called for a study of religion that engages "the moving, inconstant, spontaneous, irregular, discontinuous, non-forensic, once-only, explosive, surprise element."[25] In this extraordinary sentence, Capps issued a challenge, which still stands, to those who study religion to develop theoretical resources and methods for tracking religious mobility. Authors of studies of religion and media have taken up this challenge by reconfiguring religion as mediation, thereby enabling new understandings of imagery, sound recordings, video films, machines, and other media as material religion in motion.[26] Studies of religion and popular culture, more generally, have given new meaning to religious diffusion. Anticipated by Thomas Luckmann's "invisible religion"—independent of religious institutions, diffused through modern societies—studies of religion in and as popular culture have explored the plasticity of religion in a variety of cultural formations.[27]

More than mere metaphor, circulations range from the embodied firing of neurons and pulsing of blood to transnational migrations and global explorations, from the intimacy of tactility to the alterity of encountering alien worlds. Materialities mediate these circulations. In the tactile register of religion, caressing and shocking, intimacies of binding, burning, moving, and handling place the sense of touch, disdained by ancient authorities, at the center of modern religious circulations.[28] Emerging out of European oceanic exploration and colonization, the fetish and the cargo, disdained by economic rationality, return in the modern fetishism of commodities and the modern cargoism of "occult economies" that promise abundant wealth from mysterious sources.[29] As these brief allusions to religious tactility and occult economies can only suggest, religion is something, if it is anything, that moves from embodied intimacy to global economy in material circulations.

MATERIAL DYNAMICS

The material dynamics of categories, formations, and circulations reveal different dimensions of Marx's rendering of the "spiritual intercourse" of human beings as an "efflux of their material condition."[30] Categories reveal historical contingencies in thinking about religion; formations reveal forces at work in the emergence of religious configurations; and circulations reveal the mobility of materiality pulsating through religion in motion. Each dimension provides openings for multidisciplinary engagements in the study of religion. They can also be related to each other in exploring the intersections of categories and formations, formations and circulations, and circulations and categories.

Categories and formations: Basic categories in the study of religion can be linked to the material conditions of colonial and imperial formations. On the front lines of colonial encounter in South Africa, missionaries, travelers, and colonial agents in open frontier zones denied the existence of any religion among indigenous people; after colonial containment was secured, they discovered religious systems that mirrored colonial administrative systems for keeping people in place.[31] In the development of British imperialism during the nineteenth century from a mercantile to an administrative empire, we see a transition from an interest in the fetish as an object of indeterminate value within an empire driven by mercantile capitalism to a focus on totemism, a term encompassing religion, sexual selection, and social cohesion, within an expanding, totalizing empire of administration.[32] These intersections of discourses and forces give new meaning to the old phrase *category formation* in the study of religion by situating ways of thinking about religion in historical formations.[33]

Formations and circulations: The adoption of colonial models, which is different than conversion, resulted in all kinds of formations turning into organized human activity that looked like churches, or their structural and functional equivalents, religious institutions all over the world that circulated and recirculated basic structures of European colonial formations. For example, nineteenth-century Hindu organizations in India, such as the Brahmo Samaj and the Ramakrishna Mission, were structured to function like churches.[34] The agency animating such structures, however, was often distinctly anticolonial, moving through colonial formations in the struggle against colonialism, appropriating the Bible, for example, but with a difference, as in the case of Kwame Nkrumah's exhortation "Seek ye first the political kingdom and all other things will be added to you" (adapting Mt 6:33).[35] In many postcolonial states, the irony of liberation has seen colonial formations recirculating as new constraints, often underwritten by promises of redemption, which have further entrenched oppression.

Circulations and categories: Like race, which does not exist but is everywhere, religion has thoroughly circulated throughout the world. As suggested by Nilüfer Göle, the circulations of migrants, perhaps most evident in the movement of Muslim immigrants and refugees into Europe, have altered the very categories of the religious and the secular in both theory and practice. Circulating throughout the world, U.S. foreign policy advancing religious freedom has generated new incongruities in categorizing religion. Elizabeth Shakman Hurd has distinguished between three types of religion—expert religion, lived religion, and governed religion—that collide in the discourse and practice of international relations.[36] Transnational and global circulations, therefore, are affecting not only religion but also the categories of religion and religions, of religious difference, religious pluralism, and religious diversity, for a wide range of actors who have embraced these circulating, unstable, and often incongruous categories for thinking about religion.

What is beyond religious studies? This book indicates possibilities for studying religion beyond restricting its scope to texts and beliefs and by moving beyond stable categories to historical contingencies, beyond contexts to material formations, and beyond institutions to material circulations. As evidence of the multidisciplinary character of the study of religion, the authors of the recent books that I have highlighted in each section of this introduction are variously positioned—in a Center for Environmental Studies, a Department of African American Studies, and a nongovernmental organization dealing with diversity and corporate responsibility—but all are involved in charting the future of the study of religion. In all of these positions and possibilities, the "beyond" is already within the academic study of religion; the future is already present in the material study of religion.

MATERIALITY MATTERS

Religion: Material Dynamics focuses on material engagements as essential in the cultural processes and productions of religion, which is always constructed—invented, assembled, staged, and performed—and yet always, in a myriad of ways, consequential in the real world and often experienced as really real. As a result, we are faced with this challenge: How do human beings really fabricate the real thing? How do real things really fabricate human beings? In this material dialectic of fabrication, the being of the human being is at stake.[37]

By focusing on categories, we will see how the human is positioned in religious terms between the more than human and the less than human, between the superhuman, perhaps regarded with awe, and the subhuman animals, vegetables, and minerals that are not treated with human regard because they are treated as objects to be exploited for some human purpose.

These classifications—superhuman, human, and subhuman—are fluid and contested. We will find beings with opposable thumbs, bipedal locomotion, and an increased frontal lobe of the brain being treated as less than human, being dehumanized under categories of race, class, or gender, while we will also find superhuman power and humanlike agency in material objects.

We will encounter many objects—relics and icons, stones and feathers, papyrus and parchment, spears and guns, flowers and rice, petroleum and plastic, Tupperware and refrigerators. What are these things?

The study of material religion, according to David Morgan, "should begin with the powers attributed to objects by religious devotees."[38] Although Morgan also appreciates the capacity of objects to afford powers to people, his starting point is the attention paid by religious devotees to religious objects. An alternative starting point, however, might be objects at the intersection of different and often competing communities of interpretation, practice, and association. In this respect, religious objects are boundary objects. The notion of boundary objects can draw from the work of Susan Leigh Star and James R. Griesemer on objects that find themselves situated at the intersection of different interpretive communities. The boundary object is flexible in that it is subject to multiple interpretations, but its materiality, as an object, sustains continuity through these multiple engagements. Although Star and Griesemer meant more than interpretive flexibility in their analysis of boundary objects, the notion of objects being defined by their boundaries, and by the multiple crossing of boundaries, is a promising entry into the role of objects in religious categories, formations, and circulations

In their original formulation, Star and Griesemer define boundary objects as "objects which are both plastic enough to adapt to local needs and constraints of the several parties employing them, yet robust enough to maintain a common identity across sites."[39] Although these authors developed an analysis of scientific boundary objects, this dialectic of plastic adaptability and robust continuity captures the role of objects in religious formations. Concrete or abstract, tangible or intangible, boundary objects "have different meanings in different social worlds[,] but their structure is common enough to more than one world to make them recognizable, a means of translation," providing crucial resources, according to Star and Griesemer, for "developing and maintaining coherence across intersecting social worlds."[40] However, boundary objects can often generate more chaos than coherence, more conflict than cohesion, among competing parties engaged in disputes over the interpretation, use, and ownership of an object.

By focusing on the materiality of objects, we expand the study of religion beyond the limited scope of beliefs, doctrines, and texts, but we also run the risk of reducing the study of religion to metaphysics. What is real? An old materialism might be happy to see objects, as inanimate objects, as real, a materialism that Samuel Johnson (1709–1784) famously established by kicking a stone.[41] However, even the "new materialism" that sees agency in objects, sometimes recognizing life in stones, can seem like a new metaphysics, an alternative to an anthropocentric view of reality, perhaps, but a view of reality that humanizes objects as actors, along with human actors, in networks, entanglements, and assemblages of vibrant materiality in real worlds.

By contrast, in the real worlds made by such disciplines as law or accounting, materiality takes on a very different meaning, referring not to any metaphysics but to practical conditions and consequences that matter. In the annals of the great lawyer Perry Mason, judges are often confronted with the objection "Your Honor, that question is irrelevant, inconsequential, and immaterial!"[42] Materiality, in this legal context, refers to the conditions of a specific case, a materiality that is significant to the matter at hand and consequential to proceeding toward an outcome. Essential in criminal law, material conditions and consequences are also crucial in the negotiations of contract law.[43] In accounting, which developed out of the double-entry bookkeeping that the historian Mary Poovey has identified as the origin of the modern fact, *materiality* is a technical term of art.[44] Is any discrepancy between one side and the other of an accounting ledger material? Is it inconsequential, with no effect, or does it make a material difference that must be addressed? Auditors often operate with a "materiality figure" to guide the determination of whether the numbers under review rise to the level of materiality.[45]

These considerations of materiality in the modern practices of law and accounting move us away from the old metaphysical divide between spirit and matter, which might still be retained by new materialists attributing spirit, vibrancy, or agency to material objects, into the political economy of materiality. Moving into this practical terrain, we can ask: What are the material conditions and consequences that make materiality matter in religion?

Accordingly, this book explores categories, formations, and circulations of material religion that rise to the level of materiality. In the political economy of materiality, the material conditions of colonialism, imperialism, and apartheid matter; the material consequences of diffusions and dispersions matter. All of these conditions and consequences, which are thoroughly material in their constitution, rise to the level of materiality by making a difference in the fabrication of relations between people and things in the world.

PART I Categories

As a class of things or people with shared characteristics, a category is a necessary feature of thinking. No categories, no thinking. But where do our categories come from? How do they work? What do they do? How can we rethink our basic modes of thinking? In part 1, basic categories in the study of religion—animism and sacred, space and time—are situated in their historical formations and tested for their present viability. Incongruity, arising from the violation of categorical distinctions, is identified as itself an important category in the academic study of religion.

Chapter 1 examines the emergence of a category, "belief in spiritual beings," that drove certain "intellectualist" assumptions about the essence, origin, and persistence of religion. Essentially, as animism, religion was a primitive way of thinking about the material world as if it were inhabited by spirits. Like many terms in the study of religion in Europe during the late nineteenth century, *animism* arose through a global mediation in which an imperial theorist, in this case the father of anthropology, E. B. Tylor, relied on colonial middlemen, such as missionaries, travelers, and administrators, for evidence about indigenous people all over the world. Among other colonial sources, E. B. Tylor relied on the Anglican missionary Henry Callaway for data about Zulu people in South Africa. Drawing on Callaway's reports about Zulu dreaming and sneezing, Tylor distilled his basic definition of religion as belief in pervading and invading spirits. Against a broad imperial and colonial background, chapter 1 explores the historical emergence and ongoing consequences of the category *animism* in the study of religion.

Chapter 2 examines a category, "that which is set apart," that has been crucial for the Durkheimian tradition in the study of religion. Set apart from the ordinary, the everyday, or the profane, the sacred is set apart in such a way that it is central to social formations. Exploring the dynamics of the sacred by viewing Chris Rock's documentary *Good Hair*, which takes us from Christian hairstyling to Hindu temple rituals, this chapter shows how the sacred is produced through extraordinary attention, regular ritualization, sacrificial exchanges, and inevitable contestations over the ownership of the sacred.

After a brief review of theoretical literature on space in the study of religion, chapter 3 illustrates the production of religious space through examples drawn from Africa and India. Theories of religious space can be divided between those that focus on poetic meaning, political power, or material production. Examples from Africa illustrate how religious space can be based on structural oppositions, such as the indigenous opposition between home and wild space and the colonial opposition between land and sea. The production of religious space commonly establishes barriers, but instances of shared religious space can be found in Africa, India, and elsewhere. Competition over the ownership of a place is a recurring feature of the dynamics of religious space, as illustrated by the conflict over the site in Ayodhya identified by Hindus as the birthplace of Rama and by Muslims as a historically significant mosque. With the rise of modern nations, religious space is increasingly managed by state apparatuses, such as courts, and at the same time dispersed through transnational social networks in diaspora. Not merely meaningful, religious space is also powerful as an arena for asserting claims to access, control, and ultimately, ownership of the sacred.

Reviewing theoretical approaches to religious time, chapter 4 illustrates mythic and ritual productions of time by examples from India and Africa. Classic theories of religious time emphasize either subjective experience, social cohesion, or sacred renewal. Ritual produces regularities—

simultaneous, sequential, and hierarchical—that are coordinated by clocks and calendars. Two basic ways of producing religious time, ancestral and mythic, represent different constructions of temporal continuity. Ancestral time, relying on memory, establishes continuity between human generations of ancestors and offspring. Mythic time, transmitted in narratives of origin and destiny, establishes continuity through underlying moral, legal, or forensic relations between actions and consequences. While establishing temporal continuity, mythic time can also signal temporal ruptures in a past crisis, a present conflict, or a future apocalypse. Ritual practices and mythic narratives generate religious time, but religious timing is also crucial in other spheres of human activity, such as politics, economics, and aesthetics. Religious time, therefore, is not only or merely religious. With its regularities and regulations, its ancestral and mythic constructions of continuity, religious time is also embedded in the aesthetics, economics, and politics of time.

Chapter 5 explores the collision of categories in religious encounters, myths, and rituals. Laughter, which arises from incongruity, guides this exploration. Recalling encounters between European Christian missionaries and indigenous Africans in nineteenth-century South Africa, we find Africans often laughing at the missionary proposals to violate indigenous categories of gender, labor, hygiene, politics, and ancestral veneration. European commentators, from Christian missionaries to early anthropologists, interpreted African laughter as evidence of thoughtless ignorance. However, as an engagement with incongruity, laughter was not only a relatively uncontrolled bodily eruption; it was also a way of thinking about cultural difference. Recovering laughter as a resource for the study of religion, this chapter highlights incongruity in religious orientations and interreligious relations.

Categories, therefore, are familiar and strange, taken for granted and vulnerable to critique, in a study of religion trying to find its way in the world. The following chapters explore the material dynamics of basic categories in the study of religion.

1 Animism

Coined by the anthropologist E. B. Tylor (1832–1917), the term *animism* refers not to a type of religion but to a theory of religion. Asserting a minimal definition of religion as "belief in spiritual beings," Tylor argued that religious belief originated in the primordial mistake of attributing life, soul, or spirit to inanimate objects.[1] Although it has generally been dismissed in the academic study of religion as an obsolete term for describing the belief systems of indigenous people who hold that natural phenomena have souls or spirits, *animism* has nevertheless persisted in popular usage and academic theory to raise problems about the meaning and value of materiality in religion.

Tylor's theory of animism was premised on a kind of materialism, since he assumed that materiality by definition was "dead" matter, but his theory was also framed in terms of an ideology of European progress, underwritten by evolutionary science, which bore a strange contradiction. Although Europeans supposedly represented the pinnacle of evolutionary development, they could know that only by comparing themselves to a baseline represented by others who had supposedly not evolved. Like other social evolutionists, Tylor found his evolutionary baseline, the "primitive," in reports submitted by European travelers, missionaries, and colonial agents about indigenous people, the "savage," on the periphery of empire. While Europeans, according to Tylor's evolutionary scheme, had progressed along a developmental trajectory through animism, polytheism, and monotheism to reach the highest achievements of science, evolving from primitive to civilized, the indigenous people of the Americas, Africa, Asia, Australia, and the Pacific had supposedly been left behind by evolution, standing over as savage "survivals" of the primitive.

Although Tylor was interested in contemporary indigenous religions only as data for building a theory of the original, primordial, or primitive animism, his term caught on to such an extent that it became commonplace in European inventories of the religions of the world to identity contemporary adherents of indigenous religions as animists. A guidebook for Christian missionaries, for example, asserts that at least 40 percent of the world's population is animistic.[2] While this characterization has often been experienced by indigenous people as denigrating, it has occasionally been adopted as a term of self-identification. In Indonesia and Nigeria, for example, representatives of indigenous religions, struggling in a political arena dominated by Muslim and Christian interests, have sought formal recognition as animists. At the same time, *animism* has sometimes been adopted as a term of self-identification in New Age, neo-pagan, or environmentalist movements. While acknowledging those appropriations of the term, this chapter concentrates on the history, rationale, and consequences of animism as a theory of religion.

HISTORY OF ANIMISM

During the nineteenth century, European social scientists developed different terms—*fetishism, totemism,* and *animism*—for the original religion of humanity, but each term carried the same allegation that primitives or savages were incapable of assessing the meaning and value of material objects.

The term, *fetish*, for example, emerged out of intercultural trading relations in West Africa in which European traders argued that Africans, unlike European Christians, had no stable system of value in which they could evaluate objects. Overvaluing apparently trifling objects such as feathers, bones, and cloth used in ritual, Africans undervalued the trade goods brought by Europeans. In this context, European Christians referred to African ritual objects as "fetishes," a term derived from the Portuguese *feitiço*, referring to nefarious instruments of magic and witchcraft.[3] The term *totemism*, according to John Ferguson McLennan in publications of 1869 and 1870, referred to communal alliances under the sign of an animal or an object that combined fetishism with exogamy, mixing the inability to evaluate materiality with regulations governing sexuality.[4] Arguably, the term *animism* mixed fetishism not with human sexuality but with animal psychology. The psychology of dogs, in particular, provided the key to a theory of religion based on attributing animation to inanimate objects.

In his popular survey of human evolution, *The Origin of Civilization and the Primitive Condition of Man,* John Lubbock explained that religion originated as the result of the primitive tendency to attribute animation to inanimate objects. To illustrate this primitive "frame of mind," Lubbock cited evidence from southern Africa, relying on the early nineteenth-century report from the traveler Henry Lichtenstein that the Xhosa in the Eastern Cape assumed that an anchor cast ashore from a shipwreck was actually alive. In a footnote, Lubbock observed: "Dogs appear to do the same."[5] As Lubbock's friend and mentor, Charles Darwin, maintained, religion could be explained in terms of dog behavior. Like Lubbock, Darwin observed that dogs characteristically attributed life to inanimate objects. His dog's attention to a parasol blowing in the wind, for example, suggested to Darwin that the animal assumed that objects were alive.[6] In this animal psychology, therefore, nineteenth-century theorists had a basis for understanding animism as the primitive or savage propensity to attribute animation to inanimate objects.

EVIDENCE OF ANIMISM

In standard accounts, E. B. Tylor's theory of animism is derived from the primitive inability to distinguish between dreams and waking consciousness. When the primitive ancestors of humanity dreamed about deceased friends or relatives, they assumed that the dead were still alive in some spiritual form. Out of dreams, therefore, evolved "the doctrine of souls and other spiritual beings in general," a doctrine that was "rational," even if it was a "childish philosophy" enveloped in "intense and inveterate ignorance."[7]

Where did Tylor get his evidence to support this finding? Instead of observing dogs, Tylor collected accounts about indigenous people, the savages who appeared in reports from European travelers, missionaries, and colonial agents. Arguably, Tylor's most important source was an account of Zulu religion from South Africa, *The Religious System of the Amazulu*, which had been published under the authorship of the Anglican missionary Henry Callaway, although the Zulu Christian convert Mpengula Mbande actually provided most of the reports collected in the book.[8] Tylor praised *The Religious System of the Amazulu* for providing "the best knowledge of the lower phases of religious belief."[9]

Certainly, Tylor found evidence of an active dream life among Callaway's Zulus. Zulus often saw the shade or shadow of deceased ancestors in dreams.[10] However, Callaway's volume included a detailed account about one Zulu man, an apprenticed diviner, who had become so overwhelmed with visions of spirits that he had described his own body as "a house of dreams."[11] According to Tylor, all Zulus, as savage survivals of the primitive, were subject to dream visions, but "as for the man who is passing into the morbid condition of the professional seer, phantoms are continually coming to talk to him in his sleep, till he becomes as the expressive native phrase is, 'a house of dreams.'"[12] Although Tylor appropriated him as an archetype of the primitive, this particular Zulu man, who served Tylor as a savage survival of the original "house of dreams" from which religion originated, was James, a friend of the Christian convert Mpengula Mbande. James was torn between the Christian mission and indigenous tradition. While Mpengula went one way, becoming a catechist for the mission, James struggled in the other direction, striving to keep an ancestral dream alive under increasingly difficult colonial conditions. In this case, therefore, the "house of dreams" was not a primitive condition but a colonial situation, the product of contemporary conflicts in southern Africa.

The analysis of dreams, however, did not provide the only evidence for Tylor's theory of animism. In addition, the involuntary physical phenomenon of sneezing was central to Tylor's argument. Here again Callaway's Zulu evidence was definitive. As Tylor observed, sneezing was "not originally an arbitrary and meaningless custom, but the working out of a principle. The plain statement by the modern Zulus fits with the hints to be gained from the superstition and folklore of other races, to connect the notions and practices as to sneezing with the ancient and savage doctrine of pervading and invading spirits, considered as good or evil, and treated accordingly."[13] From Callaway's account, Tylor derived the ethnographic facts that Zulus thought their deceased ancestors caused sneezing; that sneezing reminded Zulus to name and praise their ancestors; that the ancestors entered the bodies of their descendants when they sneezed; and that ritual specialists, such as Zulu diviners, regularly sneezed as a ritual technique for invoking the spiritual power of the ancestors.[14] These Zulu concepts and practices, Tylor concluded, were remnants of a prehistoric era in which sneezing was not merely a "physiological" phenomenon "but was still in the 'theological stage.'"[15]

Much has been made of Tylor's "intellectualist" theory of religion. Although primitives suffered from primordial stupidity, Tylor argued, they nevertheless exercised their limited intellectual powers to develop explanations of the world in which they lived. Unfortunately, Tylor cited a Zulu source in support of this proposition, Callaway's catechist, Mpengula Mbande, who observed that "we are told all things, and assent without seeing clearly whether they are true or not."[16] Although cited by Tylor as evidence of savage ignorance, Mbande's point in this statement was that most Zulus had not been exposed to Callaway's new Christian gospel. Rather than offering evidence of primordial stupidity, therefore, Mbande was announcing his recently acquired Christian commitment. In any event, Tylor's theoretical work, and his use of Zulu evidence, demonstrated that his theory of the origin of religion was based on an analysis of the body as well as the mind. More animal than human, in this respect, primitive religion, as revealed according to Tylor by its survival among contemporary Zulu savages, had evolved out of a bodily process that was as simple, basic, and involuntary as sneezing. However much it might have been theologized, sneezing marked the physiological origin of religion as animism, the belief in pervading and invading spirits.

CONSEQUENCES OF ANIMISM

In building his theory of animism, E. B. Tylor intentionally disguised the colonial conditions that provided his evidence. Ignoring the social, political, intercultural, and interreligious contexts in which his evidence was embedded was not an oversight. It was a method. According to Tylor, "savage religion" had to be abstracted from its living contexts in order to be used in an evolutionary history of human culture that began with primitive animism. "In defining the religious systems of the lower races, so as to place them correctly in the history of culture," Tylor observed in 1892, "careful examination is necessary to separate the genuine developments of native theology from the effects of intercourse with civilized foreigners."[17] Any trace of more advanced religious concepts, such as ideas of deity, morality, or retribution in an afterlife, could only have entered savage religion, Tylor argued, through such foreign intercourse with "higher" races. Factoring out colonial contacts, relations, and exchanges, he stated, "leaves untouched in the religions of the lower races the lower developments of animism."[18] According to this method, therefore, animism appeared as the original religion—the earliest, the lowest—only by erasing the actual colonial situations in which indigenous people lived. As a result, the theory of animism provided an ideological supplement to the imperial project.

Although it was posed as a scientific explanation of the origin and development of religion, the theory of animism also addressed nineteenth-century European dilemmas about the meaning of materiality. Despite the expansion of scientific materialism, with its implicit challenge to religious belief, the séances of spiritualism were gaining popularity in Europe, promising material proof of spiritual survival of death. Initially, E. B. Tylor considered using the term *spiritualism* for his theory of religion, regarding contemporary spiritualist practices in Europe as a survival of prehistoric religion. Like the religious beliefs and practices of indigenous people on the colonized periphery of empire, the spiritualist séance represented an unwarranted persistence in attributing life to dead matter. As a European intellectual problem, therefore, the theory of animism can be situated in the context of nineteenth-century distress about the religious implications of scientific materialism and the scientific implications of a new religious practice such as spiritualism.[19]

At the same time, this theory of the animation of dead matter was developed in the midst of the consolidation of commodity capitalism in Europe and North America. The commodity, as Karl Marx provocatively proposed, was not dead matter, because it was animated by a "fetishism of commodities," similar to primitive religion, which attributed life to objects "abounding in metaphysical subtleties and theological niceties."[20] While supplementing the colonization of indigenous people, therefore, the theory of animism was also entangled in European struggles to understand the animation of matter in capitalism.

In the anthropology of religion, some theorists have more recently attempted to rehabilitate the theory of animism, either restating the argument that religion originated in the basic animistic propensity to project human characteristics of life, thought, and feeling onto the natural world, or redefining animism as a "relational epistemology" through which indigenous people gain knowledge by entering into humanizing relations with the natural world.[21] In literary studies, Harry Garuba has identified the animism operating in the localization of spiritual forces in African literature, while in religious studies Graham Harvey has revitalized animism as indigenous religious respect for the living world.[22] The history of the theory of animism, however, suggests that any theoretical recovery of this category will inevitably be entangled with the legacy of E. B. Tylor. So we are still left with this problem: Animism, as an account of religion and materiality, bears traces of nineteenth-century European imperialism, colonialism, and capitalism. As a result, animism represents more of a problem than a solution for our understanding of religious engagements with the material world.

2 Sacred

In the study of religion, the sacred has been defined as both supremely transcendental and essentially social, as an otherness transcending the ordinary world—Rudolph Otto's "holy," Gerardus van der Leeuw's "power," or Mircea Eliade's "real"—or as an otherness that shapes the social world, following Emile Durkheim's understanding of the sacred as that which is set apart from the ordinary, everyday rhythms of life, but set apart in such a way that it stands at the center of community formation. In between the radical transcendence of the sacred and the social dynamics of the sacred, we find ongoing mediations, at the intersections of personal subjectivity and social collectivities, in which anything can be sacralized through the religious work of intensive interpretation, regular ritualization, and inevitable contestation over ownership of the means, modes, and forces for producing the sacred.

Let us focus here, in detail, on hair as a material location of the sacred. Ordinary hair on people's heads has been rendered sacred, not only by people with hair, but also by social scientists who have linked "magical hair" with "social hair," exploring the religious, social, and psychological dynamics of what Anthony Synnott calls "the four modes of hair change (length, style, colour and additions)."[1]

Then the American comedian Chris Rock makes a documentary, *Good Hair,* raising all of these issues in the study of the sacred.[2] While focusing on African American hairstyling, the film provides ample evidence of the intensive interpretation of all the modes of hair change. We enter a thorough discussion of the multiple meanings of natural hair, styling hair, coloring hair, and perhaps most importantly, the additions to hair, the weaves that, as a $9-billion business, dominate hairstyling. But they also evoke the sacred, in Durkheimian terms, because these hair additions are set apart from ordinary contact, forbidden and tabooed—they cannot be touched, not even in the intimacy of sexual relations, as a number of male informants complain. With the development of "interlinked wigs, woven into the hair," as Synnott observes, "body contact sports are out."[3] The sacred, therefore, is not merely meaningful: it is powerful in ritualized practices of avoidance, contact, and exchange.

All of the modes of hair change are on display at the annual Bronner Bros. International Beauty Show in Atlanta, where the documentary shows hairstylists competing in a ritual drama in which four finalists demonstrate their skills. One of the finalists, Tanya Crumel, represents a hairstyling crew headed by a former winner, Kevin Kirk, who brings a specifically Christian interpretation to this ritual. Calling his hairstylists together before the event into a prayer circle, Kirk urges them to pray, fast, and sacrifice. In this evangelical Christian ritual before the hairstyling ritual, we see a charismatic invocation of the sacred in which receiving supremely transcendental rewards depends upon making personal sacrifices. "We're going to make some sacrifices," Kirk announces, calling upon his hairstyling team not only to pray for victory but also to undertake a fast that would purify them and make them worthy of such an extraordinary blessing. When a member of the team objects to going without food, Kirk retorts, "You're not a Christian?" Preparing for the hairstyling event, for Kevin Kirk, required entering the sacred through sacrifice, engaging in a transaction in which sacrificial giving would result in transcendental receiving. As Kirk later explained, he knew that his team would win, not only because of their prayers, but also through "the vision that God gave me."

Sacrificial exchange, as a quick trip to India shows, is essential for producing the raw materials that go into the rituals of hairstyling. At the Sri Venkateswara Temple in Tirupati, we learn that 10 million devotees each year sacrifice their hair, participating in the ritual of tonsure, in exchange for divine blessing. "God likes hair," one participant observes. Devotees offer their hair to God with prayers, requests, and vows. As Chris Rock explains, the ultimate meaning of this Hindu ritual of haircutting is the sacrifice of vanity, because "removing hair is considered an act of self-sacrifice." Ironically, this ritual of hair-sacrifice serves the vanity of hairstyling. Collecting, selling, and distributing this sacrificial hair is a global business, with active markets in Asia, Europe, and America. God might like hair, but as one entrepreneur exclaims, "Hair is gold." Sacred hair and profane commerce are thoroughly interwoven in the international hair exchange.

The music of worship and the noise of commerce, however, have always been related in the production of the sacred. Chris Rock's film develops the ironic juxtaposition of African American Christians weaving into their hair Hindu temple-hair, which has been "prayed upon," on the basis of an aesthetics that is simultaneously religious and commercial, creating a quasi-religious secret society, a "weave séance," a weave culture, a weave world, which accounts for up to 70 percent of the hair-care industry and depends upon a global trade in human hair that transcends race, class, gender, and national borders. Testing this religio-commercial aesthetic, Chris Rock tries to market genuine African American hair, "cut off at a Baptist temple," with no success.

Stepping out of Chris Rock's film, we find the Sri Venkateswara Temple in Tirupati, with six hundred barbers, fifty thousand pilgrims per day, a priestly monopoly on the sacrificial hair, and the ongoing transactions of auctioning, preparing, and exporting sacred hair. The entire hair-exchange is imbued with the sacred. "It is a holy business," one prominent hair exporter declares.[4] As a global business, most of the temple hair goes to China to be used in the production of keratin rather than to Europe and America for wigs and weaves. However, according to this exporter, wherever in the world the hair goes, the entire value chain—from sacrificial offering in a Hindu temple to ritualized consumption in Asia, Europe, or America—is a holy business spreading "happy hair" around the world.

The meaning, power, and ownership of the sacred are inevitably contested. When they learned that hair used in women's wigs came from Hindu temples, Orthodox rabbis in Israel ruled that any use of such hair was idolatry. Since covering their own hair with wigs was an important practice for Orthodox Jewish women, this ruling against idolatrous hair had both a religious and commercial impact. Recasting the holy business in Hindu hair as false worship, the rabbis insisted that women had an obligation to avoid such hair at the risk of incurring ritual defilement.

In response to this Jewish ban on Hindu hair, Indian entrepreneurs devised an ingenious argument that recast its sacred character. According to one prominent exporter, the hair's sacred significance was not ritual but ethical. Its sacred aura was derived not through ritual sacrifice to the temple deity but through the ethical virtue of humility. "What is ritualistic about humbling yourself in the most basic way?" this exporter asked. "In India, shaving your head equals shedding all vanity and becoming modest."[5] The ethical virtue of modesty, therefore, which was at the heart of the Orthodox Jewish injunction for women to adopt head coverings (such as wigs made out of hair from India), was asserted by this entrepreneur as the common sacred ground on which Jews and Hindus could meet and do business.

This shift from the ritual to the ethical in locating the sacred has often been identified as peculiarly Protestant. Castigating Roman Catholic ritual as idolatry, early Protestant reformers sought to dematerialize the sacred, which was found in a faith, as Luther argued, that could be accessed only by hearing, with eyes closed, while erasing all traces of idolatrous worship of objects. In his conclusion to the film *Good Hair*, comedian Chris Rock adopts this Protestant perspective on the sacred by distilling from his entire exploration of the ritual world of hair—African American, Hindu, and global—one message that he wants to give to his own daughters: "The stuff on top of their heads is nowhere near as important as what is inside their heads."

From a comedian, therefore, we learn that hair is sacred because it is a focus for extraordinary attention, the locus of ritual sacrifice, the nexus of ritualized exchanges, and the matrix of religious contestation.

First, as Jonathan Z. Smith has argued, the sacred is produced through ritualization that is essentially a way of paying attention in meticulous detail, coordinating every movement, gesture, and posture into a perfect pattern of action that factors out all of the accidents of daily life.[6] Ritual attends to incongruity, such as the gap between bad hair, which is perceived as chaotic, disorderly, and perhaps even defiling, and good hair that conforms to ritual rules of order. In this respect, classic scholarship on religious hair, which has tried to establish a basic lexicon of hair significance, such as Edmund Leach's correlation of long hair with unrestricted sexuality, short hair with restricted sexuality, and shaven hair with celibacy, can be easily challenged by counterexamples of shaven-headed religious people, such as South African President Jacob Zuma, an adherent of both Zulu ancestral tradition and evangelical Christianity, who seems to display an unrestricted sexuality.[7] Not a stable lexicon with universal correlations, the sacred is produced through intensive, ongoing, and extraordinary attention, through processes of interpretation, attending to minute detail, which are always overdetermined in their proliferation of meanings.

Second, as a recurring mode of producing the sacred, sacrifice, with its etymological root in "to make sacred," plays a prominent role in our understanding of the meaning and the power of the sacred. In the film *Good Hair*, we see sacrifice as evangelical Christian fasting and as devotional Hindu haircutting. In the earliest and perhaps most enduring theory of ritual sacrifice, *do ut des* (I give so you give), sacrificial ritual is an exchange between humans and deities, giving something ordinary for extraordinary returns. Unfortunately, in *Good Hair* the evangelical Christians lose the hairstyling competition. As we learn, however, the sacrifices of evangelical Christian hairstylists and devotional Hindu haircutters are wrapped up in a global industry in which ordinary hair does in fact produce extraordinary financial returns for entrepreneurs.

Third, as a nexus of ritualized exchanges, sacred hair circulates through global transactions that merge religion and economics. In the global hair market, we find the sacred being produced according to what anthropologists Jean and John Comaroff have identified as the prevailing milieu in late modernity, millennial capitalism, a kind of global cargo cult in which abundant wealth is expected from extraordinary sources.[8] But we also find what the perverse Durkheimian Georges Bataille calls *expenditure*, the engine of a general economy in which sacrificial destruction, loss, or waste of resources in ritual display or public spectacle must be as great as possible to certify the sacred.[9]

Finally, as a result of intensive interpretation and regular ritualization, we are left with a sacred surplus, an abundant surplus of the sacred, that is available for competing claims to ownership. Like hair, the sacred is everywhere, immediately available for meaningful interpretation and participatory ritualization, but inevitably owned and operated by someone. Who owns the sacred? In October 2009, Chris Rock was sued for appropriating the intellectual property of a filmmaker who had made a documentary about African American hairstyling, *My Nappy Roots: A Journey through Black Hair-itage*. "Let's go to India," Rock allegedly said, when he saw the film.[10] Although Rock eventually won his case, the competing claims in the dispute remind us that the ownership of intellectual property, even sacred property, is now settled in courts rather than in temples. As an appendix to his classic article "Magical Hair," Edmund Leach cited the proceedings of a court case in India from January 1957 dealing with competing claims on the hair offered by devotees at the Sri Venkateswara Temple in Tirupati, the same temple featured in Chris Rock's *Good Hair*. In that case, a secular court ruled against competing barbers by finding that only temple-authorized haircutters "were entitled exclusively to shave the heads of the pilgrim-votaries who wished to offer the hair of their heads to the deity in discharge of their vows[,] and the temple was entitled to control shaving of the heads of pilgrim-votaries and collect the hair which was endowed to the deity."[11] Certifying an exclusive claim on sacred hair, this 1950s court case established a legal monopoly on the sacred that eventually developed into a global industry and a film by an African American comedian that was ostensibly about hair but really about the permutations of the sacred.

3 Space

Religious space is produced through the labor of ritualization and interpretation. Although spatial orientations, special places, and embodied
disciplines might be imagined as given by God or handed down by tradition, religious space is created in and through the performance of ritual in
set-apart times and places and the interpretative work of making meaning. This religious labor generates a surplus of meaning and power that is
inevitably subject to competing claims on its ownership. In struggles over
the ownership of space, crucial questions are raised about access and control. In the dynamics of inclusion and exclusion, who is allowed in? Who
is kept out? Often symbolized in terms of purity, this issue of access is
entangled in the dynamics of power: Who owns the means of spatial production? How are spatial resources distributed? What are the material
locations, networks, and oppositions of spatial orientation?

POETICS, POLITICS, AND PRODUCTION

Scholars of religion have tended to emphasize either the poetics or the politics of religious space. While the poetics of space is all about meaning, the

politics of space is the dynamics in which people, along with their meanings, are positioned as above or below, as inside or outside, within the
structure of a prevailing regime of power. Developing a romantic poetics of
religious meaning, Mircea Eliade held that the sacred irrupted, manifested,
or appeared in certain places, causing them to become powerful centers of
meaningful worlds.[1] By contrast, Jonathan Z. Smith has shown how place
is sacralized through the cultural labor of ritual, in specific historical situations and political conditions, involving the hard work of attention, memory, design, construction, and control of place.[2] Not an opposition between
"insider" and "outsider" perspectives, this clash between the poetics of
meaning-making and the politics of power relations marks a recurring
divide in theories of religious space.

　　Can poetics and politics be combined? In his landmark text on the phenomenology of religion, *Religion in Essence and Manifestation*, published
in 1933, Gerardus van der Leeuw explored the implications of his substantial definition of the sacred, "power," in spatial terms. In a chapter on sacred
space, he outlined an inventory of typical sacred places that have appeared
in the history of religions. That inventory, however, was also a series of
homologies in which Van der Leeuw asserted the metaphoric equivalence
of home, temple, settlement, pilgrimage site, and human body. A home was
a temple, a temple a home. The city of Jerusalem, identified by Van der
Leeuw as sacred space in its most "typical form," was a temple in the beginning and would be a temple in the end. The pilgrimage site, as a home,
temple, or sacred settlement away from home, could ultimately be found at
the center of the body in the human heart. Sacred places, therefore, formed
a recursive series of metaphoric equivalences. In addition, Van der Leeuw
tracked a second series of homologies, identifying the core of each item in
the first series, which linked the hearth (of the home), the altar (of the temple), the sanctuary (of the settlement), the shrine (of the pilgrimage site),
and the heart (of the human body). These two series of equivalences established Van der Leeuw's basic vocabulary for an analysis of sacred places. As
they recurred in his analysis, they provided a poetics of sacred space.

　　At the same time, Van der Leeuw laced his analysis with hints of a politics of sacred space. First, he identified a politics of position. Like Eliade,
in some moments he attributed sole, transcendent, and ultimate agency to
sacred power, even holding that sacred power actually positioned itself in

the world. However, this mystifying of power was tempered by his recognition that the positioning of a sacred place was also a political act, whether that positioning involved, in his terms, selection, orientation, limitation, or conquest.

Second, Van der Leeuw suggested another political aspect of sacred space by paying attention to the politics of exclusion. A sacred place, such as a home, was a space in which relations among persons could be negotiated and worked out. Some persons, however, were left out, kept out, or forced out. In fact, the sanctity of the inside was certified by maintaining and reinforcing boundaries that kept certain persons outside the sacred place. By recognizing this process of excluding persons, Van der Leeuw raised the possibility that a politics of exclusion might be an integral part of the making of sacred space.

Third, Van der Leeuw linked sacred space with a politics of property. A sacred place was not merely a meaningful place; it was a powerful place because it was appropriated, possessed, and owned. In several important passages of his text, Van der Leeuw referred to the sacred power of property, asserting that property was the "realization of possibilities."[3] As the ultimate realization of possibilities, sacred space was inevitably owned by someone as property.

Fourth, and finally, Van der Leeuw ultimately positioned sacred space in the context of a politics of exile. He insistently highlighted a "modern" loss of the sacred, or alienation from the sacred, or nostalgia for the sacred, in his interpretation of basic data of religion. Van der Leeuw repeatedly noted that "primitives" had the sacred; some common peasant folk have retained it; but "moderns" have entirely lost it. The historical and essentially political situation of exile from the sacred entailed two theoretical implications for Van der Leeuw's phenomenology of religion: the most sacred places were remote, and the most authentic religious experience in relation to sacred space was homesickness. In the politics of exile, the sacred was positioned in relation to human beings who found themselves to be out of position.

In recent years, the study of the poetics and politics of space has been supplemented by theoretical work on the production of religious space. Following the philosopher Henri Lefebvre, Kim Knott has focused on the production of space. Beginning with the body, which provides the primary source of space, Knott has analyzed the importance for religion of spatial dimensions, properties, aspects, and dynamics. The embodied bilateral contrast between right and left hands, for example, can structure general orientations in space as well as spatial oppositions.[4] In developing a general theory of religion, Thomas A. Tweed has analyzed spatial strategies of dwelling and crossing, proposing that religious actors endeavor to "make homes and cross boundaries."[5] In this respect, Tweed has attended to productions of both domestic space, which is anchored in a specific place, and the transitional spaces of movement, migration, and diaspora in the spatial dynamics of religion. Emphasizing the material constraints on dwelling and crossing, Manuel A. Vásquez has developed a theory of spatial networks for analyzing the production of space.[6] Whether situated at home or moving on roads, deserts, or oceans, producers of religious space deal with specific material conditions and shifting social networks.

HOMES AND CAVES, LAND AND SEA

Moving from theory to practice, we turn to specific cases of the production of religious space in Africa and India. As reconstructed in the anthropological literature, the cosmology of indigenous religion in southern Africa is based on a structural opposition between "home space" and "wild space." Among the Xhosa-speaking people of the Eastern Cape, for example, the home is a sacred space, a domestic order that is built up not only through social relations of production and reproduction but also through ongoing ritual relations with ancestors. As the "people of the home" *(abantu bekhaya),* the ancestors perform vital functions—guiding, protecting, and sometimes chastising their descendants; reinforcing the authority of elders; and representing a spiritual reality beyond death—in a domestic religion designed "to make the homestead right" *(ukulungisa umzi).* While certain parts of the home, such as the hearth, the back wall, and the top of the door, are particularly associated with the spiritual presence of ancestors, the entire homestead is marked out through regular rituals as an ordered space of communication and exchange with ancestral spirits, with the cattle enclosure, or *kraal,* representing the most important site in this sacred architecture of the homestead.

The sacred space of the home, however, is also marked out in opposition to the wild, chaotic, and potentially dangerous region of the forest. In stark contrast to the space of the home, with its ancestral spirits, structured human relations, and domesticated animals, the forest contains not only wild animals but also witch familiars, the dangerous spirits deployed by witches, those antisocial agents who act to disrupt the harmony or stability of the home. The sacred space of the home, therefore, must be sustained by rituals that both invoke ancestors and protect against witches, who draw their power from the wild space.

In between the home space and the wild space, the river represents a liminal space—sometimes good, sometimes evil—in which the spiritual "people of the river" *(abantu bomlambo)* play an ambiguous role in mediating between the domestic order of the homestead and the wild forces that threaten to disrupt it. Diviners, healers, and other ritual specialists have a distinctive relationship with this liminal space of the river, since they also mediate between the spiritual order of the home and the dangers associated with the wild space.[7]

By this account, therefore, the indigenous Xhosa religion of the Eastern Cape is based on a kind of symbolic mapping, a spiritual geography grounded in the dichotomy between home space and wild space. A similar symbolic mapping has been identified in the Tswana religion in the Northern Cape in the distinction between the domestic order of the human settlement *(motse)*, which is organized and reinforced through ritual relations with ancestors, and the wild, chaotic, and dangerous forces associated with the bush *(naga)*, the domain of wild spirits and witch familiars.[8] Under colonial conditions, however, this mapping was altered by new relations between land and sea.

For both alien and indigenous people in colonial contact zones, a new orientation to the land was often articulated precisely in terms of an opposition between the land and the sea. In Africa, this opposition goes back at least to the contacts of the seventeenth century. "It is well-documented from missionary reports," as Wyatt MacGaffey has observed, "that in the seventeenth century white people were believed to live under the ocean." MacGaffey concludes that this belief "is not derived from experience but is a fundamental postulate in terms of which experience is interpreted."[9] Drawing on earlier mythic themes, this identification of Europeans with the sea became a symbolic template for interpreting the colonial encounter. Using this symbolic framework, Africans could reconfigure the encounter in terms of the spatial opposition between sea and land.

Under the impact of British colonization in nineteenth-century southern Africa, myths of the sea were reworked to make sense of the military incursions, dispossession of land, and new relations of power. In response to the British incursions and depredations of the early nineteenth century, for example, the Xhosa chief Ngqika (r. 1775–1829) observed that since the Europeans were people of the sea—the "natives of the water"—they should have stayed in the sea. They had no business coming out of the sea onto the land.[10] The Xhosa religious visionary and war-leader Nxele (d. 1819), also known as Makana, the Lynx, developed this observation about sea and land into an indigenous theology that identified two gods, Thixo, the god of the white people, who had punished white people for killing his son by casting them into the sea, and Mdalidiphu, the god of the deeps, who dwelled under the ground but had ultimate dominion over the sea.[11] Similarly, during the first half of the nineteenth century, a Zulu emergence myth was reconfigured in terms of this colonial opposition between land and sea. In the beginning, according to an account recorded in the 1850s, uNkulunkulu created human beings, male and female, but also black and white. While black human beings according to this myth were created to be naked, carry spears, and live on the land, white human beings were created to wear clothing, carry guns, and live in the sea.[12] For these African religious thinkers, therefore, the mythic origin of the world was clearly located in the new colonial era that produced the crucial spatial opposition between people of the sea and people of the land.

After the advent of postcolonial and postapartheid democracy in 1994, South Africans still struggled over the ownership of religious space. In the Caledon Valley of the Free State, in a region known as the Conquered Territory, a chain of cave shrines formed a spatial network for new forms of religious coexistence.[13] Displaced and denied land ownership in the territory, Africans had also been prevented from visiting ancestral graves or sites associated with powerful chiefs and diviners of the past. After 1994, however, pilgrims began traveling to the caves overhanging streams and springs in the territory, marking out a series of sites that stretched over sixty kilometers. Although the caves were located on white-owned farms, neither the landowners nor the government prevented the pilgrims from gaining access to the cave shrines. White farmers might assert their claims to ownership, based on the sanctity of property, by charging admission fees. But the performance of ritual also asserted a claim to ownership. Overcoming decades of exclusion, Africans pursued religious pilgrimage as an avenue for performing spiritual rituals of healing, purification, possession, and empowerment while implicitly asserting African claims to ownership of the land.

In the largest site, Badimong, "among ancestors," the caves above a riverbed became locations for building altars, small enclosures, and temporary housing for pilgrims. A diverse array of religious practices coexisted at Badimong, with adherents of ancestral religion, initiates of traditional divination, and members of independent and mainline Christian churches all sharing the same space. Displaying fluidity in which a Christian feast of thanksgiving could shift into ancestral divination or possession, religious practices mixed and merged in the ritual observances of the cave shrines. As a vortex drawing together diverse rituals, Badimong was a rare instance of a shared religious space.

MOSQUES AND TEMPLES, NATION AND DIASPORA

Although rare, sharing religious space has occurred elsewhere in history.[14] During the fourth century in Palestine, the shrine of the sacred oak at Mamre, near Hebron, was a place for regular ritualization and intensive interpretation by Jews, Christians, and pagans. Mamre, which was identified by Jews as the place where three angels visited the patriarch Abraham (Gen. 18:1–22), was interpreted by Christians as a site at which Christ, the second person of this trinity, appeared in the world. While Mamre attracted Jewish and Christian pilgrims, the sacred oak was also a pagan shrine, the site of an annual festival at which pagan celebrants invoked the angels, poured out wine, burned incense, and sacrificed animals. Although the Christian emperor Constantine tried to assert an exclusive Christian ownership of Mamre, alternative claims on the site continued to be advanced by Jews and pagans through ritual.[15]

India also holds examples of shared religious sites. Thomas Christians, tracing their lineage back to the apostle Thomas from Syria, who, according to tradition moved to India in the first century, found a home within a broadly Hindu environment in southern India. Christians and Hindus shared temple precincts, street processions, and ritual regalia. The Christian shrine of Mylapore, the site of the martyrdom of Thomas, was also revered by Hindus and Muslims. Until captured by the Portuguese in 1517, Mylapore remained an interreligious site for adherents of different religions.[16] In the city of Ayodhya in northern India, Muslims and Hindus worshipped together in the Babri Masjid, the mosque built in 1528 on the site of the presumed birthplace of the Hindu deity Rama, an avatar or manifestation of Vishnu. Under the impact of British colonialism, conflict between Muslims and Hindus developed at this site, inspiring the British administrators to erect a fence separating Muslims worshiping in the mosque from Hindus worshiping on a raised platform.[17] Although divided by a barrier, Hindus and Muslims continued to perform rituals within the same sacred precinct of Ayodhya.

In the production of space, the fence was as much a part of the religious built environment of the precinct as the architecture of the mosque or the platform for ritual observances. Certainly, Muslims and Hindus developed different interpretations of the precinct's significance within larger sacred geographies. For Muslims, the Babri Masjid, like any mosque, was an inviolable sacred site for prayers, sermons, and devotion to Allah. Although adherents were directing prayers to God toward Mecca, the mosque established a spatial orientation, which might be called a utopian orientation, that revolved around a God who was everywhere. By contrast, Hindus interpreted the site not only as the birthplace of Rama but also as the "head" of the body of Vishnu that formed a geographical network made up of seven pilgrimage sites, or *tirthas*, distributed throughout India.[18] In this spatial orientation, which might be called a locative orientation, God might ultimately be everywhere but also necessarily anchored in specific sites or particular places of a sacred geography.[19] The fence reinforced the division between these two religious orientations in space, a division further entrenched by British colonial administration, the partition of India and Pakistan, and religious rivalry over contested territory.

For Hindus, the network of *tirthas*—the dwellings of deities and the crossing of worlds—created a symbolic map of a unified India linked together by pilgrimage sites. Taking up this ritual construction of space,

Hindu nationalists advanced the ideology of *hindutva*, the sacred bond between Hindus and Bharat Mata, Mother India. During the 1980s, Hindu nationalist campaigns focused on Ayodhya. Securing a secular court decision over Muslim objections in 1986, Hindu nationalists were granted the right to enter the Babri Mosque to perform ritual *puja* to Rama. In 1989, during a national election, Hindu nationalists focused on Ayodhya for political mobilization by asserting ritual claims to the space in laying the foundation stone for a new temple to Rama. Placed next to the mosque, the foundation stone was consecrated by water from all the sacred rivers and earth from all the pilgrimage sites of India. On December 6, 1992, in an extraordinary act of desecration, as many as 150,000 Hindus participated in the demolition of the mosque, brick by brick, to claim ownership of the space. In this ritualized destruction, the Muslim mosque became a locative space, a specific, highly charged location for the sacred, while the Hindu temple proposed for this location, remaining unbuilt for decades, became a utopian space for Hindu national aspirations.[20]

A nation, which Ernest Renan characterized as "a soul, a spiritual principle," can be based on utopian religious space, but a modern state in Max Weber's classic definition is the monopoly on the exercise of legitimate violence over a territory.[21] What counts as "legitimate," of course, is the crucial problem in this definition of the state, but the spatial demarcation of territory is also at stake in the formation of the modern state system. In the production of religious space within this system, ritual rights are increasingly subject to the jurisdiction of state functions such as secular courts, civil administration, and public policing. In the case of Ayodhya, secular courts tried to adjudicate religious space for Hindu nationalists by ruling for their ritual access to the mosque in 1986 but ruling against their plans for the ritual destruction of the mosque in 1992. As events unfolded, the state clearly did not hold a monopoly on the exercise of violence in the production and destruction of religious space.

While modern secular states have been involved in producing religious space—adjudicating ritual rights, access, and ownership—transnational circulations of people have produced new spatial orientations. Diaspora, or dispersion, has generated new interpretations and ritualizations of a sacred home that can be engaged only away from home. In the African diaspora, practitioners of Haitian Vodou, descendants of Africans who underwent the middle passage across the Atlantic Ocean into slavery, perform rituals that link Haiti with Africa, pouring libations on the ground, for example, that will cross the ocean to the motherland.[22] For the Hindu diaspora, which extends throughout the world, domestic rituals connect practitioners with Bharata Mata, Mother India.[23] In these ritual transactions in diaspora, local space, whether in Haiti or Trinidad, is reproduced as the utopian sacred space of a lost but recoverable home in Africa or India.

RELIGIOUS SPACING

Although we have considered cases from Africa and India, we can draw more general conclusions from these illustrations about the production of space in the history of religions.

First, as we have seen, structured oppositions, such as the oppositions between home and wild, or sea and land, are important features of the production of meaningful and powerful religious space. Perhaps derived from the left-right axis of the human body,[24] the primary space of religious production, structural oppositions—inside and outside, up and down—are deployed in producing spatial orientations of religious purity and power: religious purity through rituals of exclusion and religious power through rituals of subordination, subjection, and extraction of human and material resources.

Second, in between structured oppositions, liminal space, like the river that is neither home nor wild, signals the importance of possibility in the religious production of space. Not fixed in place on one side or the other, the liminal space is open to new things. In the colonial relations between sea and land in southern Africa, the liminal space was the frontier zone, the contact zone, in which anything might happen. As religious resources were drawn into configuring the meaning and power of this in-between space of intercultural contact, new spatial orientations toward the land and sea emerged. These reconfigurations of space in liminality, contact, and mediation between land and sea have been crucial to the production of religious space in colonial and postcolonial worlds.[25]

Third, religious space is directional, directing attention but also directing people to move. Space is a medium for motion. People move through space, whether pushed or pulled, in ways that produce space. Characteristically, religious motion in space is either centripetal, drawing into a center, or centrifugal, moving out from a center, which suggests that people move between centers and peripheries in a kind of Newtonian social physics of religious space. However, in religious diasporas we find a post-Newtonian field of circulations in which relations between centers and peripheries are constantly being renegotiated.

Fourth, in a Newtonian social physics, since no two points can occupy the same space, conflict is inevitable between any two or more religious groups who try to inhabit the same site. Certainly, we can find instances of mutual coexistence, but conflict seems to be the norm. Although conflicts might not be primarily or exclusively religious, fighting over space seems to be a recurring feature of the production of space in the history of religions. Not merely meaningful, space is also powerful as an arena for asserting claims to access, control, and ultimately ownership of the sacred.

As the ongoing religious work of ritualization and interpretation produces a surplus of meaning and power, significance and energy, a surplus that arises out of space but also overflows any place, no assertion of privileged ownership of the sacred can ever be final. Inviting and resisting assertions of ownership, the materiality of space confounds all religious claims. Accordingly, struggles continue over the ownership of religious space as it is produced and reproduced at the intersections of competing communities of interpretation.

4 Time

Religious time is produced through the labor of ritualization and interpretation, but it is also subject to disciplinary regulation by clocks, calendars, and other instruments for coordinating different temporalities. In time, embodied rhythms such as inhaling and exhaling, stillness and motion, might be spontaneous or accidental. Integrated into religious disciplines, however, these rhythms can be coordinated with temporal regularities and regulations that merge personal subjectivities, lived in time, with social collectivities that evoke a sense of timelessness. By enacting traditions supposedly handed down from time immemorial—for example, rites of passage that turn death into new birth, or liturgies that transform temporal succession into a succession of eternities—ritual and interpretive labor can be orchestrated in producing religious time.

Embodied time and social time come together in religious time. Adapting terms from the philosopher John Locke, we can distinguish between two basic types of religious time—ancestral time that establishes *cognitive* continuity through memory, and mythic time that establishes *forensic* continuity by linking actions with consequences.[1]

While cognitive continuity is based on remembering, forensic continuity can be established, even if no one remembers, by linking actors with the effects of their actions. Although the term *forensics* is familiar from modern criminal investigations, we can, by following Locke, who proposed that *personal identity* is a forensic term, see how religious discourse and practice often establish forensic links between actions and consequences. Myth, in particular, relies on forensic continuity to draw personal identity into social narratives that no one personally remembers, because these stories are situated in time immemorial. Nevertheless, in mythic time, everyone is implicated. In the absence of personal memory, the basis for cognitive continuity, myth provides forensic terms and conditions for holding everyone accountable. Religious time, therefore, does not merely take place in time. Through ritual regularities and mythic narratives, through cognitive continuity and forensic continuity, religion produces time.

RITUAL, REGULARITIES, AND REGULATION

By contrast to the philosopher Henri Bergson, who analyzed the subjective experience of time as an indivisible flow,[2] theorists of religion have argued that myth and ritual break up the flow of time. A student of Emile Durkheim, Henri Hubert undertook a preliminary study of religious representations of time by outlining the ways in which rituals create intervals and interventions in time. As a result, the sacred "seeds itself within time."[3] Interrupting the flow of everyday, ordinary, or profane time, sacred time marks out a field of temporal regularities that are also collective representations of society. Sharing sacred time, in this rendering, is sharing social cohesion.

Adopting this distinction between profane and sacred time, Mircea Eliade developed a theory of religion as the repetition of paradigmatic or archetypal events that happened in the beginning, as reenacting a sacred model initiated by gods or ancestors in a time of origins. Religious practices, according to Eliade, enable people to break out of ordinary time into a mythic world, "periodically becoming contemporary with the gods."[4] As a religious interruption of ordinary time, sacred time in Eliade's theory is placed in opposition not only to the everyday temporal flow but also to history or the "terror of history."[5] In a formulation that has been generally rejected in subsequent scholarship, Eliade contrasted the circular time of myth, which enables renewal, reactualization, and eternal return, with the linear time of history. If religion provides ways in which "time can be overcome," Eliade's notion of transcendence involved overcoming both profane time and historical time.[6]

Against history, Eliade nevertheless developed a kind of theory of religious history based on erasure and nostalgia. As an example of historical erasure, when considering "primitive" millenarian movements, he found that historical factors and forces could be neglected by scholars of religion because "there is no need to dwell on the political, social, and economic character of these movements."[7] As an example of historical nostalgia, when reflecting on the loss of the sacred in modern politics, society, and economy, he asserted that "the secularization of work is like an open wound in the body of modern society."[8] Eliade's poetics of sacred time, based on a metaphoric equivalence between now and then, between ritual and origins, also bore traces of a politics of nostalgia.

Without sharing Eliade's nostalgia for the sacred, many anthropological theorists of religious time have based their analyses on distinguishing between two different kinds of time.[9] In his analysis of time reckoning among the Nuer, E. E. Evans-Pritchard distinguished between natural ecological time and social structural time.[10] Claude Lévi-Strauss opposed statistical or historical time to mechanical or structural time.[11] Clifford Geertz contrasted quantitative time to the qualitative time cycles he observed in Bali, where "they don't tell you what time it is. They tell you what kind of time it is."[12] Maurice Bloch distinguished between "durational" time and the "static" or "cyclic" time derived from ritual.[13] In a significant theoretical intervention in these dualisms, Edmund Leach argued that two kinds of time—the irreversible processes of aging, entropy, and death; and the repetition observed in rain falling, clocks ticking, rhythmic drumming, and the recurrence of days, months, and seasons— are brought together under the same term, *time*, only because of religion.[14] By turning irreversible processes into regularities, religious ritual produces not only sacred time but also the very notion of time that has been inherited in the West.

Temporal regularities include the simultaneous, the sequential, and the hierarchical.[15]

First, simultaneous regularities are produced by everyone doing the same thing at the same time. Whether the activity is prayer, meditation, chanting, listening, singing, drumming, or dancing, the synchronization of bodies in time creates a sense of presence in the present. Simultaneity depends upon rhythm and repetition, moving in time, but its coordinated timing evokes a sense of timelessness by staying on the beat.

Second, sequential regularities are produced by moving through prescribed stages in a liturgical ordering of time, attending to each stage, step by step, in a temporal progression. A single ritual, a series of rituals, or a large ritual cycle can create sequential regularity. Paying attention to each stage in the sequence, enacting the ritual choreography in its proper timing, duration, and transitions, officiants and participants enact not only a temporal sequence but also a connection with previous enactments. In the process, sequential regularities produce a link between present and past.

Third, hierarchical regularities are produced in many rituals by marking transitions between lower and higher status. A recurring feature of religion, rites of passage mark transitions in the life cycle—birth, adulthood, marriage, and death—as a production of time that mediates between past and future. Following the pattern identified by Arnold van Gennep, rites of passage enact a symbolic death, a liminal period of seclusion, and a symbolic rebirth, but they are also a hierarchical ordering of time.[16] Although the in-between, or liminal, stage of transition might be a time of uncertainty, the timing of the ritual process links an abandoned past with a better future.

All of these regularities, which can overlap and intersect in any ritual production of time, inevitably come under the jurisdiction of the owners of clocks and calendars, those instruments of temporal regulation.[17] Although many ancient societies developed methods of timekeeping, the clock in the West arose directly from religious ritual as an instrument for regulating the observance of monastic prayer.[18] For Roman Catholic monasteries in the European Middle Ages, the clock was a technique of religious regulation, timing the observance of a daily cycle of prayers to which monks or nuns were bound. Under the auspices of an ecclesiastical hierarchy, the monastic clock regulated a division of time into prayer, work, and leisure. As the historian E. P. Thompson argued in "Time, Work-Discipline, and Industrial Capitalism," this division of time became a division of labor in the rise of capitalism.[19] The owners of capital found that time is money, but workers were subjected to a temporal discipline in which all of their time was regulated by the clock.

Owners of calendars, as well, have been instrumental in regulating religious time.[20] Every calendar is authorized—the Julian calendar by an emperor, the Gregorian calendar by a pope—in order to regulate observance and obedience in time. The diversity of calendrical calculations, which might place this year in relation to the birth of Christ, the creation of the world, the *hijrah* of the Prophet, or the Mayan apocalypse, is never merely a matter of mathematics. By appropriating the religious production of time, with its simultaneous, sequential, and hierarchical regularities, political agents can regulate time and thereby entrench the regulation of people in time.

ANCESTRAL TIME

In religious time, continuity is crucial. Ritual enactments establish a sense of continuity. They generate sensory experiences and practical repertoires that can be retained in memory. Following Endel Tulving, we can distinguish between two kinds of memory, the episodic memory of distinct events, full of sensory content, and the schematic memory of basic patterns, recalling the way things usually happen.[21] While episodic memory might be intense, fleeting, or even lost, schematic memory is relatively stable. The anthropologist Harvey Whitehouse has drawn upon this analysis of memory in distinguishing between two types of rituals, those of high sensory intensity that are infrequently performed and those of low intensity that are frequently performed. Rituals of high intensity and low frequency, such as many rites of passage, tend to be retained in episodic memory; rituals of low intensity and high frequency, such as daily prayer or weekly liturgy, are held in schematic memory as general patterns.[22]

Schematic memory is essential for performing rituals for the dead. In Hindu *śrāddha* rituals, memory is activated not only by recalling episodes from the life of the deceased but also in following the sequential timing of prescribed ritual observances. According to one account, on the day after sacrificing the body through cremation the son of the deceased began a ritual sequence designed to form a new spiritual body by shaping a ball of cooked rice, a *piṇḍa*, which was treated with reverence as the temporary body of the deceased. Placed on an altar of dirt about half an inch high by a small lamp, the *piṇḍa* was honored with prayers, incense, flowers, and white threads symbolizing clothing. While offering prayers for the deceased, the son poured a mixture of water and sesame seeds from a clay cup over the rice ball, signifying the nourishment and strengthening of a new body for the deceased. For ten days this *piṇḍa* service, the *sapiṇḍīkaraṇa*, was repeated. Each day, however, the number of cups of sesame-seed water was increased, until on the tenth and final day of the sequence ten cups were poured over the rice ball. Although the process was interpreted as producing a new body for the deceased, creating the head on the first day, the neck and shoulders the second day, then the heart and chest, the back, the stomach, the thighs and bowels, the lower legs and skin, the knees and hair, the genitals, and finally on the tenth day the power of digestion, the sequential regularity of the ritual also produced a temporal continuity between present and past.

During the ten days after death, the deceased lingered in an interim state as a ghost *(preta)* who had not yet become an ancestor *(pitṛ)*. On the eleventh and final day of the ritual, sequential timing culminated in a hierarchical transition from ghost to ancestor. In that final ceremony, attended by priests representing ancestors, the son laid out rice balls representing the lineage of the deceased's father, grandfather, and great-grandfather. Reciting prayers, the son performing the ritual cut the rice ball representing the deceased into three portions and blended each into the rice balls of the ancestors. Calling on each by name, the son invited the deceased to join his ancestors. Finally, as all rice balls were blended into one, the ritual marked the integration of the deceased as a revered ancestor in heaven.[23] Replicating the Hindu lunar calendar's tenth-month gestation period for human birth, the ten-day ritual sequence turned death into rebirth, culminating in a hierarchical transition from an abandoned past to an ancestral future.

In Zulu tradition in South Africa, ancestral time was also produced out of ritual sequencing and transformation. The great Zulu dramatist H. I. E. Dhlomo compared the indigenous Zulu ritual of death to the sequencing of a five-act play. "In this great ceremony," he observed, "there are five divisions or five 'acts': Death, Burial, Mourning, Ihlambo (Cleansing), and Ukubuyisa (the bringing back of the spirit of the deceased)."[24] In this "great, tragic performance," ritual timing involved simultaneity in sharing temporal regularities of silence, wailing, humming, fasting, sharing in a sacrifice, and refraining from work, while the entire sequence extended over one year between death and *ukubuyisa*, the final bringing back of the deceased as an ancestor in the household. The beginning of the sequence was marked by reversals of conventional behavior, such as walking backward when carrying the corpse, wearing clothing inside out, using the left hand, and adopting a special language in which "no" means "yes" and "yes" means "no," which signaled a disruption of the conventional structure of ordinary time. As in the Hindu *śrāddha* ritual, the deceased lingered in an interim status, suspended in time, until the ritual sequence culminated in the final integration of the deceased into the generations of ancestors. The Zulu ritual of *ukubuyisa*, a festive occasion of sacrifice, feasting, and celebration, marked the presence of the ancestor in the ongoing life of a household. Ultimately, therefore, ancestral time links the past with an unbroken continuity, unbroken by death, which extends into the future.

In ancestral ritual, time is regulated by clocks and calendars, by hours, days, months, and years, but time is also produced as dynamic relations between past, present, and future. The primary medium of timekeeping in ancestral ritual is food—preparing, cooking, and eating food. Ritual recipes take time and make time. While *śrāddha* rituals marked sacred time by the preparation of rice balls and the pouring of sesame water, Zulu rituals of death marked sacred time by the eating of sacrificial meat and drinking of sanctified beer. In ongoing relations with an ancestral spirit, food is essential. The ritualized feeding of the ancestor is the crucial link between generations in many religious traditions. In this regard, the end of a funeral cycle can mark the beginning of an ongoing commitment to nourishing and sustaining ancestors through the ritual timing of offering and sharing food, suggesting that religion is often more like cooking than like philosophy.

MYTHIC TIME

Mythic time is narrative time, the temporal ordering of sacred stories about universal creation and destruction, human origin and destiny, and dramatic disruption and redemption. These powerful narratives produce a sense of continuity that is different than the continuity entailed by the ritual observances of ancestral time. While memory establishes continuity in ancestral time, mythic time is ruled by forensics, by legal accountability and moral responsibility, by acts and their consequences. As the temporal subtext of myth, a forensic dimension runs like a unifying thread through religious stories about time.

The Hindu conception of time related in the ancient *Laws of Manu* moves from infinitesimally small units—the twinklings of an eye that make a second, the seconds that make a minute, the minutes that make an hour, and the hours that make a cycle of day and night—to extraordinarily vast ages, the *yugas*, that are the day and night of Brahma. Encompassing a time span of 4,320,000 human years, the four *yugas* mark a sequence of degeneration from the golden Krita age to the current Kali age of iron, in which the human condition has worsened dramatically. When the current age ends in destruction, the creative process begins again, as Manu observed, because "the creations and destructions (of the world are) numberless; sporting [or playing], as it were, Brahman repeats this again and again."[25]

The forensic subtext in this mythic time is karma, the consequences of past actions, which bind a person, as the same person, to the cycle of birth, death, and rebirth through eternity. Shared by Hindus, Buddhists, Jains, and others, this understanding of temporal continuity does not depend upon the cognitive capacity of memory; it is fashioned out of a forensic link between past actions, present consequences, and future prospects. Liberation from the cycle of rebirth, from the eternity of creations and destructions, promises timelessness. In the meantime, however, temporal continuity is measured by the enduring karmic law governing acts and consequences.[26]

A Christian conception of the temporal duration of the world, drawn from biblical tradition, encompasses a comparatively brief timespan, extending perhaps less than six thousand years, following Augustine of Hippo, from the original creation of the world to its final destruction in the apocalypse.[27] Although Christian mythic time is often regarded as linear, directional, and even historical, it can also be circular, based on a single temporal cycle of fall and redemption. Here the forensic thread linking past, present, and future in a temporal continuity is sin, which, like karma, measures time by connecting actions with consequences. Even if sin is not

inherited unconsciously as original sin, human acts, desires, and dispositions are embedded in a mythic time that extends from origin to eventual
redemption or damnation. In this understanding of time, which is generally shared by Christians, Jews, and Muslims, mythic time is again driven
by forensic continuity.

In counterpoint to temporal continuity, mythic time also deals with
dramatic ruptures in time.

First, myth can focus on a rupture in the past. In the beginning, according to a Nuer myth, God gave cattle to the good human being, Nuer, but
the cattle was stolen by the wicked human being, Dinka. This original
theft, which disrupted the divine order instituted by God in the beginning,
justified Nuer warriors in raiding cattle from the neighboring Dinka people. In the moral economy of mythic time, cattle-raiding was not stealing
but restoring. For their part, the Dinka told the same story, except with
the roles reversed.[28] Focusing on a rupture in the past, mythic time can
provide a warrant for actions in the present.

Second, myth can focus on a rupture in the present. Under colonial
conditions in South Africa during the 1860s, the Zulu Christian convert
Mpengula Mbande related the "account which black men give white men
of their origin."[29] According to this creation myth, black men emerged
first from the *uhlanga*, the place of the origin of all nations, coming out,
however, with only a few things. They emerged with some cattle, corn,
spears, and picks for digging the earth. Arrogantly, with their few possessions, the black men thought that they possessed all things. When the
white men emerged, however, they came out with ox-drawn wagons bearing abundant goods and able to traverse great distances. By displaying this
new, unexpected use for cattle, the whites demonstrated a superior wisdom that had been drawn from the *uhlanga*. In relation to the power and
possessions of white men, black men recognized that they were defense-
less. The wisdom, wealth, and virtue that whites had drawn from the
uhlanga were sufficient to overpower the black people, who reflected
among themselves, as Mbande reported, that "these men who can do such
things, it is not proper that we should think of contending with them, as,
if because their works conquer us, they would conquer us by weapons."[30]
In this mythic account, Mpengula Mbande recorded an indigenous religious rationale for submission to the colonial government and its Christian

mission. Obviously, this myth was not an ancient Zulu cosmogony. It was a critical reflection on the contemporary Zulu colonial situation.

Third, myth can focus on a rupture in the future. Millenarian myths, anticipating an imminent, dramatic, and collective redemption, are recurring features of mythic time. In the Eastern Cape of South Africa during 1856, a millenarian movement arose on the basis of the prophecy of a young woman, Nongqawuse, that the ancestors were returning. Against the background of decades of British colonial warfare, this prophecy was a promise of future redemption, a vision of an ancestral return that would drive away the white invaders and restore land, cattle, and prosperity to the people. Mediated by her uncle, Mhlakaza, who had spent time with the Christian mission, and adopted by the Xhosa chief Sarhili, Nongqawuse's visionary promise came at a price: all surviving cattle that had not been taken by the British or lost to an epidemic of lungsickness had to be killed to open the way for the return of the ancestors. In this millennial ritual of destruction, the majority of Xhosa homesteads responded to the prophecy by sacrificing their cattle and destroying their crops. An estimated four hundred thousand head of cattle were sacrificed in expectation of the imminent return of the ancestors. In the failure of the prophecy, which brought death, indentured labor, and the destruction of any political independence for the Xhosa, many observers labeled the Xhosa cattle-killing as national suicide or suicidal millennialism.[31] However, with its focus on temporal rupture in the immediate future, this millenarian movement can also be seen as an attempt, perhaps a desperate attempt, to restore a just order in the moral accounting of mythic time.

RELIGIOUS TIMING

Ritual practices and mythic narratives generate religious time, but religious timing is also crucial in other spheres of human activity, such as politics, economics, and aesthetics.

First, in the politics of religious time, political power can be legitimated by privileged claims on origins, whether those claims are certified through ancestral or mythic time. Like the Nuer myth that asserted an original ownership of cattle, religious timing can be engaged in underwriting claims on territory, resources, and people. Originality, in these assertions of power, is inevitably contested. Although the Christian convert Mpengula Mbande developed a mythic rationale for the political subordination of the Zulu, the participants in the Xhosa millenarian movement anticipated an imminent return of their ancestors that would restore their original political sovereignty. In the politics of religious time, beginnings and endings are negotiated in the present, an expanded present that embraces memories of an origin and anticipations of a future. Since those memories and anticipations are multiple, conflict arises over who can establish claims on being there first and being there in the end.

Second, in the economy of religious time, temporality is measured by money, debt, and credit. Although the science of economics defines money as a unit of accounting, a store of value, and a medium of exchange, money is also a system of symbols that generates profound moods and motivations and cloaks those dynamics of desire and agency in an aura of factuality to make them seem uniquely real.[32] Money is time—the timing of debt and its repayment, credit and its duration, interest and its multiplication of value. In an economy of religious time, the term for "sin" can be derived from debt, the term for "merit" can be derived from credit, and the accumulation of interest can be transformed from the sin of usury to the virtue of capital investment. While the term *redemption* is derived from the process of paying a debt, millenarian movements generally anticipate the destruction of the prevailing system of accounting.[33] Religious time, therefore, can be embedded in a religious economy.

Finally, the aesthetics of religious time cultivates the embodied, sensory engagement with the lights and colors, the bells and music, the incense, flavors, and rhythms of time. Not only regulated by clocks and calendars, religious time is mediated by the senses, drawing personal subjectivity into the temporal regularities of a social collectivity. Although the discipline of the senses in focusing attention is crucial for religious timing, the derangement of the senses through synesthesia, trance states, or spirit possession can create a sense of timelessness in productions of religious time.

Religious time, therefore, is not only or merely religious. With its regularities and regulations, its ancestral and mythic constructions of continuity, religious time is also the aesthetics, economics, and politics of time.

5 Incongruity

Religion, according to the great psychologist of religion William James, "signifies always a *serious* state of mind." As a serious mentality, religion "says 'hush' to all vain chatter and smart wit"; it is "hostile to light irony." Emotionally, as James observed, "there must be something solemn, serious, and tender about any attitude which we denominate religious. If glad, it must not grin or snicker; if sad, it must not scream or curse. It is precisely as being *solemn* experiences that I wish to interest you in religious experiences." Clarifying his definition of religion as a response to whatever human beings might regard as divine, James insisted that the "divine shall mean for us only such a primal reality as the individual feels impelled to respond to solemnly and gravely, and neither by a curse nor a jest."[1]

Humor, of course, appears in religious and every other human activity, especially evident in cursing and jesting, confronting and celebrating irony, and laughing in, through, and at contradictions.[2] The great scholar of religion and humorist Ninian Smart was attentive to the dynamics of laughter in the study of religion, observing, for example, that religion deals with paradoxes. However, "if paradoxes were all intended to point to the inexpressible, they could be of any sort (like 'Ultimate reality is both a tomato and a banana')."[3] Laughter is also a recurring feature of intercultural relations. In South Africa during the 1780s, for example, when the French traveler François Le Vaillant read an account of Khoisan customs to a group of Khoisan people, the traveler recounted, "They openly laughed in my face."[4] What does laughter signify for the study of religion?

CONTACT

On the front lines of intercultural encounter, nineteenth-century Protestant missionaries in South Africa were often confronted with African laughter. For example, Robert Moffat, representative of the London Missionary Society among Tswana-speaking people, found that laughter represented a serious challenge to the claims of his mission. On one occasion, Moffat recounted, a Tswana chief gathered together thirty men to tell them what the missionary had said about religion. While the missionary had taken an indigenous Tswana term for mysterious power, Morimo, as the name for the Christian God, he had insisted that Tswana ancestral spirits, their *barimo*, were actually demons. After recounting Moffat's gospel of God and demons, sin and salvation, the chief asked his people: "Did you ever hear *litlamane* (fables) like these?" That question "was followed by a burst of deafening laughter," Moffat recalled, "and on its partially subsiding, the chief man begged me to say no more on such trifles, lest the people should think me mad!"[5] Therefore, Tswana-speaking people apparently compared the missionary's curious appropriation of their religious vocabulary to a kind of madness. By manipulating their cultural symbols, he had produced a crazy joke.

Moffat's religious claims were often met with laughter. When he related his "fables" to the chief of the Ndebele, Moffat noticed that Chief Mzilikazi thought he was joking. "He would stare at me," Moffat recalled, "to see if I maintained my gravity."[6] Apparently, the chief was waiting for Moffat to join in the laughter. Like his religious discourse, Moffat's interventions in African gender relations, division of labor, and hygiene also produced laughter. When he told a group of Tswana women that they should convince their husbands to do the agricultural work, an arrangement that would have violated their gendered division of labor, Moffat found that his suggestion "set them all into a roar of laughter."[7] Moffat's insistence that people should wash their bodies with soap and water, instead of lubricating them with animal fat and red ochre, "contributed to their amusement in no small degree." On one occasion, Moffat told his Tswana cook to turn the meat on the fire with a stick or fork instead of his greasy hands. "This suggestion made him and his companions laugh extravagantly," Moffat recalled, "and they were wont to repeat it as an interesting joke wherever they came."[8] Although Moffat also repeated this joke by publishing it, he took no delight in the interplay of its humor. In the midst of African laughter, the missionary managed to maintain his gravity.

Along with other missionaries in South Africa, Robert Moffat seemed to have been particularly sensitive about Africans laughing at the strange religious notions and unconventional social initiatives introduced by the Christian mission. In his frequent complaints about this practice, Moffat interpreted African laughter as evidence of an ignorant, stubborn resistance to his Christian gospel. Out of inveterate ignorance and intractable opposition, he concluded, Africans ridiculed the mission with the sound of their laughter. However, Moffat was not only worried about the laughter of Africans. He also looked back over his shoulder at those scoffers in Europe who have "laughed to scorn every article of our creed, and have died martyrs to atheism!"[9] Clearly, the missionary displayed a strong apprehension about being mocked by laughter. As a result, perhaps, he could only experience laughter as mockery.

Certainly, instances of mockery occurred. In some cases, Africans engaged in humorous mimicry of the mission, imitating its practices for comic effect. James Chapman observed that people in one Tswana town used to "laugh at Livingstone telling them about God, mimic him preaching and singing," and that "the chief and his councillors fill the air with shouts and yells."[10] During his mission to the Ndebele of Chief Mzilikazi, John Mackenzie learned "that the chief, after we left his presence, proceeded, amid the merriment of his attendants, to draw a ludicrous picture of the state of Matabele [Ndebele] society were the Christian views adopted."[11] In these cases, the mimicry of the mission was an occasion for humorous reflection on difference. At the very least, such jokes, mimes, and satires suggested that the comparison of different religious ways of life could be fun.

The missionaries, however, followed a much more serious agenda. In the face of African laughter, they could draw some consolation from contemplating the ultimate revenge that would be enacted on anyone who laughed at their religion and culture. When the missionary Thomas Hodgson warned the Tswana chief Sefunelo that God would punish people who presumed that they could affect the rains through ritual acts, Sefunelo responded with laughter. "He laughed," Hodgson reported, "at the idea of the Almighty being angry with him for attempting such a presumptuous act." The African chief might respond with laughter, but the missionary anticipated that in the end he would have the last laugh, as Hodgson informed Chief Sefunelo "that he would see things in a different light when he died."[12] Obviously, therefore, from the Christian missionary perspective, comparative religion was no laughing matter.

Only rarely did a European observer suspect that laughter was evidence of comparative religion. At the beginning of the nineteenth century, the traveler Henry Lichtenstein reported that the Tswana people were always in a good mood, laughing easily and loudly at anything that surprised them, especially if they wanted to show their appreciation. As Lichtenstein observed, the missionaries were distressed by African laughter. He noted that the missionaries "maintained that they could achieve nothing because the Beetjuanas ridiculed divine service and laughed about the teachings of Christianity." However, instead of interpreting this laughter as a symptom of stubborn resistance or inveterate ignorance, Lichtenstein proposed that people laughed because they were comparing Christianity to their own beliefs. If that was the case, their laughter indicated that Africans might after all hold "a kind of religious conviction."[13]

In raising this possibility, Lichtenstein suggested that laughter might be understood as evidence of an African practice of comparison. In the juxtaposition of different beliefs and practices on the frontier, laughter might be a reflex that registered the existence of a kind of comparative religion. Although Moffat interpreted this laughter as ignorant and stubborn resistance to his gospel, it might be better understood as the expression of a basic comparative observation. Laughter suggested that Africans recognized that the missionary's religious and social interventions involved crazy, illegitimate transpositions of the fundamental symbolic categories of their culture. In the play of difference, people smiled. In the recognition of incongruity, they laughed and shouted at the absurdity. Since intercultural relations required people to reflect upon alternative realities, some of the alternatives provoked laughter. Humor played a critical, reflective role in intercultural contact. From the sudden peal of mirth to the satirical mimicry, African comparativists advanced critical responses to the intercultural encounter of different religions. Amid the widespread confusion of cultural categories, laughter attended the comparison of different religious beliefs, practices, and forms of social organization on South African frontiers. This way of interpreting laughter, as an index of comparison, has been one of the lost opportunities of comparative religion.

HUMANS, ANIMALS, AND MACHINES

The human being, according to the classic formulation, is the only animal that laughs. But why do human beings laugh? Theories of laughter have tended to provide either physiological or social answers to this question. As an example of the first approach, Herbert Spencer explained laughter as a biological mechanism for the discharge of surplus nervous energy.[14] As an example of the second, the French philosopher Henri Bergson argued that laughter was a significant feature of social relations. In his book-length analysis of laughter, Bergson proposed that people laugh when they observe human beings behaving like machines. The fundamental basis of laughter, he argued, is the sudden, surprising perception of incongruity that occurs whenever human beings are observed acting with the inflexibility or absentmindedness of a mechanical object. In this analysis, Bergson located the source of humor in the contradiction that arises whenever humans behave in unconscious, automatic, or inflexible ways like machines.[15]

We can find direct evidence of this phenomenon on South African frontiers. For example, the London Missionary Society agent John Campbell complained in 1815 that Tswana boys and girls followed him, asked him questions, and laughed at him as he continued walking without answering. "I was grieved I could not understand a single word," Campbell recalled, "but this very circumstance afforded them much entertainment."[16] In this case, the children laughed at the missionary because he failed to enter into the human interchange of communication. This failure registered not only as antisocial but also as mechanical. Inflexibly and absentmindedly, therefore, the missionary provoked laugher by acting like a machine.

However, the identification of European Christians with machines was actually an important feature of Tswana reflections on religious difference. As Moffat recalled, the Tswana *ngaka,* that "wily rainmaker," inspired the delight and applause of the people by relating an alternative to the missionary's fables about Morimo and the creation of human beings. According to this "rainmaker," the Supreme Being who made humans first produced the "Bushmen" but did not like them, because they were so ugly and their speech sounded like frogs. So the Creator then made the "Hottentots," but did not like them any better than the "Bushmen." Using all his knowledge and skill, the Creator next made the "Bechuanas," the Tswana-speaking people that he found to be a great improvement but still not the end of creation. Finally, the Supreme Being produced white people and sent them out into the world with ox-drawn wagons and ox-drawn plows. Moffat perceived this story as a countermyth, a direct challenge to his own account, because he expressed disgust that the "wily rainmaker's" story "received the applause of the people, while the poor missionary's arguments, drawn from the source of Divine truth, were thrown into the shade."[17] Like the "wily serpent" in the Garden of Eden, the Tswana rainmaker, according to Moffat, had transposed "Divine truth" to serve "Satanic" ends.

In the Northern Cape, however, such appropriations and transpositions of religious elements defined the local practice of an intercultural comparative religion. In counteracting the missionary's fables, the Tswana sacred specialist adapted an indigenous emergence myth to the conditions of the colonial frontier situation. In the beginning, according to that myth, all human beings had emerged from a hole in the ground with their distinctive sacred animal emblems. Sacred animals defined a system of allegiances, cutting across chiefdoms, which bound people together under the sign of a common object of communal reverence, honor, and praise. The term for praise, *seboko* (pl. *liboko*), was often used for the sacred animal. Or the animal was called *seano* (pl. *diano*) to indicate a sacred object of reverence. To have a sacred animal was to dance *(go bina)* that animal. At the same time, the object of reverence was also guarded by avoidances, particularly by the prohibitions of people under a particular *seboko* from killing or eating their sacred animal. European observers tried to document this system of animal praise and avoidance. According to one account, the Bakuena had the crocodile *(kuena)*; the Bataung, the lion *(taung)*; the Batloung, the elephant *(tlou)*; the Batsueneng, the baboon *(tsuene)*; the Batlokoa, the wild cat *(quabi)*; the Bapedi, the porcupine *(noka)*; and so on.[18] Bushmen in the region apparently developed their own sacred animal, the goat, as a focus for ritual attention and communal identity.[19] In these terms, therefore, human beings were identified by their sacred animal emblems.

In thinking about intercultural relations of difference in the colonial situation, the system of sacred animals posed a problem for the Tswana. Here was a network of differences, distinguishing people on the basis of animal emblems, that seemed to have no counterpart in the Christian mission. African comparativists must have asked: If the Bakuena *bina* the crocodile, and the Bushmen *bina* the goat, what do the European Christians *bina?* One solution to this problem in comparative religion on the northern frontier was posed by the Tswana *ngaka* recorded by Robert Moffat. In his creative improvisation on a traditional origin myth, Moffat's adversary suggested that the white people had emerged from the hole in the ground, like other human beings, with their particular sacred animal. In the beginning, they came out of the hole with the ox-drawn wagon or the ox-drawn plow. According to the "wily rainmaker," therefore, the sacred animal of Europeans was the wagon or plow. Clearly, Robert Moffat regarded the plow as a sacred emblem. He was fond of declaring that Africa would be regenerated by two sacred objects, the Bible and the plow.[20] The ox-drawn wagon could also be regarded as a European sacred animal. As many Africans recalled, their first impression upon seeing an ox-wagon was that it comprised a single, composite animal.[21] In the emergence myth told by the Tswana *ngaka*, that animal was represented as a sacred emblem of Europeans. In the beginning, Europeans had emerged from the hole in the ground under the sacred sign of a mechanical device, the wagon or the plow. They were, accordingly, the people of the machine.

In the interplay of intercultural relations, therefore, Europeans provoked laughter because they behaved in ways that were as inflexible and automatic as any machine. Although they might be powerful and dangerous, Europeans were also funny because they did not act like human beings. Africans noticed. They laughed. In the sound of their laughter, significant questions about what it might mean to be a human being were put into play in the practice of frontier comparative religion.

JOKES, MYTHS, AND RITUALS

These basic classifications—humans, animals, and machines—generated considerable confusion in the intercultural relations of nineteenth-century South African frontiers. But they also provoked laughter. Both confusion and laughter were confrontations with incongruity. As many theorists of humor have held, laughter depends upon a perception of incongruity. In the eighteenth century, James Beattie proposed that humor involves "the union of two or more inconsistent, unsuitable, or incongruous parts or circumstances . . . united in one complex object."[22] During the twentieth century, James Kern Feibleman held that humor arises from the incongruity between a perfect, ideal order and the actual disorderly state of the world; John M. Willmann argued that humor expresses "the union of two ideas which involve some sort of contradiction or incongruity"; and Jerry M. Suls proposed that "humour derives from experiencing a sudden incongruity that is then made congruous."[23] In frontier relations, incongruity, from different perspectives, was constantly being encountered. In many respects, incongruity was the defining feature of intercultural relations on South African frontiers. If incongruity generates humor, it should not be surprising that people laughed.

More can be said, however, about frontier laughter. On psychoanalytic and linguistic grounds, Sigmund Freud's researches into the dynamics of laughter are suggestive. In his 1905 study *Jokes and Their Relation to the Unconscious,* Freud based his psychoanalytic theory of humor on incongruity, but with a particular poetic twist, since he reduced humor, in effect, to the tropes of metaphor and metonymy. He did so by arguing that laughter was induced by two kinds of incongruity, the effects of metaphoric condensation, in which two ideas are fused into a single word, phrase, or act, and metonymic displacement, in which emphasis is displaced from one idea to another, from the expected to the unexpected, from the relevant to the irrelevant, or from the normal to the abnormal.[24] Certainly, condensation and displacement operated in the intercultural relations of the frontier. For the most part, Moffat's fables, as well as his interventions in local culture, must have registered as unexpected displacements from the normal. In the creation myth of the "wily rainmaker," however, we find both condensation and displacement at work. On the one hand, ox-drawn wagons or plows were condensed into a single composite animal that could stand as a sacred animal emblem, like the crocodile, lion, elephant, hyena, or goat, that had emerged from the hole in the ground during the original creation of all human beings. On the other hand, the essential identity of Europeans was displaced onto their machines when their sacred animal, the defining emblem of their identity, was revealed to be a mechanical object. Therefore, by redeploying a traditional creation myth in the colonial situation, the Tswana *ngaka* had produced a complex and revealing joke.

At this point, however, we must admit that the dividing line between jokes and myths is unclear. This distinction is blurred, not only because the "wily rainmaker" devised a mythic joke, but also, more profoundly, because the basic structures of both jokes and myths necessarily involve incongruity. Obviously, both rely upon metaphoric condensation and metonymic displacement for rhetorical effects. But sacred narratives, like jokes, also juxtapose an ideal or perfect order with the actual disorderly state of the world. From a structural perspective, as the anthropologist Edmund Leach argued, any ordered system of classification, when violated, can produce laughter.[25] Myth also confronts order with its violation. Historian of religions Jonathan Z. Smith has shown how myths, particularly in colonial situations, can be media for dealing with incongruity. For example, the myth of Hainuwele, which circulated widely throughout Melanesia, relates the story of a young woman who excreted valuable manufactured goods from her anus—new symbols of wealth, coming from a strange place. According to Smith, this story served as a template for thinking about the economic, social, and political contradictions of the colonial situation. In this case, Smith has argued, myth was, among other things, a way of "working with this incongruity."[26] As a product of situational incongruity, therefore, myth provided a kind of narrative resolution. But did it also provoke laughter? Was the Hainuwele myth, like the story of the "wily rainmaker," met with the "applause of the people" because it, too, was perceived as funny?

Along with myth, we might also consider religious ritual as a way of dealing with incongruity. Staying with the work of Jonathan Z. Smith, we find a theory of ritual that is also based on situational incongruity. As Smith has argued, "Ritual gains force where incongruency is perceived and thought about." In his central example, Siberian bear sacrifice, Smith has shown how that specific ritual provided a practical resolution for the "incongruity between the hunters' ideological statements of how they *ought* to hunt and their actual behavior while hunting."[27] The dissonance between ethical obligation and actual behavior, therefore, could be harmonized through the annual ritual enactment of a perfect hunt. In that sacrificial ritual, incongruity could be resolved. But did the participants laugh? Was laughter provoked by this ritual occasion for perceiving and thinking about incongruity in human affairs?

In South Africa, ritualized relationships based on laughter have received a special designation in anthropological literature as "joking relationships." Identified by A. R. Radcliffe-Brown in 1940, joking relationships are structured social interactions in which the humor of satire, ridicule, and verbal abuse is required but not taken literally. Rather, it seals the closeness of relationships. In such cases, as Radcliffe-Brown put it, joking fuses the "pretense of hostility and real friendliness."[28] Mixing condensation and displacement, therefore, a joking relationship acts out mock hostility in the interest of a real alliance. In the structured relations between mother's brother and sister's son, or, if we follow Andrew Apter's analysis of Swazi royal ritual, between subjects and king, this joking relationship can provide a ritualized means for dealing with the incongruities of closeness and distance in interpersonal, social, or political relations.[29]

However, the missionaries, as we have seen, insisted upon a "no-joking relationship." Maintaining their gravity, they saw nothing funny in the situational incongruity produced by intercultural relations in South Africa. Rather than entering into a ritualized joking relationship, they repressed laughter, only allowing it to mark a sign or symptom of ignorant and stubborn resistance to Christian civilization. In this interpretation, the missionaries enforced a particular reading of the human body. As anthropologists Jean and John Comaroff have argued, the civilizing mission of the nineteenth century was directed not only at the soul but also at the body. The conversion of the body, through European clothing, productive labor, new gender relations, hygiene, and other embodied disciplines, defined a range of practical interventions by the Christian mission in African life.[30] In the context of these new restraints on the body, laughter registered as an undisciplined bodily eruption, a body language that was the opposite of rational speech.

As Norbert Elias has documented in his classic work *The Civilizing Process*, civility in western Europe came to be constituted by a repertoire of specific controls over the body.[31] Targeting relatively uncontrolled bodily eruptions such as sneezing, coughing, nose blowing, farting, urinating, and defecating, a civilized discipline of the body required their meticulously rationalized management and control. Those "elite" standards of civility were mobilized against what Mikhail Bakhtin called the European popular culture of laughter.[32] The carnivalesque features of that culture of laughter, with its bawdy and often rude deportment of the body, were countered by a rational discipline of the body. In the process, body discipline revealed not only civility but also the presence of reason, a rationality that could be demonstrated only in and through the civilized deportment of the body. As agents of the "civilizing process" in South Africa, the missionaries interpreted African laughter as an uncontrolled bodily eruption. As such, laughter, like other "uncivilized" embodied behavior, signaled an absence of rationality. Laughter was the opposite of reason.

LAUGHTER, PAIN, AND THE STUDY OF RELIGION

The academic study of religion has inherited this humorless legacy. By the early twentieth century, this linkage between laughter, "uncivilized" behavior, and irrationality defined the very notion of "primitive mentality." While Bergson's philosophical analysis of laughter was being serialized in the *Revue de Paris,* his compatriot the anthropologist and philosopher Lucien Lévy-Bruhl was pursuing research that culminated in 1910 in the publication of his first book on "primitive mentality," *Les Fonctions mentales dans les sociétés inférieures.* Analyzing "how natives think," Lévy-Bruhl proposed that "primitive" people "do not seem to us to rise to the level of what we properly term 'thought.'"³³ Instead, they displayed a "pre-logical" or "mystical" mentality. Although he collected evidence from all over the world, Lévy-Bruhl made considerable use of South African data in building his model of "primitive mentality." In the process, Lévy-Bruhl reinscribed the reports of nineteenth-century travelers, missionaries, and other colonial agents into his scientific theory of primitive religion and thought. For example, as proof of the existence of a "prelogical" mentality in Africa, Lévy-Bruhl repeated the assertion by London Missionary Society official John Philip that South Africans lived in a complete "state of ignorance."³⁴ By the term *ignorance*, of course, Philip only meant to indicate that the indigenous people of South Africa resisted conversion to Christianity. In the hands of Lévy-Bruhl, however, this missionary invective was transformed into a finding of social science.

According to Lévy-Bruhl, African ignorance was demonstrated by their propensity for laughter. In arguing that Africans, like other "primitives," were incapable of abstract thought, Lévy-Bruhl invoked the testimony of the missionary Thomas Arbousset. "In the midst of the laughter and applause of the populace," Arbousset had reported, "the heathen inquirer is heard saying: 'Can the God of the white men be seen by our eyes? . . . and if *Morimo* (God) is absolutely invisible, how can a reasonable being worship a hidden thing?'"³⁵ Certainly, the laughter in this case could be subjected to various interpretations. Was it inspired by a shared percep-tion of incongruity in the context of an interreligious argument? Was it a reasonable response to the perceived irrationality of the mission? Was it a psychological defense against the encroachments of a Christian mission that was confusing and was disrupting indigenous cultural categories? Or was it simply a popular response to a playful joke at the expense of the missionary? Taking sides with the missionary, however, Lévy-Bruhl froze African laughter by concluding that it was only evidence of a "lack of seri-ous thought and an absence of reflection."³⁶ Instead of recognizing laugh-ter as a significant comparative impulse, and therefore as an act of rational reflection on cultural and religious difference, Lévy-Bruhl perpetuated the seriousness of the missionaries. Like Robert Moffat, he maintained his intellectual gravity by refusing to hear any rationality in the sound of African laughter. Ironically, therefore, while Henri Bergson was arguing that people laugh at human beings who act like absentminded machines,

Lucien Lévy-Bruhl insisted that "primitives" laugh only because they are themselves essentially absentminded.

However, Africans did not only laugh; they also experienced pain in their encounters with Europeans. Lévy-Bruhl cited a report by the naturalist William J. Burchell about his African companion, stating that "abstract questions of the plainest kind soon exhausted all mental strength and reduced him to the state of a child whose reason was yet dormant. He would then complain that his head began to ache."[37] Similarly, as Lévy-Bruhl noted, the missionary and ethnographer Henri-Alexandre Junod recounted that abstract thought caused pain among Africans. "When requiring reasoning," Junod observed, "it is a painful occupation."[38] In citing and repeating these claims by travelers and missionaries, Lévy-Bruhl concluded that "primitives" avoided thinking because it was painful. Although encounters with Europeans actually caused real pain and suffering for Africans, Lévy-Bruhl used their pain as evidence of an absence of rational thought. Pain provided further proof that Africans did not rise to the level of rationality. By their laughter and pain, therefore, Africans were incorporated in the academic study of religion.

"Perhaps I know best why it is man alone who laughs," Nietzsche asserted. "He alone suffers so deeply that he had to invent laughter."[39] As Ninian Smart has proposed, suffering lies at the heart of religious reflection on the human condition, from the Buddha to the Christ, "who were both keenly aware of suffering."[40] Out of the depths of human suffering, whether that suffering is located in sin or desire, whether it is constituted by existential anxiety or colonial oppression, laughter inevitably surfaces. Of course, this strange linkage of suffering and laughter presents us with a paradox. How can the pain of suffering produce the pleasure of laughter? In Ninian Smart's terms, however, the juxtaposition of suffering and laughter is a revelatory paradox, a contradiction that apparently stops thought but actually stimulates new insights into the nature of reality.[41] In this respect, the paradoxical union of suffering and laughter captures something important about the way in which religion operates. Certainly, religion can transform suffering into laughter. But laughter, as we have seen, can also pose a problem for religion, especially if it registers as the unspoken sign of an absence of rationality. But what if laughter were also a way of thinking? Like religious symbols, myths, and rituals, laughter might provide resources for confronting, mediating, and thinking through incongruity.

For the future of the study of religion, this paradox of suffering and laughter is crucial. If Nietzsche and Ninian Smart are right, we cannot have one without the other, since both laughter and pain define what it is to be human within the human project, the human product, or the human problem that we call religion. As a humanistic discipline, the study of religion can nurture empathy for the diversity of religious configurations of human suffering. But it also can cultivate a critical analysis of the conditions and contradictions under which pain and laughter arise. As students of laughter have found, any joke confronts us with multiple possibilities by highlighting the incongruity between different ways of being in the world. Often, the joke confronts us with an incongruous juxtaposition between a normative and an alternative pattern of conduct. According to Mary Douglas, "The joke affords opportunity for realizing that an accepted pattern has no necessity. Its excitement lies in the suggestion that any particular ordering of experience may be arbitrary. It is frivolous in that it produces no real alternative, only an exhilarating sense of freedom from form in general."[42] In this sense, the academic study of religion is a joke. It is an occasion for exploring alternative possibilities for being human in the world. Instead of imposing a necessary form, the study of religion produces an exhilarating sense of freedom in the play of possibilities.

However, as a critical discipline, the study of religion also investigates the conditions of possibility under which pain becomes laughter and laughter becomes pain. Some of those conditions have become so familiar—colonial oppression, racist domination, class struggle, and gender discrimination—that they seem to define the character and composition of the modern world. However, as Ninian Smart observed in the late 1950s, we need to constantly confront the familiar features of this modern ideological landscape with alternative possibilities because "familiarity banishes surprise."[43] In the study of religion, as in other human and social sciences, theory is the intellectual instrument of surprise. In all of his work, Ninian Smart has encouraged us to cultivate this capacity for surprise. By making the strange familiar and the familiar strange, he has stimulated surprising insights into the play of possibilities in the human enterprise of religion. However, the laughter that arises from that playful engagement with possibilities must also be connected to the pain that is suffered by human beings who live under impossible conditions. Laughter can arise from an engagement with multiple worlds, but pain, as Elaine Scarry has argued, can entail the collapse of worlds as human reason, discourse, and possibility dissolve under the searing, excruciating effects of the body in pain.[44] Poised between laughter and pain as a science of incongruity, the academic study of religion studies the making and unmaking of worlds.

PART II   Formations

In the specific sense that the term is used here, *formations* signifies configurations of power in which religious symbols, discourses, practices, and institutions emerge. Not merely contexts, formations exercise forces, compelling and repelling forces, centripetal and centrifugal forces, that draw people inside and push people outside of a religious domain. Operating within material cultures and cultural economies, religious formations are complex assemblies of meaning and power. After examining general features of culture and economy in religious formations, chapters in this section explore religious formations within modern colonialism, imperialism, and apartheid.

Chapter 6 engages material culture in the study of religion. Referring to bodies, objects, and places, material culture in religion is the sacred vitality of things. Living extensions of the human body can become sacred, while inanimate objects can become lively. Rejecting the division between spirit and matter, soul and body, recent research on religion and material culture has attended to the senses, embodied practices, meaningful objects, built environments, and the material possibilities and constraints of technology, with special attention to the communication technology of media. As an entry into the study of religion and material culture, this chapter focuses on the relic and the icon as material objects in religious practice; on the fetish in the Atlantic World and the cargo in the Pacific World as focal points for conflicts over the meaning, power, and value of objects; and on the material conditions of religious media, from the senses to audiovisual media, which in their materiality create different capacities and constraints for religion.

Chapter 7 explores possibilities for locating religious formations at the intersections of culture and economy. Not solely the preserve of professional economists, *economy* is a term that has expanded in scope to include economies of signs and desires that generate values beyond the pricing mechanisms of the modern capitalist market. To illustrate how religion can be situated in a cultural economy, this chapter focuses on animated cartoons that might be regarded as sacred texts of the modern religion of the market, valorizing conformity but also promising redemption. One animated film, *Destination Earth* (1956), sponsored by the American Petroleum Institute, illustrates a political economy of the sacred in which the oppression of communist collectivism is opposed to the freedom promised by American free-market capitalism. The sacred secret at the center of this promise of redemption is revealed to be oil. Viewing this film provides an occasion for highlighting three features of the political economy of the sacred: mediations between economic and sacred values; mediations between economic scarcity and sacred surplus; and mediations among competing claims to legitimate ownership of the sacred.

Chapter 8 situates religious formations in the contact zones and power relations of colonial situations. Referring to the settlement of a distant territory by foreigners, colonialism entails the use of military force and political power to create and maintain a situation in which colonizers gain economic benefits by exploiting trade, raw materials, and the labor of indigenous people. For the study of religion, colonialism calls attention to the role of religion in intercultural contact; the force of religion in the conquest and control of indigenous populations; and the changing character of religious subjectivity and agency, especially in relation to the inherent violence of colonialism. These issues are examined by relying primarily on the analysis of anticolonial theorists and activists, such as Mohandas K. Gandhi, Frantz Fanon, and Eduardo Mondlane. While colonialism has played an important role in the history of religions, it has also shaped the study of religion to the extent that colonial situations have contributed to the emergence of the modern categories of religion and religions.

Chapter 9 extends the analysis of religious formations in colonial situations. As critical research on religion, the study of imperialism and religion directs attention to religious creativity within the asymmetrical power relations of contact zones, intercultural relations, and diasporic circulations. Starting with the imperial ceremony of the 2012 London Olympics, which featured a pageant of the imperial myth of progress from savagery to civilization, this chapter recalls how the Shakespearean drama of the imperial Prospero and the colonized Caliban has been a template for analyzing religion under colonial conditions. Like Shakespeare's enchanted isle, colonizing and colonized religion have been shaped by oceans, with the Mediterranean, Atlantic, Indian, and Pacific worlds emerging as crucial units of analysis. By attending to imperial and colonial formations, this chapter indicates some of the important landmarks, sea changes, and possibilities in the study of imperialism and religion.

Chapter 10 suggests that *apartheid*, a term meaning "separation"— which was operative in South Africa between 1948 and 1994 as a force of exclusion and incorporation, excluding people from citizenship and exploiting people as labor—was formative for certain ways of thinking about religion. One of the architects of apartheid, the anthropologist W. M. Eiselen, was a leading expert on indigenous religions in South Africa. Eiselen's writings on African religion illustrate three overlapping types of comparative religion—a frontier comparative religion based on denial and containment; an imperial comparative religion assuming evolutionary progress from savagery to civilization; and an apartheid comparative religion creating and reinforcing boundaries to keep people apart. Although apartheid was formally established as a racist policy of separation in South Africa, the making and maintaining of boundaries has been a recurring feature of religious formations.

By locating religion within cultural, economic, and political formations, these chapters identify forces animating religion, not in any simple relation of cause and effect, but in complex configurations of discourses and power relations. Shaping subjectivities and collectivities, religious formations give substance to the material dynamics of religion.

6 Culture

In the study of religion, *material culture* refers to the stuff of religion, the bodies, objects, and places of religious life that are animated through practices of sensory engagement, economic exchange, and technological mediation. Material culture is the cultural activity of things. Human beings engage things in many ways, not only by finding, making, using, exchanging, consuming, and destroying them, but also by thinking about them, interacting with them, and ritually attending to them in religious ways. In recent research on religion and material culture, an earlier division between spirit and matter, soul and body, has been rejected. Research has been redirected by interests in embodied religion, with attention to the senses, gender, sexuality, life, and death, as embodied religion intersects with material religion, the solidity, opacity, animation, biographies, and social lives of material objects.

The study of religion and material culture might be defined against the background of a religious materialism, going back to the German philosopher Ludwig Feuerbach, who argued that human consciousness is not an independent spiritual essence, aloof from the material world of objects. Against any idealist rendering of humanity, Feuerbach argued that human beings were constituted by their reciprocal engagements with material objects. "Man is nothing without an object," Feuerbach asserted, "but the object to which a subject essentially, necessarily relates, is nothing else than this subject's own, but objective, nature."[1] This formulation of humanity raised two risks, reification and alienation. By reifying objects, as if they were more real than human beings, humans sacrificed their humanity to their own projections, including the supreme projection of a God, reified in the image of a human being. By mistaking projections for reality, human beings suffered alienation from their own material ground of being.

Without reducing religion to reification and alienation, historians of religions have found materiality a productive source of religious creativity. While Mircea Eliade found matter at the origin of religion, as human beings engaged with the solidity of stone, the fluidity of water, and the expanse of sky, Charles H. Long has directed attention to the materiality of signification, focusing on the materiality of signs, their material transmission, and the modes of human imagination, orientation, and formation that have directly engaged materiality.[2] The imagination of matter, as Long has argued, is not confined to an original primordial ontology or defined by an enduring poetic phenomenology. Rather, the imagination of matter can be historically situated in the contacts, relations, and exchanges of the colonial era, at work and at stake within colonial situations that provided the material terms for significations of meaning and power. In the intercultural encounters of colonial situations, arguments arose about the value of objects, the spirit of matter, the social life of things, the cultural promiscuity of things, the intractable materiality of the fetish, and the secret of the cargo, all shadowed by the circulation of the commodity, eventually operating in what has been called the global religion of the market.

Mediation has emerged as a central concept in the study of religion and material culture. Religion has been recognized as a human activity that does not merely use media but is a process of mediation in which relations among the human, the less than human, and the more than human are materially transacted. In the science of mediology established by the French Marxist Régis Debray, which is dedicated to the disciplined investigation of culture, communication, and media, religion registers in gestures of symbolic efficacy that are required by the material organization of any collectivity. Identifying symbolic efficacy as "religious materialism," Debray argued that mediology investigated not the meaning but the power of signs, the "becoming-material" forces of symbolic forms. Taking mediation as his subject, Debray focused on the materiality of signs and technologies of signification. Basically, Debray argued that material organization is necessary for the organization of matter in any transmission of culture. Attention to the materiality of material culture raises these questions: How do signs produce effects? How does saying or showing become doing? In the science of mediology, these are questions of both material and religious importance. Observing that Marx's problem was that he had not studied the history of religions, Debray developed a materialist analysis of symbolic efficacy that holds implications for the study of religion as material culture.[3] From a variety of disciplinary perspectives, many other researchers have attended to material mediations of religion. Since 2005, the journal *Material Religion: The Journal of Objects, Art, and Belief* has been at the forefront of charting new theoretical developments in the study of religion, media, and material culture.[4]

MATERIAL OBJECTS: RELICS AND ICONS

Relics, the physical remains of holy persons, act as powerful objects in many religious traditions. Whether defined as the remnant (from the Latin, *relinquere*) or the essential ingredient (from the Sanskrit, *dhatu*), relics have not been regarded as dead matter, parts of corpses, but as animate objects, living presences, endowed with life. In Buddhist practice, the allure of relics has resided in the perceived presence of sacred power within them instead of their capacity to symbolically represent holy persons.[5] For Roman Catholicism during the European Middle Ages, constructing a church as the meeting place between the living and the dead required the physical remains of saints. Since they acted as patrons, protectors, and intercessors between the material and spiritual worlds, the saints had to be present in a church. In fact, their bones had to be located within the most sacred center of the church, the altar, in order for the building itself to be sanctified. Not only necessary for sanctifying an altar, relics were also used for swearing oaths, for rituals of healing, and for religious devotions that brought pilgrims from great distances to be in the presence of a holy patron.

As this practice was followed throughout Europe, churches and monasteries embarked on a quest for relics, developing new methods for acquiring the physical remains of saints. Certainly, relics might be simply discovered, as the empress Helena had found relics in fourth-century Jerusalem, but this method became extremely rare in medieval Europe. As the European demand for relics increased, a class of professional relic merchants emerged to serve the expanding international trade in the bodies of saints. Relic salesmen acted as middlemen in sacred exchanges between Rome and the rest of Europe. Although relic merchants assured their customers that the bones they were purchasing were genuine, the question of authenticity was ultimately settled in practical terms. If the bones worked miracles, inspired the faithful, attracted pilgrims, secured funds from donors, and added prestige to the community, then they had to be regarded as authentic relics. Better than buying relics, however, was stealing them. By stealing the body of a saint, a community could be assured not only of the authenticity of the relic but also of the blessing of the saint, since saints would certainly not allow their bodies to be moved without their spiritual approval. The bones of Saint Benedict, for example, were stolen from his monastery, Monte Cassino, in Italy and taken to the Fleury monastery on the Loire River in France. To certify their claim on the spiritual power of Saint Benedict, the monks of Fleury told elaborate stories about stealing the bones, with the implicit permission of the saint, and transferring them to France, where they subsequently conveyed their miraculous power. Throughout medieval Europe, similar accounts of stealing relics, known as *translationes*, certified local claims on the bodies of saints and martyrs.[6] As living material objects, relics played significant roles in mythic narratives of the origin of a community; in regular rituals of display, procession, and celebration; and in attracting pilgrims to be in the presence of the physical remains of a holy person.

Like the relic, in many religious traditions, visual images, or icons, have often been perceived as imbued with sacred power that is presentational rather than representational, a power engaged not only by the gaze but also by kissing, touching, and carrying them in rituals of procession. By the sixth century, icons had assumed an important role in the religious practices of Eastern Orthodox Christianity. In general terms, holy images were used for education, veneration, and protection. Although icons were often characterized as if they were a visual scripture, the Bible of the illiterate, their pedagogical role was superseded by their status as sacred objects effectively conveying the spiritual power of holy persons. Although great value was placed on the accuracy of a representation, an icon was more than a mere likeness; it was a presence. Through ritual acts of veneration—bowing, kneeling, and kissing the image—devotees could gain access to the spiritual power present in the image. By such acts of veneration, Christians entered into ritual exchanges with Jesus, Mary, and the saints, the heavenly "prototypes" of the material images. As they came to be widely used in personal devotion, church liturgy, public processions, and even in defending a city against invaders, icons emerged as crucial intercessors between heaven and earth.

During the eighth century, however, the Orthodox Church entered a period of crisis regarding the image. Known as the iconoclastic controversy, this crisis called into question the legitimacy of venerating icons. To a certain extent, this controversy was waged in the broader context of an interreligious argument about images among Jews, Muslims, and Christians. Generally, Jews and Muslims rejected the use of visual images in their own religious worship. Although their criticisms of Christian practice were taken seriously, the iconoclastic controversy was primarily an internal argument among Christians who agreed on regarding Jesus Christ as divine. According to the defenders of icons—the "icon lovers," known as iconophiles—the merger of spiritual and material in these holy images corresponded directly to the merger of divinity and humanity in the incarnation of Christ. However, the opponents of images, who became known as iconoclasts, were convinced that icons had drawn Christians into violating the biblical commandment prohibiting the worship of any "graven image" (Exodus 20:4). Not only idolatrous, the veneration of icons was useless, because these images were inanimate objects. In place of the holy images, iconoclasts directed Christian attention to the text of the Bible, the bread and wine of the Eucharist, and the triumphalist sign of the True Cross. Only these objects, they argued, could be regarded as bearing the spiritual power of Christ.[7] The iconoclastic controversy, therefore, was an argument about the material location of the sacred.

MATERIAL RELATIONS: FETISH AND CARGO

As the mediation of sacred presence in material forms, religious material culture also engages objects in motion, since objects circulate in a variety of transactions with religious significance. Such transactions bear multiple meanings. A sacrificial offering, for example, might be understood as a gift, a communal meal, an act of sanctification, or a rule-governed manipulation of objects. In all these respects, material objects in motion are central actors in the meaning of the ritual.

During the modern era of colonization, imperialism, and globalization, two religious objects have been particularly important for the study of religion and material culture: the fetish in the Atlantic world and the cargo in the Pacific world. As research on the history of the fetish has shown, the term emerged in West Africa during the fifteenth century within intercultural trading zones.[8] In these mercantile trading networks, Portuguese, Dutch, and English traders in West Africa dealt with African Christians, Muslims, and "fetishists," who, according to the European observers, had no religion at all. From this European Christian perspective, fetishists, allegedly lacking any trace of religion, had no stable system of value to assess material objects. Without religion, African fetishists were supposedly unable to evaluate objects. They overvalued trifling objects—a bird's feather, a pebble, a piece of cloth, a dog's leg—by treating them as fetishes for ritual attention, but they undervalued trade goods, showing a lack of interest in acquiring what European traders were interested in selling. Fetishism, therefore, emerged in the fifteenth century as a European mercantile theory not of the origin but of the absence of religion. In the context of incommensurable values in these intercultural trading relations, Europeans developed the stereotype of "fetishism" to characterize Africans who had no religion to organize the necessary relations of meaning, power, and value between human beings and material objects and thereby to organize relations among human beings in the exchange of objects. The discourse of fetishism, which cast Africans as incapable of properly valuing objects, could also be deployed to turn Africans themselves into objects, rendering them as suitable commodities for the slave trade. As the discourse of fetishism has been turned back on the West through Marxist critiques of commodity fetishism or Freudian analysis of sexual fetishism, the fetish has endured as an argument over the meaning, power, and value of objects.

In the Pacific world, the cargo has played a similar role in arguments over the material culture of religion. As Melanesian islanders developed complex beliefs and practices in relation to the material goods brought by white merchants, missionaries, and colonial administrators, the cargo emerged as a new location for negotiating meaning, power, and value. The history of cargo movements illustrates different religious strategies in relation to the material goods brought by European explorers, colonizers, and missionaries. Engaging Christian myth, ritual, and institutions, cargo movements emerged that reconfigured indigenous religious resources to make sense out of the new world of material goods. In some cases, people embraced the Christian church as the road to the cargo. The Christian gospel of the cargo, however, turned out to be a great disappointment. Many Christian converts in Melanesia were convinced that white men hid the secret of the cargo. They say, "Work for it," but you do not get it. They say, "Pray for it," but you do not get it." With the failure of wage labor and religious ritual to deliver the cargo, the only remaining way to get it was to steal it. According to many cargo myths, the secret of the cargo was the truth of theft: long ago, whites had secured the cargo by mistake—in effect, by stealing it—from its original producers and rightful owners, the deities and ancestors of the island people. In the colonial situation, therefore, the secret of the cargo revealed that private property was theft. The cargo millennium promised to redress that act of original theft by restoring material goods to their rightful owners.[9] Like the fetish, the cargo has been turned back on the West. Critiques of the spiritual materialism of the global market have rendered the market as a religion, as a millenarian capitalism expecting material wealth to mysteriously appear from extraordinary sources. This mystery of the market resembles the religious material culture of cargo movements.

MATERIAL MEDIATIONS: SENSES AND MEDIA

As the primary media in the material culture of religion, the senses have received considerable attention in recent research that focuses on what Marx called "sensuous human activity" in religious practice. In practices of seeing and being seen, sight has been studied in religious visual culture, the sensory embrace of images, and the variety of religious ways of looking. The sense of hearing, which has also been studied in terms of practice, focusing on religious practices of listening, which in many religious traditions cultivate a disciplined ethics of listening, has inspired research on religious soundscapes as an important feature of the material culture of religion. While the fragrance of sanctity, the stench of sin, and the taste of salvation employ sensory metaphors, smell and taste are important aspects of religious practices, especially if we regard religion as more like cooking than like philosophy. Finally, focusing on the sense of touch, some researchers have argued that tactility is the most important religious sense, the most integrative sense, incorporating the entire corporeal field of the body in pleasure and pain, in handling and manipulating objects, and in the kinesthetic motion of all religious activity. Often, religious media are synesthetic, engaging many senses simultaneously, creating an intense, unified, and perhaps even transcendent sensorium, while some religious media narrow the perceptual field to one dominant sense, such as the sense of hearing in practices of listening to sermons or maintaining silence. In any case, attention to the senses shifts emphasis from the design and function of material objects to embodied experience in the material culture of religion.

Mediating physical environments feature prominently in the material culture of religion, whether the natural environments of deserts, rivers, or mountains or the built environments of religious architecture. In places of religious gathering, such as churches, mosques, temples, or synagogues, religion is materialized in wood and stone, iron and glass, but also in the directing of religious attention, the staging of religious performance, and the alignment of individuals with a collectivity.[10] In its design, religious architecture can contain in material microcosm an entire religious world. For indigenous religion in South Africa, the cattle enclosure was a sacred place, the site for sacrificial offerings to ancestral spirits, but it was also the material embodiment of a religious worldview that depended upon ongoing material transactions between humans, domesticated animals, and ancestors. These transactions built up the homestead as a human place but also protected the homestead against antihuman forces associated with the wild space of the forest or the desert that harbored dangerous wild animals and wild spirits. Entering the cattle enclosure, therefore, was to enter this world of spiritual and material relations. Likewise, a temple can materially embody the meeting point between heaven and earth, a cathedral can provide entry into the cross of Christ, and a mosque can direct religious devotion toward Mecca. These ideal patterns, however, are not simply revealed in religious architecture; they are intensively interpreted, regularly ritualized, and inevitably contested by competing claims on their ownership. Interpretation and ritualization are obviously required for sacralizing a place; contestations among competing interests are often overlooked. Material culture, therefore, also entails the mediation of conflicts over ownership and access, inclusion and exclusion, within the built environments of religion.

Crucial to the transmission of religion, communication media have been thoroughly material in the history of religions. Against the background of face-to-face oral communication, Régis Debray has charted the shifts from writing to printed texts to audiovisual media as comprehensive reorientations in the materiality of religious communication.[11] First, in the *logosphere* of writing, techniques were developed—pictographic, ideographic, and phonetic—to create material traces of words. Writing on stone, whether a pyramid, a stela, or a stupa, necessarily fixed those traces in a specific location. The sheer weight of their material grounding signaled a locative orientation to the religious significance of that place or an assertion of religiopolitical authority over that place. By contrast, collecting the material traces of words on papyrus and, later, vellum or parchment signaled a greater degree of religious mobility, supporting a utopian orientation in which sacred words were portable, capable of being carried to places far beyond their material point of origin. However, despite this increased mobility, the materiality of written texts still placed limits on their circulation. Parchment, for example, was extremely expensive, made from the hides of sheep, goats, or calves. Writers on parchment had to calculate the number of animals required for each text. As a result, writing and reading was the preserve of people in specified religious roles who drew their textual authority from the material and organizational base that was created to sustain this costly technology.

Second, initiating the *graphosphere* of the printed text, the sixteenth-century Guttenberg revolution in movable metallic type radically altered the material conditions for the circulation of words. As this technology increased the accessibility of the written word, religious reformers embraced the printing press as a divine intervention. Celebrating the printing press as God's latest and greatest gift, the Protestant reformer Martin Luther sacralized a communication technology as a divine instrument for transmitting "true religion" to all nations of the earth. Certainly, his printed words circulated widely, but the material technology of printing also led to unanticipated consequences of skeptical scholarship and secular publics organized around printed publications. Nevertheless, the technology of printing provided a new material base for individual engagements with religion.

Finally, the *videosphere*, animated by audiovisual media, has dramatically increased the pace and scope of the circulation of religious signs. While some critics, following Walter Benjamin, have argued that mechanical reproduction deprives these signs of their "aura," their sacred significance that was previously grounded in a specific religious architecture or ritual practice, others have recognized the proliferation of sacred significance in photographs, radio, films, television, and the Internet. Nevertheless, these media also place material constraints on religion. Religious broadcasts on television can engage the eyes and ears, displaying spectacle, proclaiming words, and performing music, but they cannot convey the fragrance of incense, the taste of holy food, or the embrace of congregants. Furthermore, like the expense of parchment, the cost of broadcasting exerts material constraints on audiovisual media, which has coincided with the emergence of a new spirituality of money that not only promises prosperity to viewers but also advances a new religious devotion to fund-raising for religious broadcasting. In all of these spheres of communication, therefore, spirituality has been thoroughly infused with materiality.

7 Economy

Modern economists, who claim specialized expertise in the scientific study of the capitalist economy, have no privileged role in defining or deploying the keyword *economy* in the study of religion. They certainly have expertise in establishing generally accepted principles of accounting, in calculating profit and loss in a balance sheet, in assessing risk and reward in unstable markets, and in charting economic trends in global financial markets that are usually overtaken by unforeseen, surprising events. In the study of religion, rational choice theory, based on the premise that people act to maximize profit and minimize loss, has drawn on the expertise of modern economists.[1] But the very notion of economy has a much broader scope in cultural studies and religious studies.

Within cultural studies, economy has been integrated into a wider field of practices that are simultaneously material and symbolic. In his *Outline of a Theory of Practice*, the influential French sociologist Pierre Bourdieu insisted that we must "abandon the dichotomy of the economic and the non-economic," because the conventional assumption that the economy can be distinguished from its wider field of symbolic, material, and social relations "stands in the way of seeing the science of economic practices as a particular case of a general science of the economy of practices."

Dissolving this dichotomy promised radical results. Modern economic science, with its laws of supply and demand, financial interest, exchange value, market competition, and so on, could be recast as a particular set of symbolic practices in a social field. Social practices, including religion, the arts, and media, could be recast as "economic practices directed towards the maximization of material or symbolic profit."[2] This notion of symbolic profit, which could be produced by symbolic labor and realized as symbolic capital, effectively integrated economic practices into the entire field of meaningful cultural productions.

At the same time, cultural practices, including the practices of cultural media for the storage, transmission, and reception of information, could be incorporated within this expanded understanding of economy. Meaning-making enterprises, such as religion and media, emerged as economic practices of production, circulation, and consumption. Although modern economic theories, such as rational choice theory, might seek to explain the proliferation of cultural meanings within a conventional economic framework, the cultural meanings of *economy* have dramatically expanded within recent cultural theory to such an extent that they cannot be so easily contained.

Religion, mediating the transcendent and the sacred, ostensibly situated beyond or apart from these economic considerations, is intimately embedded in the symbolic and material economy of media, culture, and social relations. Although institutionalized as a separate domain in modern social arrangements, *religion* is a keyword, or focusing lens, for directing our attention to productions, circulations, and contestations of transcendent claims and sacralizing practices that operate within any network of social relations. For the study of media and culture, this broader understanding of religion is crucial. It allows us to explore not only the ways in which religion, organized within distinct religious institutions, relates to media but also the ways in which religion, as mythic traces of transcendence, ritualized practices of sacralization, and orientations in sacred time and space, might permeate or animate a cultural field. This broader but also rigorously theorized understanding of religion, which recognizes religion as mediation and media as incorporating discursive and ritualized practices of religion, fits the broader understanding of *economy* that has emerged in cultural analysis.

Pierre Bourdieu wanted to develop a "political economy of religion" that would advance "the full potential of the materialist analysis of religion without destroying the properly symbolic character of the phenomenon."[3] The study of religion, materiality, and media, however, necessarily requires us to attend to the dynamics of symbolic and material mediations within an economy that I call the political economy of the sacred.

EXPANDING ECONOMY

In academic analysis and ordinary language, the keyword *economy* continues on its long history of expansion to incorporate and encompass more and more of human life. In Greco-Roman antiquity, the term had a relatively narrow focus, referring to the management of a household. During the eighteenth century, however, with the rise of modern states, the term was redeployed to refer to the management of resources and the accumulation of wealth within a larger collectivity that Adam Smith called "the great body of the people." Economy, in this sense, was political economy, the power relations within which a society "arranges to allocate scarce resources with a view toward satisfying certain needs and not others."[4] Within this expanding scope, the political economy of capitalism could be described as a system for the production, distribution, exchange, and consumption of wealth through the management of scarce resources and potentially unlimited needs. However, this political economy could also be subjected to critique, most notably by Marx and Engels, as a system of alienation that appropriated labor value as a surplus for satisfying the needs of a privileged social class.

Both of these approaches to political economy, the descriptive and the critical, differ from the modern science of economics, which bases its calculations on the notion of abstract individuals who are motivated by a desire for goods that are regulated by the pricing mechanisms of the market.[5] However, these modern understandings of the economy, whether they focused on political order, contending social classes, or atomized individuals in a free market, all participated in what Max Weber identified as the modern differentiation of specialized social institutions. As a result, the economy could be regarded as a separate domain that certainly affected any network of social relations but was in principle independent of other spheres of human activity such as religion or aesthetics.

During the twentieth century, critical theorists of political economy challenged any privileging of the economic as a separate sphere. In a variety of critical interventions, accounts of economy were developed that embraced basically aesthetic categories of display and reciprocity in a gift economy,[6] of excess, extravagance, and sacrificial loss in a general economy,[7] of desire in a libidinal economy,[8] and of representation, circulation, and interpretation in a symbolic economy.[9] In a dramatic and influential reevaluation of economy, Jean Baudrillard's political economy of the sign proposed that late capitalism was essentially a signifying practice, circulating signs, rather than primarily a mode for producing material goods.[10] As sociologists Scott Lash and John Urry argued, "What is increasingly being produced are not material objects, but signs."[11] Economy, therefore, was increasingly being recast as an economy of meaning.

In this expanding economy, which embraced aesthetics, desire, and imagination as an economy of signification, the aesthetics of cultural media, in all of its various forms, could also be rendered as an economy of production, circulation, and consumption. On the production side, during the 1930s the critical theorist Theodor Adorno called attention to the "culture industry," the machinery of mass cultural production in a capitalist economy.[12] As cultural production becomes an industry, the artwork is transformed into a commodity that is created and exchanged for profit. In the process, all cultural productions bear what Adorno called "the stigmata of capitalism."[13] In this production-oriented model, popular culture serves the interests of capital—profitability, uniformity, and utility—by entangling people in a culture industry in which a character like "Donald Duck in the cartoons . . . gets his beating so that the viewers can get used to the same treatment."[14]

On the consumption side, the popular reception of cultural forms, styles, and content calls attention to the many different ways people actually find to make mass-produced culture their own. Following the critical theorist Walter Benjamin, many cultural analysts argue that the reception of popular culture involves not passive submission but creative activity. Recognizing the capitalist control of mass-produced culture, Benjamin nevertheless found that people develop new perceptual and interpretive capacities that enable them to transform private hopes and fears into "figures of collective dream, such as the globe-encircling Mickey Mouse."[15] Where Adorno insisted that the productions of the culture industry were oppressive, Benjamin looked for the therapeutic effects, such as the healing potential of collective laughter, and even the redemptive possibilities in the reception of popular culture. In the case of Mickey Mouse, for example, Benjamin suggested that audiences were able to think through basic cultural categories—machines, animals, and humans—by participating in a popular form of entertainment that scrambles them up. As Benjamin observed, Mickey Mouse cartoons are "full of miracles—miracles that not only surpass those of technology, but make fun of them." For an audience "grown weary of the endless complications of everyday living," Benjamin concluded, these "miracles" promise a kind of "redemption" in an extraordinary world.[16]

In between cultural production and consumption, the space of media and popular culture is a contested terrain. Popular culture is a landscape in which people occupy vastly different and often multiple subject positions, subjectivities grounded in race, ethnicity, social class, occupation, region, gender, sexual orientation, and so on. As the cultural theorist Stuart Hall has established, popular culture is a site of struggle in which various alternative cultural projects contend against the hegemony of the dominant culture. While subcultures develop oppositional positions, perhaps even methods of "cultural resistance," social elites work to appropriate and assimilate the creativity of alternative cultural formations within the larger society. Not a stable system of production and consumption, popular culture is a battlefield of contending strategies, tactics, and maneuvers in struggles over the legitimate ownership of highly charged cultural symbols of meaning and power.[17]

These struggles over interpreting and appropriating highly charged, perhaps even sacred, symbols look a lot like religion. In trying to understand the expanding economy, many analysts have found that religion has reentered the picture, not merely in relation to economic activity, such as the "elective affinity" Max Weber traced between Calvinism and the rise of capitalism, but also in the inherently religious character of capitalism.[18] From Walter Benjamin's reflections in the late 1920s on "capitalism as religion" to recent debates about the "religion of the market," the expanding economy of capitalism has been engaged as if it were a religion, emerging in Europe, developing in North America, and now global.[19]

If the capitalist economy is a religion, its sacred texts, its canonical scriptures, might very well be discovered in animated cartoons. Both Adorno and Benjamin, for different reasons, found Disney cartoons revelatory in reinforcing capitalism's ethos of conformity and promise of redemption. Although all modern media are entangled in these cycles of production, consumption, and contestation, animation is a particularly plastic medium for testing and transcending limits, for taking a beating, like Donald Duck, but also for playing with transformations, like Mickey Mouse, in an alternative world that is "full of miracles." To illustrate these animations of the constraints of the culture industry and its miraculous promises of redemption, I focus here on one animated film, *Destination Earth*.

SECRET, SACRED

Destination Earth (1956) is a thirteen-minute animated cartoon, brilliantly illustrated by a team of creative animators, produced by John Sutherland, and financed by the American Petroleum Institute, in which Martians learn the secret of American power.[20] Opening with an expansive display of planets in outer space, with traces of a whizzing spacecraft, the film settles into a stadium, where the supreme Martian leader, Ogg the Exalted, announces that all Martians are "commanded—er, invited—to attend." Accordingly, the stadium, Ogg Memorial Stadium, in the city of Oggville, with its Oggmart, Ogg Café, and many other Ogg enterprises, is filled to capacity with subservient, obedient Martians cheering their "glorious leader, Ogg the Great," in response to prompters instructing them to cheer and applaud on cue. Surrounded by banners that herald the glorious Ogg as "friend, leader, crusader," the Great Ogg begins by thanking the people for their "unsolicited testimonial" to his greatness.

This gathering was convened to hear the report from a Martian who had recently returned from outer space. Ogg announces, "By special permission of the commander-in-chief—me—here is Mars's first space explorer, Colonel Cosmic." As the colonel explains to the crowd, he was sent into outer space by Ogg the Magnificent because the supreme Martian leader had become dissatisfied with the speed and efficiency of Ogg power, coerced slave labor, "which runs most of our industry." Particularly, the great Ogg was frustrated that his official limousine was too slow if drawn by slaves and too dangerous if propelled by explosives. Therefore, as Colonel Cosmic explains, he "ordered our first expedition into space to bring back the secret of how other planets got their state limousines to run smoothly."

Undertaking this interplanetary mission, Colonel Cosmic had headed for Earth, finding himself in "a country of Earth called the United States of America," where he was immediately astounded by all of the "Earthmobiles" driving around as if they were state limousines. These vehicles, he soon discovered, were fast, efficient, and owned by everyone. Searching out the secret of all this power, he went into a library, read a few books, and found that Earth's "code was remarkably easy to break."

Here was the secret: oil. Power was drawn from drilling oil, transporting oil, refining oil, and, through the "magic of research," transforming oil into a "whole galaxy of things" that made life in America better "than in any country on the whole planet."

But this secret would have remained locked deep under Earth's crust had it not been liberated by the key of free-market competition. As Colonel Cosmic discovered, the competition of entrepreneurs, taking risks, exploiting opportunities, and seeking competitive advantages against each other, necessarily turned scarce resources into surpluses. Market competition, he found, was not only the key to success in the oil industry but also in "almost every successful business enterprise in America."

In concluding his speech to the Martian rally in Ogg Memorial Stadium, Colonel Cosmic announces that his exploration of Earth had revealed that the "big secret is of course oil, which has brought a better life to all the people in the U.S.A. But the key to making oil work for everybody is competition." Over the Great Ogg's objection that competition was "downright un-Martian," the rally breaks up as Martians start rushing around drilling for oil under new signs such as "Martian Oil Explorers" and "Martian Oil Pioneers." Even the old Ogg Café is suddenly reopened, "under new management," as Joe's Café.

Against the background of this explosion of oil drilling and free enterprise all over Mars, the Martian dictator explodes, somehow easily blown up by a push of a button, as Colonel Cosmic says to the Great Ogg: "You are through." In the coda for the film, the colonel addresses a wider audience, extending from Mars to Earth, by drawing out the obvious moral of the story: "Yes, the real secret is not only a great source of energy but also the freedom to make it work for everybody. And if you have both of these things, any goal is possible. It's destination unlimited!" As the music expands and swells and the film displays this new banner—"Destination Unlimited!"—we learn again, in the rolling credits, that this beautifully animated and richly entertaining film was presented by the Oil Industry Information Committee of the American Petroleum Institute.

Nothing in this film, we might think, has anything to do with religion. We see no churches, mosques, temples, or synagogues. We hear no priests, imams, gurus, or rabbis. Therefore, this film is not religious, as religion is conventionally defined, as it is commonly understood as something located in specialized religious institutions, arbitrated by recognized religious leaders, and adhered to by religious followers. Based on such a conventional definition, the analysis of religion and media is straightforward. We look for media representations of religion and religious uses of media. However, as the historian of religions Jonathan Z. Smith has observed, such a conventional, commonsense definition of religion is circular: religious organizations, with their religious leaders and followers, are religious because they are engaged in religious activities.[21] So, we are left with the problem of thinking more carefully about what we want to mean by *religion*, for purposes of analysis, for our struggles in trying to understand the material and symbolic economy of religion, media, and popular culture.

If we define *religion*, following Emile Durkheim, as beliefs, practices, and social relations revolving around the sacred, that which is "set apart," we find that religion is set apart at the center of personal subjectivities and social formations.[22] In the context of the expanding economy, we can explore this definition of *religion* as a political economy of the sacred in order to understand the ways in which the sacred is produced, circulated, engaged, and consumed in media. Not merely given, "the sacred" is produced through the religious labor of interpretation and ritualization as both a poetics of meaning and a politics of power relations.

In exploring the political economy of the sacred, we need to identify the means, modes, and forces involved in the production of sacred values. In *Destination Earth*, these features of production were explicitly represented—industry run by Ogg power was contrasted with industry running on oil; communist collectivism was opposed to capitalist competition; and a Martian (or Marxist) totalitarian dictatorship was overthrown by the liberating spirit of American freedom. Since the late 1940s, producer John Sutherland had been animating these themes for early Cold War America. *Make Mine Freedom* (1948), for example, depicted a group of Americans rejecting the promises of a snake-oil salesman, Dr. Utopia, selling bottles of "Ism," because their capitalist system gave them the freedom for "working together to produce an ever-greater abundance of material and spiritual values for all."[23] In the conclusion to this film, Sutherland directly referred to the production of spiritual values, but the spirit of capitalism was also present as a transcendent force of production in other films by Sutherland Productions, such as *Going Places* (1948), *Meet King Joe* (1949), and *What Makes Us Tick* (1952). Clearly, capitalist competition was invoked in *Destination Earth* as a spiritual mode of production.

Of course, we must notice the role of material forces of production in these films. *Make Mine Freedom* was sponsored by a former chairman of General Motors, *Destination Earth* by the American Petroleum Institute, so the oil and auto industries were clearly driving these productions. But their instrumental and interested roles were mystified in these films by rendering capitalism not only as spirit but also as secret, a sacred secret at the heart of America. The capitalist production of material and spiritual values, *Make Mine Freedom* reveals, "is the secret of American prosperity." In *Destination Earth*, as we have seen, the entire storyline is premised on discovering, decoding, and deploying a secret. Colonel Cosmic was sent to "bring back the secret"; he found that the "code was remarkably easy to break"; and he concluded that "the real secret" was oil and competition, a source of energy and an economic system.

Secrecy plays an important role in the production of sacred values within any political economy of the sacred.[24] Even open, public secrets, such as those displayed in the films of John Sutherland, are important in generating the mystery that invests values with a sacred aura. Scarce resources, like oil, are heavily invested with secret, sacred meaning. But a secret, sacred aura attaches to all the commodities of the capitalist market. As Karl Marx observed, the political economy "converts every product into a social hieroglyphic," a secret code that might not always be so easy to break as "we try to decipher the hieroglyphic, to get behind the secret of our own social products." According to Marx, capitalism made deciphering the secret meaning of products difficult by transposing relations among human beings into mysterious relations among things, as if commodities, "abounding in metaphysical subtleties and theological niceties," were animated objects, with a life of their own, which enveloped human beings in an economy that resonated with the "misty world of religion."[25]

THE POLITICAL ECONOMY OF THE SACRED

As a counterpoint to modern economics, anthropological accounts of economic relations in small-scale, indigenous societies, formerly known as "primitive," have found systems of exchange based on the reciprocity of the gift, a ritualized regime of gift giving that entails sacred obligations rather than economic debts. Durkheim's colleague Marcel Mauss outlined this contrast between primitive and modern economies in his classic book *The Gift* (1924). As the anthropologist E. E. Evans-Pritchard observed, this investigation of alternative economic relations showed "how much we have lost, whatever we may have otherwise gained, by the substitution of a rational economic system for a system in which the exchange of goods was not a mechanical but a moral transaction, bringing about and maintaining human, personal, relationships between individuals and groups."[26] Although gift giving persists under capitalism, it is subsumed within an overarching economic rationality.

Entertainment media are poised between sacred gifts and economic calculations. In the animated world of *Destination Earth,* with its corporate sponsors and capitalist propaganda, the secret, sacred gift, oil, is celebrated as the ultimate standard of value. Oil is represented as a gift, as something that is just given, as a natural resource that is available everywhere for anyone and everyone. Although the film draws a stark opposition between the economic systems of totalitarian communism and free-market capitalism, *Destination Earth* actually represents a gift economy, an economy based on "moral transactions" of competition that promise to transform "relationships between individuals and groups" from oppressive conformity into liberating and unlimited freedom.

While invoking the moral, transformative, and even redemptive power of the gift, the entire range of media operating in a capitalist economy also celebrates the power of extravagant expenditure, which the Durkheimian theorist Georges Bataille identified as the heart of a general economy that was based not on production but on loss, on a sacrificial expenditure of material and human resources. For Bataille, the general economy of capitalism was ultimately about meaning, but meaning had to be underwritten by sacrificial acts of expenditure, with the loss as great as possible, in order to certify authenticity.[27]

Obviously, entertainment media thrive within this general economy of expenditure. Big-budget extravaganzas, exorbitant publicity, and transgressive superstars all participate. But this sacrificial economy, based on loss, also demands sacrificial victims. Underscoring this point, Georges Bataille proposed to revitalize the society and economy of France in the 1930s by officiating over a human sacrifice in Paris. Although he found a volunteer, Bataille was frustrated by the Parisian municipal authorities, who refused a permit for this sacrificial ritual. In nationalist rhetoric and popular media, however, this impetus of redemptive sacrifice is a common, recurring motif, with many heroic individuals, from Jesus to Bruce Willis, willingly sacrificing their own lives so that others might live. But the sacrificial victim does not have to be a willing victim. In *Destination Earth*, as we have seen, the dictator, Ogg, is killed, effortlessly but necessarily, in order to bring freedom to his people by liberating their oil.

In these mediations of the gift and the sacrifice, we find traces of religious economies that cannot be contained within rational economic calculations of self-interest and market exchange. The gift and the sacrifice evoke powerful and pervasive religious practices of receiving and giving. But these religious resources, with their deep histories, are not immune from commodification. Like art, poetry, music, and other creative human enterprises, religion operates within a productive economy. Official spokespersons for religion and other cultural productions might insist on their autonomy from market relations, but in a mediated world religion has no such pure place in which to stand.

Under the conditions of a capitalist economy, religion intersects with electronic media in producing the multiple mediations of a political economy of the sacred. Intending to be suggestive rather than exhaustive,

I point to some of the basic features of three mediations in this political economy—the mediations between economic and sacred values; the mediations between economic scarcity and sacred surplus; and the mediations among competing claims on the legitimate ownership of the sacred.

First, electronic media are engaged in symbolic labor by mediating between economic values and sacred values. As we have seen in *Destination Earth,* an animated film can celebrate an economic system as if it were a religious system of sacred or spiritual values for human flourishing and ultimately for human liberation. Clearly, many American films and television shows, even when they are not so blatantly designed as propaganda, can be read as reinforcing free-market capitalism as a sacred orientation.

Money, at the heart of this mediation between economic and sacred values, is itself a medium, a medium of exchange. Although it is also a store of value and a unit of accounting, money is a meaning-generating medium invested with a sacred aura. As a medium for religion and electronic media, money has been a nexus for transactions between economic and sacred values. Enthusiastically, the popular evangelist Reverend Ike, broadcasting on radio and television, proclaimed a gospel of money based on the principle that "the lack of money is the root of all evil." Cynically, the Church of the Profit$, appearing on the Internet, has claimed to be the only honest religious group in America because it openly admits that it is only in it for the money.[28]

In between these extreme cases, electronic media are inevitably involved in a cycle of symbolic labor mediating between contingent and changing economic relations and enduring values that must appear to be stable, unchanging, and perhaps even eternal. Assessing the production and consumption of values, the fetishism of commodities, which must also include commodified media productions, has often been cited as the engine that drives this apparent stability of values by transposing human relations into exchange relations among objects. But the very notion of the fetish, which arose in the intercultural and interreligious trading relations of fifteenth-century West Africa, was originally invoked by Europeans to signal the absence of any stable system of value for mediating exchange relations among people of different religions.[29] As the term developed in Europe

during the nineteenth century, it was turned back on the instability of values in the capitalist economy by Marx and the sexual economy by Freud,
signaling for both a gap within the reality of modernity.

Although Marx and Freud worked against religion, they identified an
economy of desire, alienated and perverse desire, perhaps, but with profound religious resonance. Every religious form of life has a logic of desire.
For example, the Christian economy outlined in Dante's *Divina Commedia*
was based on directing desire toward God and away from the world. The
Bardo Thödol of Tibetan Buddhism was based on eliminating desire. In
both cases, however, sin was defined as perverted desire.[30] Electronic
media, as multisensory, self-involving mediations of desire, are engaged in
a kind of religious work by mediating the gaps between contemporary
economic relations that are based on the manipulation of desire and the
desire for sacred values.

Second, electronic media are engaged in building symbolic capital by
mediating transformations of economic scarcity into sacred surplus. In
Destination Earth, the finite and nonrenewable geological resource of
petroleum is revealed as an infinitely available surplus. But scarcity can be
transformed into surplus only through the spirit of free-market capitalism. In that spirit of capitalism, a scarce resource becomes miraculously
transformed into a sacred abundance of unlimited wealth and power.

As anthropologists Jean and John Comaroff have observed, religious
life all over the world, struggling to adapt to globalizing capitalism, has
been drawn into "occult economies," economic beliefs and practices based
on the expectation of abundant wealth from mysterious sources.[31] During
the twentieth century, cargo movements in Melanesia, which developed
myths, rituals, and spiritual preparations for the miraculous arrival of
wealth, anticipated this development under conditions of colonial oppression. Now, in a global economy, where the locations of production are dispersed and the rituals of consumption seem to add value, many people
find themselves in a cargo situation.[32]

If cargo movements provide a precedent, we must recall that they went
through three basic stages as adherents attempted to access the sacred
surplus. First, when colonial administrators told indigenous people of the
islands to work for wealth, they worked but did not get it. Second, when

Christian missionaries told the people to pray for wealth, they prayed and did not get it. Although people sometimes found new ways to combine work and prayer by building piers, docks, and flagpoles and integrating indigenous and Christian ritual, the failure of work and prayer to produce the cargo left a third option: steal it.[33]

This truth of theft is a recurring theme in the history of religion and economy, from Prometheus stealing fire from the gods to the butter-thief Krishna, even if it has not necessarily been underwritten by the Marxist generalization that all private ownership of property is theft. Electronic media, however, with their immediacy, availability, and propensity for personal engagements, place the ownership of sacred surplus in question and at stake. A popular guidebook for screenwriters and filmmakers, *Stealing Fire from the Gods,* explicitly invokes the truth of sacred theft in its title.[34] But the problem of theft is more widespread and more profound in the economy of religion, media, and culture: Who owns the sacred surplus?

Third, electronic media are engaged in mediating conflicts over the legitimate ownership of the sacred. As we saw in *Destination Earth,* this question of legitimacy was easily, quickly resolved in favor of private ownership in a competitive environment. But this principle of legitimate ownership could be certified only by eliminating the central symbol of opposition, Ogg the Magnificent. An undercurrent of violence, therefore, runs through these mediated negotiations of legitimacy. However, the question of violence can also be easily, quickly resolved by distinguishing between us and them, by highlighting their illegitimate acts of violence, such as Ogg's tyrannical rule, coercive manipulation of public opinion, and exploitation of his people as slave labor, in order to draw a stark contrast between their violence and our judicious exercise of legitimate force in killing the tyrant, liberating the oil, and freeing the people to participate in a competitive economy based on private ownership.

Modern media, from news media to entertainment media, are actively engaged in these contestations over the legitimate ownership of sacred symbols. Drawing on the insight of literary theorist Kenneth Burke into the cultural process of the stealing back and forth of symbols, we can enter into the economy of religion, media, and culture as an ongoing contest over the stealing back and forth of sacred symbols.[35] Not only made meaningful through interpretation, sacred symbols are made powerful by ongoing acts of appropriation. But no appropriation goes uncontested. Therefore, the field of religion, media, and culture is contested terrain, a conflictual arena in which competing claims on the ownership of sacred symbols are asserted, adjudicated, and reasserted. Since no claim can be final, the struggle over the legitimate ownership of sacred symbols continues to be negotiated through religion, popular culture, and their intersections with media.

8 Colonialism

Drawn from the Latin word, *colonia,* for a farm or settlement established by Roman citizens in a distant territory, while the settlers retained their Roman citizenship, *colonialism* signifies contacts, relations, and exchanges between alien intruders and indigenous inhabitants of a place. For the study of religion, colonialism focuses our attention on critical problems of analysis—the dynamics of contact, the relations of force, and the processes of change—that arise not only in colonial situations but also at any intersection of religious meaning and political power.

Taking a long view, we can recognize a very long history of colonial settlements, a history perhaps as old as humanity itself, since according to the "out of Africa" hypothesis of human evolution *Homo sapiens* emerged from Africa to settle all over the world. As recent research has shown, their encounters with Neanderthals resulted in both exchange through trading and sexual relations and conflict through fighting, killing, and displacing these indigenous inhabitants of Europe. During what has been described as long-term genocide, *Homo sapiens* developed new forms of cultural knowledge and practice that were performed in relation to Neanderthals. Developing techniques for inducing trance states, which might be regarded as the origin of shamanism, humans also pioneered new forms of social organization, ritual practices, and cave art, which represented both their cognitive capacity and cultural superiority over indigenous people.[1] Colonialism, therefore, might have been instrumental in the evolution of religion, as *Homo sapiens* developed innovative cultural repertoires in the face of other species to signify their superiority and certify their claims on territory.

People have moved from place to place for what we might regard as religious reasons, either to change themselves through pilgrimage or to change other people by seeking converts through missionizing. Colonialism has borne traces of both religious motives, since colonizers have sought to transform themselves on pilgrimage—including the armed pilgrimage of crusade—to distant lands, and to change others in the missionary quest to convert indigenous people to conform to their alien religious identity, economic interests, and political allegiance. Although colonialism might have an ancient history, its modern forms have been the primary locus for research on religion and religions under colonial conditions. European colonization, beginning with the discovery of the New World at the end of the fifteenth century, proceeded under the auspices of Christian legitimacy, whether Catholic or Protestant, as Spain, Portugal, Britain, France, the Netherlands, and other European nations conquered and settled distant lands. As Americans, Africans, or Asians became colonized, European cities became imperial metropoles, establishing relations between imperial centers and colonized peripheries in global circulations of religion.

As an entry into how the term *colonialism* has been related to religion in the modern era, we will focus here on the work of anticolonial theorists, with special attention to Eduardo Mondlane (1920–1969), leader of an anticolonial struggle against the Portuguese colonization of Mozambique. Although Mondlane grew up in southern Mozambique among the Gaza, "absorbing the traditions of my tribe," as he recalled, he also absorbed Christianity, education, and nationalist ideals from the Protestants of the Swiss Romande mission. Accordingly, he is representative of the contacts, relations, and exchanges between indigenous and alien religion under colonial conditions. Mondlane identified the basic features of colonialism as the imposition of a centralized administration, a policy of divide and rule, the creation of foreign-owned companies to exploit natural resources, the extraction of forced labor from indigenous people, and the alliance of all of these practices of domination and exploitation with the religious authority of the Catholic Church. As a result, opposition to Portuguese control over land, labor, and life in Mozambique required a critique of the role of religion in colonialism. As his opening aphorism in *The Struggle for Mozambique*, Mondlane invoked a familiar African saying: "When the whites came to our country we had the land, and they had the Bible; now we have the Bible and they have the land."[2] From this anticolonial perspective, religion was an integral feature of the colonizing project, justifying conquest, legitimating dispossession, and underwriting control over native populations.

CONQUERING

As a prelude to colonial settlement, European conquest was justified by religious doctrines, such as the Roman Catholic division of the New World into Spanish and Portuguese spheres or the Protestant notion of *vacuum domicilium* (uninhabited land) or *terra nullius* (empty land), developed by John Locke, which deemed any territory empty of human habitation and available for European possession if the land was not being cultivated through settled agriculture. Enacting these religious ideas, Catholics planted crosses, Protestants planted gardens, as ceremonies of possession in establishing new colonial settlements in distant lands.[3]

Mondlane's critique of the role of religion in colonialism highlighted three stages in the colonizing process—religion was corrupted by colonialism; religion was deployed by colonialism in conquest; and religion was utilized by colonialism in pacifying the natives. Recalling the initial contacts of the seventeenth century, Mondlane acknowledged that Catholic missionaries, first Dominicans, then Jesuits, might have been motivated by the "pure" religious objectives of proclaiming their gospel and saving souls in Africa. However, these purely religious aims were quickly entangled with Portuguese political ambitions and economic interests. As a result, whatever religious success the early missionaries might have achieved in converting Africans was destroyed "by the corrupting effects of the alliance between the commercial, religious and political activity of Church and State." Therefore, according to Mondlane, colonialism was a corruption of religion, a denigration of religion by sacrificing its spirituality for economic gain and political power in a subjugated territory. This corruption of religion, he proposed, was central to the colonizing process, since the "alliance between Church, State and commercial interests dates back to the very beginning of colonial expansion."[4]

Because religion has always been not only spiritual but also political and commercial, we do not necessarily have to subscribe to Mondlane's indictment of corruption. Nevertheless, we can see that his focus on the interrelation of religion, politics, and economics in a colonial situation calls for attention to the conjunctures and disjunctures of these fields. On the one hand, the British imperial slogan "Christianity, Commerce, and Civilization" exemplified this alliance in Africa. On the other hand, dealing with new colonial realities, indigenous people found ways to adapt Christianity to their own economic interests, adopting the Bible and the plow, for example, to enter commercial agriculture, while adapting Christianity to advance egalitarian or revolutionary political projects. Colonialism, therefore, focuses our attention on the intersections of religion with economics and politics.

Recalling the consolidation of the colonization of Africa by European states at the Berlin Conference of 1884–85, Mondlane critiqued the role of religion as an ideological cover for military violence. Christianity, during this stage of colonization, was deployed to pacify the natives, with "the Christian faith offered as a lullaby, while the Portuguese military forces occupied the land and controlled the people."[5] Not merely an opiate of the masses, religion, in this rendering, was part of the military strategy of colonization. In collusion with the Portuguese military and colonial administration, according to Mondlane, the Catholic Church assumed "the responsibility for spiritual 'pacification' of the people."[6] Religion, in this respect, was an ideological supplement to conquest.

Colonialism, therefore, directs our attention to relations between religion and violence, especially in asymmetrical power relations. Clearly, colonial interventions were violent in killing, displacing, and dispossessing indigenous people, in controlling, containing, and exploiting native populations. Anticolonial strategy and tactics have also been violent, even embracing revolutionary violence as a quasi-religious redemption of people subjugated by colonial violence. As Frantz Fanon (1925–1961) insisted in relation to French colonialism in Algeria, anticolonial violence was a means for recovering humanity from dehumanization, the "thingification" of colonized human beings under colonial domination. In the colonial situation, where the violence of oppression has institutionalised the dehumanization of the oppressed, according to Fanon, collective violence against the colonial system can represent "the veritable creation of a new man." For him, the structural violence of the colonial order of domination represented "violence in its natural state," a normalized order of violence based on both coercive force and dehumanization that "will only yield when confronted with greater violence." Accordingly, violent acts were necessary to break the colonial order. As Fanon advised, "Decolonization, which sets out to change the order of the world, is, obviously, a programme of complete disorder." When undertaken in the interests of human liberation, "decolonization is always a violent phenomenon." Far from seeing violent resistance as structurally dysfunctional or illegitimate by definition, he argued that anticolonial violence was necessary for the legitimate recovery of humanity from dehumanizing conditions.[7] Not merely justifiable, revolutionary violence was required to fashion a new humanity that was whole, unified, pure, and free in its liberation from the violent domination of the colonial order.

By contrast, anticolonial strategy and tactics have also been based on principled nonviolent resistance, most notably in Mohandas K. Gandhi's (1869–1948) commitment to *satyagraha*, "soul force" or "truth power," in his opposition to British colonialism in India. Where Fanon found religion to be an "imaginary haze" enveloping the violence of colonialism, Gandhi drew on religious resources to forge an anticolonial spirituality, supposedly shared by all Indians, that could be contrasted with British colonial materialism. Gandhi recast religion as a generic spirituality, which could be found not only in Hindu tradition but also in the spirituality of all religions in India. Adopting an ascetic spirituality of nonviolence, or harmlessness *(ahimsa)*, he sought to spiritualize the Indian political struggle against British colonialism.[8] While Fanon invested revolutionary violence with quasi-religious significance in redeeming the full humanity of the colonized, Gandhi spiritualized religion, invoking an indigenous Indian spirituality that would overcome the material superiority of the colonizer.

MODERNIZING

Once the colonial regime had been established, religion featured as an instrument for "civilizing" the natives, not only through religious conversion, but also through institutions of colonial education. Missionary religious institutions and colonial educational institutions, according to Mondlane, formed an alliance in Mozambique to shape the subjectivity of the natives. For its part, the Catholic Church undertook not only "to Christianize and educate" but also to "nationalize and civilize the native populations."[9] Here the linkage between Christianity and the civilizing process was mediated through education; but nationalization assumed a specifically colonial meaning: to inculcate loyalty among the natives to Portugal. To nationalize, in this sense, was to cultivate among the natives a sense of identification with an imperial nation, which would cut across any tribal divisions of language, culture, or religion. As Mondlane observed, the Portuguese colonizers trusted the Catholic Church with the responsibility of educating the natives for this kind of national unity, while distrusting foreign missionaries, especially Protestants, such as the Swiss Romande missionaries who taught him, because they were suspected of "denationalizing the natives." While such Protestant missionaries could not be trusted to sustain national loyalty to Catholic Portugal among the natives, they were also accused of giving rise to new ideas of nationalism that threatened Portuguese colonialism in Mozambique.[10] Reinforcing the Portuguese imperial mandate to define nationalism as loyalty to Portugal, the educational institutions of the colonial state were mobilized to meet the challenge of any emerging native nationalism. Here also, religion played an important role in education. "On the assumption that political unity is founded upon a moral unity," Mondlane observed, "the Portuguese have attached great importance to religion in African education."[11] In the field of education, therefore, we find an alliance between religion and state in educating indigenous people for loyalty to a foreign power.

As colonialism has ranged from the extraordinary violence of conquest to the ordinary socialization of colonized subjects, religion has played a crucial role in the formation of subjectivities in colonial situations. Although colonialism has signified military, economic, and administrative power, it has also shaped religious consciousness, practices, and everyday life among both alien colonizers and indigenous colonized. The colonization of southern Africa gave rise to new religious attention to physical bodies, clothing, gender relations, sexuality, labor, house construction, and time management, all of which were invested with religious meaning for Christian missionaries, African converts, and Africans resisting the Christian colonizing project.[12] Likewise, in the Dutch colonization of Indonesia, new religious understandings of time, human agency, and the meaning of material objects were negotiated in colonial relations.[13] In both cases, Protestant Christianity, with its emphasis on the interiority of personal belief, was recast in opposition to indigenous religious practices, with special attention to attacking the religious materiality of indigenous religions. These interreligious engagements in colonial situations reshaped subjectivities of both colonizers and colonized. Colonialism, therefore, was not only a military, administrative, and economic project; it was also a cultural intervention that produced unexpected consequences in forming new senses of self and other in a changing interreligious environment.

Informed by his critique of religion and nationalism, Mondlane imagined a new nationalism for Mozambique that bore the deep imprint of its colonial experience and carried enduring traces of religion under colonialism. A new nation, he recognized, could never emerge out of any precolonial nation, out of "a stable community, in history a linguistic, territorial, economic and cultural unity." No such national unity had ever existed; it could not be recovered and restored. Instead, a new nation had to emerge out of the shared experience of "colonial domination." A new national unity had to be "born out of the experience of European colonialism."[14] If colonialism was the furnace in which an indigenous nationalism might be forged, religion could provide a template for national redemption, as we find in the motto of Ghanaian liberator Kwame Nkrumah: "Seek ye first the political kingdom and all other things will be added to you" (adapting Mt 6:33).

In the struggle for an anticolonial nationalism, Mondlane observed that traditional religious resources were being deployed. Indigenous religious forms of poetry, songs, dances, and art were being revived. They were being mobilized in resistance to colonialism. But they were also being recast under colonial conditions of interreligious contact in entirely new modes of engagement. Traditional woodcarvers, the Makonde, were performing their indigenous art by appropriating and transposing Christian symbols. As Mondlane recounted, these traditional artists were representing Christ as a demon, priests as animals, and the suffering of the crucifixion as a call for revenge. In these wood carvings, "a Madonna is given a demon to hold instead of the Christ Child; a priest is represented with the feet of a wild animal, a pieta becomes a study not of sorrow but of revenge, with the mother raising a spear over the body of her dead son."[15] Here we find a kind of wild religion, employing indigenous art, but intervening in the colonial contest over religious meanings by appropriating, distorting, and reconfiguring a colonizing religion.

This kind of hybridity, mixing and merging, appropriating and subverting, religious signs has been a recurring feature of colonial situations. The anticolonial theorist and strategist Frantz Fanon observed that a kind of wild religion emerged under colonial conditions to evoke powers more terrifying than the colonizer. In the *Wretched of the Earth*, Fanon largely ignored religion, whether Islam in Algeria or Christianity, Islam, and indigenous African religion in West Africa, but he did reflect on recurring revivals in Africa of this type of wild religion, with its "terrifying myths" populated by maleficent spirits, the "leopardmen, serpent-men, six-legged dogs, zombies," which generated an imaginary world of spiritual powers and prohibitions that were "far more terrifying than the world of the settler."[16] The hybrids identified by Mondlane, however, were more terrifying to the settler because they appropriated the settler's religion.

Appropriations and reappropriations of religious symbols, myths, rituals, and traditions have characterized colonial relations. In southern Africa, where Christian missionaries appropriated indigenous religion as evidence of demonic beliefs and practices, Africans engaged Christianity in a variety of ways, resisting, converting, and making Christianity into an indigenous African religion. Colonized Africans found ways to own Christianity. In northern Nigeria, where British colonial policy tried to use Islam for the containment and surveillance of the population, attempting to bring Islam under British control, African Muslims developed a range of arguments for resistance, alliance, or temporary accommodation with colonialism. Colonized Muslims found ways to own British colonialism by incorporating its interventions into Islamic jurisprudence.[17] One of the most striking instances of religious appropriation under colonial conditions is found among the cargo movements of Melanesia, where islanders developed religious beliefs and practices based on the premise that Europeans had stolen material goods, military weapons, and even Christianity from the ancestors of the indigenous people of the islands. Anticipating an imminent return of their ancestors, which would restore these material and spiritual goods to their rightful heirs, cargo movements asserted indigenous ownership of the political, economic, and religious power of the colonizers.

Modernity, as Bruno Latour has argued, is based on classifications, distinctions, and divisions of labor designed to purify the world of all hybrids.[18] This modern sense of purity, especially as it has been cast as national unity, has also been important to anticolonial national projects. In opposition to the colonizer, the colonized emerges as a unity, despite linguistic, ethnic, cultural, and religious differences, because the colonizer had established a Manichaean dualism. This Manichaean construction of colonialism, with reference to Mani, the third-century Persian religious visionary who divided the world into separate spheres of light and dark, good and evil, suggests that all of the contacts, relations, and exchanges in colonial situations are polarized. As Mondlane observed, colonialism established a "line of demarcation between colonizer and colonized" in which each side of the line could be imagined as if it were a unified front. In this confrontation, the colonized "views himself as a dominated whole and sets himself up against another whole, the colonizing group, with which he contests for power."[19] As a Manichaean opposition between the forces of light and dark, this colonial construction of unified domination and unified subjugation provided one kind of model of colonialism. This notion of colonialism as binary opposition generated ideals of Pan-Africanism, Pan-Asianism, and Pan-Islamism, all unified, despite obvious diversity, by opposition to European colonialism.

While embracing modernity, anticolonial projects have also tried to forge unity out of diversity. As Eduardo Mondlane observed, given the "heterogeneous nature of the membership," coming from different religious, ethnic, and linguistic backgrounds, his anticolonial movement had to unify itself, making a "conscious effort to preserve unity" against colonial opposition, with its policy of divide and rule, by trying "to combat tribalism, racism and religious intolerance." However, echoing the colonial project for nationalizing the natives, Mondlane noted that in forging a new anticolonial unity "the main form this took was education." An anticipation of the postcolonial state, his revolutionary movement, the Liberation Front of Mozambique, FRELIMO, embodied a modern division of labor between the religious and the secular, as Mondlane stated: "FRELIMO is an entirely secular body; within it all religions are tolerated, and a great variety are practiced."[20] Anticolonial nationalisms, therefore, could adopt modern approaches to the secular management of religion, trying to create national unity out of linguistic, cultural, and religious diversity.

Although the preceding discussion has focused on the colonialism advanced by European empires, whether Catholic or Protestant, other modern empires, including the Russian, Ottoman, Japanese, and U.S. empires, have colonized indigenous people, all drawing on religious justifications for conquering, dispossessing, and controlling native populations. In establishing relations of domination and resistance, accommodation and hybridity, colonialism has had a profound effect on religion in the modern world.

CATEGORIZING

Colonialism has also been instrumental in producing the modern categories of religion and religions. Under colonial conditions, indigenous religions have been subjected to denials of their status as religions, with these denials underwriting explicit or implicit definitions of religion. In southern Africa, European observers entered contested territory by asserting that Africans had no religion. According to European reports, the Khoisan had no religion; the Xhosa had no religion; the Zulu had no religion; the Tswana had no religion. Instead, they allegedly lived in a world of superstition. Once they were conquered and contained within a colonial administrative system, however, each of these African groupings was found to have an indigenous religious system. On the Eastern Cape frontier, for example, every European intruder, whether traveler, trader, missionary, or colonial agent, consistently found that the indigenous Xhosa people of the region lacked any trace of religion, allegedly living, by contrast, in a world of superstition. These reports about the absence of any Xhosa religion continued until Xhosa political independence was destroyed and they were placed under the authority of a colonial administrative system. In 1858, the colonial magistrate J. C. Warner reported on the "religious system" of the Xhosa who had been shattered by colonial warfare and contained within the colonial "village system." With the imposition of this colonial administrative system for native control, surveillance, and tax collection, Warner discovered that the Xhosa actually had a religion, even a religious system, that counted as a religion because it fulfilled the two basic functions of any religious system by providing a sense of psychological security and reinforcing social stability. According to this proto-functionalist in the Eastern Cape, therefore, the Xhosa had a religious system that could be reduced to these psychological and social functions— security and stability—that oddly duplicated the aims of the colonial administrative system in keeping people in place.[21]

Rather than representing an advance in human recognition, this discovery of an indigenous religious system was a strategy of colonial containment that mirrored the structure of the magisterial system, location system, or reserve system. With the destruction of the last independent African polity in the 1890s, when every African was in principle contained within an urban location system or a rural reserve system, European observers found that every African man, woman, and child shared the same religious system, called "Bantu religion," which fulfilled psychological and social functions that kept people in their place.[22] While the European denial of the existence of any African religion was a strategic intervention in a contested frontier, the discovery of indigenous African religions in nineteenth-century southern Africa served the management and control of local populations.

From a variety of vantage points, the history of the study of religion has been rendered in colonial and postcolonial perspectives. Asian religions, according to earlier scholarship, were "discovered" in Europe, with the British discovery of Hinduism, Buddhism, and other Asian religions providing the premise for stories about internal intellectual developments within European philological and historical research. By contrast, attention to colonial situations has demonstrated the ways in which European discoveries were embedded in the power relations established by the conquest and control of colonized populations. A variety of Buddhisms, for example, were not simply discovered but effectively invented under different colonial conditions from Sri Lanka to Tibet. Situated in colonial contexts and demystifying earlier accounts of heroic European discoveries, new narratives of the history of the study of religion have included colonial agents, from administrators to missionaries, in the production of "knowledge" about the religious traditions of Asia.

However, these histories of invented traditions might still give too much credit to European imperial ambitions. Under colonial conditions, religious categories were not simply discovered or purely invented by outside observers. They emerged through complex interrelations, negotiations, and mediations between alien and indigenous intellectuals. In recent research on the invention of Hinduism, for example, analysts have argued that Europeans in India encountered religious category formations that were already shaped by distinctively Indian cultural, social, and political interests. But this new emphasis on indigenous agency retains the earlier insights into the invention of traditions by arguing that the category of "Hinduism" actually emerged out of both indigenous and alien inventions in an ongoing process of intellectual production. Similarly, the emergence of the academic study of Chinese and other Asian religions in Europe depended upon Asian and European intellectuals discovering each other in relations of reciprocal reinvention.[23] In these changing narratives of the history of the study of religion, moving from discoveries through inventions to intercultural mediations under colonial conditions, we are gaining greater insight into the complex formation of basic categories in the academic study of religion.

9 Imperialism

On July 27, 2012, at the opening ceremony of the London Olympics, directed by filmmaker Danny Boyle, the world watched a tribute to Great Britain that bore traces of imperialism, colonialism, and religion. Following a single tone from the Olympic Bell and patriotic hymns, a pageant unfolded that displayed the four-stage stadial model of human progress. Developed in the European Enlightenment, this stadial model was adopted by liberal imperialists during the nineteenth century as a warrant for the British Empire. Beginning with the savagery of hunter-gatherers, human development proceeded through the barbarism of pastoralists and the culture of agriculturalists to culminate in urban civilization.[1] In the Olympic opening ceremony, this stadial theory was illustrated by savage drumming, the migration from farms to cities, and the revolution of commerce and industry. This tableau of human evolution was launched by the actor Kenneth Branagh playing the part of the great civil engineer Isambard Kingdom Brunel, the pioneer of the Industrial Revolution, the architect of modern Britain, who recited from Shakespeare's *The Tempest:*

> Be not afeard. The isle is full of noises,
> Sounds, and sweet airs, that give delight and hurt not.
> Sometimes a thousand twangling instruments

Will hum about mine ears, and sometime voices
That, if I then had waked after long sleep,
Will make me sleep again. And then, in dreaming,
The clouds methought would open and show riches
Ready to drop upon me, that when I waked,
I cried to dream again. (III.ii.133–41)

Strangely, the Olympic ceremony Brunel, representing the magician of urban civilization, the modern Prospero, appropriated the words of Prospero's "savage and deformed slave," Caliban.[2] Originally performed in 1611 when the English were colonizing Virginia and Guyana, *The Tempest*, as Peter Hulme has observed, "has its finger on what is most essential in the dialectic between colonizer and colonized."[3] Under the spell of Prospero's magic, the indigenous Caliban was dispossessed of the island he inherited, exploited for his labor, forced to speak (and curse) in an alien language, and subject to new dreams of redemption. While the psychoanalyst Octave Mannoni developed a problematic theory of inherent colonial dependency in *Prospero and Caliban*,[4] anticolonial theorists, especially in the Americas, adopted the master-slave dialectic in *The Tempest* as a template for analyzing colonial situations. Under colonialism, as Barbara Bush has noted, "'Prospero and Caliban,' colonizer and colonized, were locked in complex spirals of power and dependence, collaboration and resistance."[5] By stealing Caliban's lines, Brunel introduced an imperial display of colonizing power, which was underwritten by an ideology of human progress from savagery to civilization. This imperial performance was finalized in the closing ceremony, in which Caliban's same lines were repeated by Winston Churchill before the athletes from all the nations of the world filed into the stadium to fit within the pattern of the flag of the United Kingdom.[6]

What does any of this have to do with religion? The founder of the modern Olympics, Pierre de Coubertin, was clear that his International Olympic Committee was presiding over a religion, a *religio athletae*, a Muskelreligion, to be celebrated through a recurring sacred festival.[7] In the era from Brunel to Churchill, which has often been regarded as an age of secularizing modernity, many new "religions" emerged in Great Britain. John Stuart Mill, for example, promoted the "religion of humanity" proposed by Auguste Comte, the father of scientific positivism, who traced an evolutionary progression from magic, through religion, to science, which would culminate in a religion of humanity based on altruism.[8] The religion of humanity, Mill argued, "is not only entitled to be called a religion: it is a better religion than any of those which are ordinarily called by that title."[9] Making a religion out of science, Thomas Huxley proclaimed himself as the bishop of the church scientific, while Francis Galton argued for a religion of eugenics, led by "prophets and high priests of civilization," which would purify and thereby redeem the human population.[10] Making a religion out of imperial expansion, devotees of the British Empire could equate imperialism with religion, as in Alfred Milner's religion of empire or John Buchan's "church of empire," which also promised universal redemption.[11] On the colonized peripheries of empire, this implicit religion of the United Kingdom was often displayed. In Africa, as the historian Terence Ranger has observed, "the 'theology' of an omniscient, omnipotent and omnipresent monarchy [was] almost the sole ingredient of imperial ideology as it was represented to Africans."[12] Imperial mastery, in this sense, was not legitimated by religion; it was religion.

Imperialism, which Edward Said defined as "the practice, the theory, and the attitudes of a dominating center ruling a distant territory," is necessarily related to colonialism.[13] Imperial practices celebrate the power of a dominating center over colonized peripheries. During the five hundred years of European colonization of the world, imperial pageantry has been displayed in rituals of power, those ceremonies of possession that provided a sacral warrant for the political domination, economic exploitation, territorial containment, and missionizing imposition of alien beliefs, practices, and values on indigenous people. Like Prospero's magic book, the Bible, the "white men's magic," was an instrument of colonizing power, giving rise to the common anticolonial aphorism, which Eduardo Mondlane invoked in opening *The Struggle for Mozambique:* "When the whites came to our country we had the land, and they had the Bible; now we have the Bible and they have the land."[14] In colonial situations, religion was invoked to certify ownership of land, from the Roman Catholic division of the New World into Spanish and Portuguese spheres through the Protestant doctrine that land was "empty" if it was not developed by settled agriculture. "This island's mine by Sycorax, my mother," Caliban exclaimed, asserting his indigenous ancestral ownership against Prospero, "Which thou tak'st from me" (I.11.331–2). Prospero had taken control through the power of his book.

The opposition between Prospero and Caliban, colonizer and colonized, has often been rendered as a dualism. "The colonial world is a Manichaean world," Frantz Fanon held.[15] Recent research on religion and colonialism, however, has explored the complex ways in which religion has been fashioned and refashioned in the asymmetrical power relations of colonial contact zones. In southern Africa, for example, while Christian missionaries redefined their gospel in opposition to indigenous practices of initiation, polygyny, and ancestral sacrifices, Africans sacralized their ancestors in reinforcing indigenous claims on land that were under threat by colonialism.[16] In southwestern Nigeria, under colonial conditions, Yoruba ethnic, cultural, and religious identities were made in Africa and remade in the Atlantic world.[17] In Madagascar, where the Malagasy revolt in 1947 against French colonial rule provided the impetus for Mannoni's *Prospero and Caliban*, ancestral rituals have continued to mediate the history and memory of colonialism, as Jennifer Cole has observed, embodying and enacting "the creative ways in which Malagasy in different parts of the island reacted to colonial intrusions and transformations alike."[18] These relational strategies of religious self-fashioning were worked out in local negotiations over meaning and power. Not a Manichaean dualism, these relations were hybrid, simultaneously alien and indigenous.

As religion in motion—crossing seas, entering new territories—imperial religion was not imported as a pure product to be consumed; indigenous religion was not inevitably destroyed, damaged, or defiled by the colonial encounter. Certainly, colonial violence against indigenous religions, such as the aggressive "extirpation of idolatry" in the Americas, has featured in this history of interreligious engagement. In the name of a civilizing mission, colonization might directly attack local religious beliefs and practices, as in the case of Prospero, at least as rendered by the great Shakespearean scholar G. Wilson Knight, who celebrated him as an emblem of Great Britain's "colonizing, especially her will to raise savage peoples from superstition and blood-sacrifice, taboos and witchcraft and the attendant fears and slaveries, to a more enlightened existence."[19] But recent research has moved beyond the stark opposition between submission and resistance, which poised Caliban between either conversion to the religion of the book or adherence to ancestral heritage, to explore the dynamics of religious creativity under colonial conditions.

For anticolonial activists in the Americas, Caliban has been recast as the hero of the colonial encounter, a hero of hybridity, "our mestizo America," according to the Cuban philologist Roberto Fernández Retamar in his influential essay "Caliban" (1971),[20] and a hero of diaspora, an African slave struggling for liberation as he appears in *Une tempête* (1969) by the Martinican poet and politician Aimé Césaire.[21] Not creating Calypso Calibans, with a Caribbean flavor, these recastings have been political interventions in imperial and colonial mythmaking. Explaining his project as a dramatic revision of the opposition between the civilized and the primitive, Césaire observed,

> I was trying to "de-mythify" the tale. To me Prospero is the complete totalitarian. I am always surprised when others consider him the wise man who "forgives." What is most obvious, even in Shakespeare's version, is the man's absolute will to power. Prospero is the man of cold reason, the man of methodical conquest—in other words, a portrait of the "enlightened" European. And I see the whole play in such terms: the "civilized" European world coming face to face for the first time with the world of primitivism and magic. Let's not hide the fact that in Europe the world of reason has inevitably led to various kinds of totalitarianism.[22]

While Césaire's Caliban refused Prospero's image of him as a savage and rejected the legitimacy of Prospero's civilizing mission, Césaire deconstructed the colonial opposition between the primitive and the civilized by having Caliban proclaim, "Uhuru!" change his name to "X," and invoke the Yoruba deity Shango. At the play's conclusion, Prospero remains on the island as if imprisoned, and Caliban X is heard singing, "FREEDOM HI-DAY FREEDOM HI-DAY!"[23]

The opposition between the savage and the civilized might have been established by imperial theory and colonial practices, but it was constantly being undermined by the fluid nature of colonial encounters and exchanges that generated new ways of remythifying the relations between Prospero and Caliban in colonial situations. Césaire's Caliban suggests some of the important ways in which religion has been linked with anticolonialism in new nationalist movements, transnational connections, and diasporic circulations. Under the slogan "Uhuru," anticolonial struggles for liberation in Africa often announced new dreams of redemption. Adopting the name "X" in solidarity with Black Muslims in the United States indicated how a history of colonialism, enslavement, and oppression could be sublated, simultaneously erased and retained in memory, while providing a basis for new forms of interreligious solidarity beyond colonial borders. The Yoruba god Shango, god of storms, who was interpreted by W. E. B. Du Bois as a deity of African political sovereignty, stronger in Africa than the Aryan Thor or the Semitic Jehovah, has circulated widely throughout the Atlantic world, demonstrating diasporic religious creativity as an important legacy of colonialism.[24]

Shakespeare's enchanted isle in *The Tempest,* an island of indeterminate location in both the Mediterranean and the Atlantic worlds, was actually made out of migrations and circulations, exiles and shipwrecks, across oceans. For the study of religion, imperialism, and colonialism, the ocean has become a crucial unit of analysis. Like the fetish in the Atlantic world, which emerged out of mercantile and eventually colonial encounters in West Africa, the cargo in the Pacific world, with all its dreamlike riches, has served as an emblem for the creativity and contestation of religion under colonial conditions. As Sugata Bose has proposed, the Indian Ocean is the basic unit of analysis that must be adopted for understanding religion under British colonialism in South Asia.[25] By focusing on the land, scholars have developed revealing insights into the imperial and colonial impact on religion in India. Drawing historically informed generalizations, Partha Chatterjee found that the political, public, and material force of British colonization had inspired Hindus to emphasize the "inner" or "spiritual domain" of their religion, while Gauri Viswanathan has argued that the British colonial administration entrenched a legislated social identity for religion that for Hindus diminished the importance of private religious belief or experience.[26] Both of these generalizations, apparently contradictory, might be true. Under colonial conditions, Hindus worked out new spiritual aspirations and social allegiances. However, perhaps too much weight has been given to the spirit of empire and the social engineering of colonialism. As Bose has argued, before the arrival of the British the Indian Ocean had long been a region of "multiple and competing universalisms."[27] Not simply a confrontation between a universalizing Christian civilization and local traditions, the colonial encounter introduced another universalism into the mix of religious discourses, practices, and associations. Beyond imperial control, religious life under colonial conditions circulated in the Indian Ocean.

As critical research on religion, the study of religion, imperialism, and colonialism might be nothing more or less than the study of religion. After all, as Raymond Williams noted, the keyword *culture*, from the Latin root *colere*, is etymologically linked with *colonus* and *cult*, with inhabiting a colony and honoring with worship.[28] Culture, religion, and colonization, therefore, might be aspects of the same mix. That configuration might run deep in human prehistory, perhaps appearing as early as *Homo sapiens* confronting Neanderthals in Europe, but it is definitely central to European claims on the imperial heritage of ancient Rome. In one of Shakespeare's principal sources, *The Aeneid*, the Roman gods are honored by the "great-souled" Aeneas because he will "crush wild peoples and set up laws for men and build walls" (I.63–4). Overseen and underwritten by religion, colonization has often been exacted upon "wild peoples" but also undermined by indigenous renegotiations of alien impositions.

In the colonial contact zones between imperial ambitions and indigenous responses, religious creativity has been generated out of the "long conversation" between colonizers and colonized, the reevaluation of agency, words, and things in colonial exchanges, and the many ways in which people have found to be modern in a world that includes gods and spirits.[29] Attending to asymmetrical power relations, research on religion and colonialism has been a fertile field for linking meaning and power, not by reducing meaning to structures of domination, but by analyzing meaning in networks, webs, or arteries of circulation, on land and at sea, in which religious discourses, practices, and associations have been both enabling and disabling. As an imperial term, the very word *religion* must also be a focus of critical research interrogating the term's colonial productions and deployments against the background of its imperial aspirations.[30] But we also can attend to the many different ways in which indigenous people in colonial situations have made something out of the keyword *religion* for their own intellectual, social, and political projects.[31] At the very least, such critical investigation of religion will depart from the stadial theory of human progress from savagery to civilization enacted in the opening ceremony of the London Olympics and the implicit opposition between the subhuman savagery of Caliban and the human civilization of Prospero, Brunel, and Churchill. By *depart,* here, I mean to reject, but I also mean to return to, these theories of structural opposition and temporal progression as points of departure for critical analysis in the study of religion.

10 Apartheid

The term *apartheid*, meaning "separation," became notorious in South Africa as a political policy of exclusion and incorporation, a policy for excluding the majority black population from citizenship while incorporating black people as exploitable labor within a capitalist economy. Drawing on earlier British colonial policies of racial segregation, urban townships, native reserves, and indirect rule through African chiefs, the white Afrikaner nationalists who came to power in 1948 sought to transform all of South Africa into separate spheres that were defined not only on the basis of race but also by differences of language, ethnicity, culture, and religion.

Economic historians have argued that apartheid secured a labor supply for white-controlled mining and manufacturing, for white-controlled farming and banking, and for competing interests among different factions of white Afrikaner nationalists who were struggling for control over the South African economy. At the same time, apartheid was underwritten by ideological justifications that ranged from an apartheid theology of racial separation, through scientific racism, to moral appeals for respecting the right to self-determination of separate nations, languages, cultures, and religions. Although some advocates of apartheid were influenced by the racism of Nazi Germany, others were informed by the history of racial discrimination and segregation of the United States.[1]

For our purposes in thinking about theory in the study of religion, we can regard *apartheid* as a term of exclusion and incorporation: a term of exclusion in marking, making, and policing boundaries, and a term of incorporation in absorbing everyone into an all-encompassing system of classification. On this basis, we can understand apartheid comparative religion to refer to the intellectual work of distinguishing among separate and perhaps even pure religions within an overarching system of classification for identifying distinct and separate languages, cultures, and religions. However, we will need to refine this preliminary definition of apartheid comparative religion.

On the one hand, we must situate it within a local history of engaging religious difference in South Africa. As I have argued elsewhere, intercultural contacts, relations, and exchanges in South Africa resulted in a proliferation of comparisons about religion within contested frontier zones.[2] For European travelers, explorers, missionaries, soldiers, settlers, and administrators, frontier comparative religion generally began with denial, with the insistence that indigenous Africans lacked any trace of religion. Once a frontier was brought under European control, however, colonial agents discovered that Africans had a religious system, just like a colonial administrative system, that kept them in place. Accordingly, apartheid comparative religion needs to be understood against the background of this longer history of colonial denial, discovery, and containment.

On the other hand, we must situate apartheid comparative religion within broader European and even global developments in the academic study of religion. In the emergence of the study of religion in Britain, we can discern an imperial comparative religion that its putative founder, Friedrich Max Müller, advanced under the slogan "Classify and conquer."[3] Here also was a system of classification based on distinguishing separate languages, cultures, and religions. Although it was global in scope and produced through complex mediations between imperial centers and colonized peripheries, this imperial comparative religion lacked the local policing power that is one of the defining features of apartheid comparative religion. Although apartheid theorists incorporated many aspects of imperial theory in assuming an animistic core of primitive religion, an evolutionary progression from primitive to civilized, and a general classification of separate and distinct world religions, they applied these theoretical principles by directly intervening in political policy, social engineering, education, and other areas of public and personal life.

Along these lines, I propose that we consider *apartheid comparative religion* as a generic term for making and enforcing separations. As Daniel Boyarin has observed, this understanding of apartheid comparative religion can be useful in understanding the making and enforcing of the separation between two distinct religions, Christianity and Judaism, in late antiquity. Second-century religious theorists, such as Justin Martyr, deployed the term *heresy* to mark distinctions but also to police new boundaries between the two religions. These new border lines, Boyarin has argued, were produced through a kind of apartheid comparative religion in which the "heresiologists of antiquity were performing a very similar function to that of students of comparative religion of modernity." In their intellectual work of identifying "pure" religions, and their political work of legislating against religious mixtures or exchanges as illicit syncretism, experts on heresy policed the emerging border lines separating Judaism and Christianity. Accordingly, as Boyarin concludes, their marking and policing of heresy should be understood as "a form of apartheid comparative religion, and apartheid comparative religion, in turn, is a product of late antiquity."[4]

While appreciating Daniel Boyarin's analysis of the deep history of apartheid comparative religion in late antiquity, here I focus on South Africa, recalling the historical roots and extensions of apartheid in the study of religion and concluding with postapartheid prospects.

FRONTIER, IMPERIAL, AND APARTHEID COMPARATIVE RELIGION

In the emergence and implementation of apartheid in South Africa, the anthropologist Werner Eiselen played a prominent role. An expert on indigenous African religion, Eiselen was an apartheid theorist and administrator, marking and enforcing boundaries. As South African anthropologist Isaac Schapera recalled in an interview at the end of the 1980s, "Eiselen [was] the son of a missionary in the civil service. He became

Secretary for Native Affairs and drafted the original blueprint of apart-heid."[5] Fifty years earlier, however, Schapera had praised Eiselen for his in-depth knowledge of the indigenous religious beliefs and practices of Africans in South Africa. As Schapera noted in the 1930s, "Eiselen is now engaged in writing a book on the religious life of the Southern Bantu which . . . should make this aspect of Bantu life one of the best known."[6] Although this book was never written, Eiselen nevertheless wrote exten-sively on African religious life, trying to recover its "primitive" forms and endeavoring to assess the impact of Christianity and civilization. In his research findings, Werner Eiselen replicated a history of frontier denials and imperial assumptions about social evolution that fed into apartheid comparative religion in South Africa.

Within open and contested frontier zones, European observers had consistently reported that Africans lacked any trace of religion. Although they might have an abundance of superstition, the defining opposite of religion, Africans allegedly had no religion. This denial, repeated over and over again by European travelers, missionaries, and colonial agents, was a comparative observation that served to call into question the full human-ity of Africans and thereby challenge their human rights to land, livestock, or control over their own labor within fluid and contested frontier zones. During the 1920s, Werner Eiselen, expert on African religion, began with such a denial as his point of departure, insisting that Africans actually did not have beliefs and practices that should be designated as religion. Claiming that the term *religion* should be reserved only for people of an "elevated culture," Eiselen found that Africans did not qualify. Since they lacked the "higher" culture supposedly developed by Europeans, Africans could not be credited with such a cultural accomplishment as religion. Accordingly, he argued, Africans might very well have "forms of belief" (*geloofsvorme*); but they had no religion (*godsdiens*).[7] In his earliest research, therefore, Eiselen argued that Africans had no religion, recast-ing the frontier denial of African religion and culture.

Drawing on imperial comparative religion, however, Werner Eiselen found that Africans were not merely an absence of religion; they also repre-sented a point of origin for the evolution of religion. A variety of British imperial theorists, developing this evolutionary theme, had traced the ori-gin of religion back to primitive fetishism, animism, or totemism. For example, John Lubbock, in 1870 in his *Origin of Civilization*, had tracked a developmental sequence—atheism, fetishism, totemism, shamanism, idolatry, polytheism, and theism—in the origin and evolution of religion.[8] Eiselen was interested in positioning indigenous African religion within such an evolutionary trajectory from the primitive to the civilized. Placing Africans in South Africa on this scale, Eiselen observed, "The Bantu is no longer primitive in the true meaning of the word." Although this might at first glance seem to be a positive judgment, Eiselen only meant to suggest that he had detected some evolutionary progression from a primitive origin to totemism. "The level of development that he has reached," Eiselen went on to say, "we usually call the Totem-culture."[9] Having advanced one stage above fetishism, the primitive and promiscuous worship of objects, Africans in South Africa according to Eiselen had evolved to the next evolutionary stage of worshipping emblems of collective identity or tribal solidarity. In this finding, we can only suspect, Werner Eiselen was anticipating the importance of the totemic group, the *volk*, in the blueprint of apartheid.

As an architect of apartheid, Eiselen claimed that he intended only to facilitate "the creation of effective arrangements for the peaceful existence of different ethnic groups."[10] The policy of "separate development," which created fictional nations for African ethnic groups, was an integral part of this apartheid plan for peaceful coexistence. But Eiselen's policy bore traces of both the frontier and the imperial heritage of comparative religion in South Africa.

Maintaining frontier denials, Eiselen's research denigrated Africans as if they represented an absence. The Bantu, according to Eiselen, were not rational. For evidence of this alleged lack of rationality, he compared European and African methods in agriculture. According to Eiselen, white Afrikaans-speaking farmers made use of rational techniques, such as irrigation and storage, although they might also draw on religious resources of prayer. African farmers, however, not being rational, knew nothing of such rational techniques, so they only resorted to prayer or its functional equivalent, rainmaking ritual.[11] Ironically, this apartheid denial seemed to reverse the frontier assertion that Africans lacked religion. Instead, Africans allegedly only resorted to religion. But South African frontiers did not only produce denials; they also resulted in discoveries that Africans had religious systems, perhaps irrational systems, that kept them in place. Clearly,

Eiselen and other ideologues of apartheid were interested in assigning, maintaining, and enforcing separate places for Africans in South Africa.

At the same time, drawing on his own missionary background and the Christian interests invested in apartheid, Eiselen recast the evolutionary scheme of imperial comparative religion. Accordingly, when he outlined the next stage of African evolution, he foresaw an evolutionary trajectory guided by Christian civilization. "Christian education," he concluded, "is the only way to make [the African] a useful inhabitant of our Union."[12] This version of evolutionary progression, turning Africans into "useful" subjects of a Christian state, was symptomatic of an apartheid comparative religion based on denigrating but also incorporating people in theory and practice.

BEYOND APARTHEID

As it was developed by Werner Eiselen and other apartheid ideologues in South Africa, apartheid comparative religion drew upon earlier ways of understanding religion, including frontier denials and containments; imperial theories of primitive mentality and social evolution; and even Emile Durkheim's thesis that religion reflects society. Making explicit reference to Durkheim, Eiselen argued that "the South African tribes had a very rigid structure and so we can expect to find a fairly clear replica thereof in the structure of their religion."[13] Rigid and unchanging, African religion supposedly reinforced a "tribal solidarity" that kept everyone in their place. As secretary for native affairs, Eiselen played a crucial role in carrying out apartheid policies of exclusion and incorporation, marking and enforcing spatial boundaries, such as separate urban areas defined by race and separate African "homelands" defined by tribal solidarity, while also seeking to incorporate everyone within the domain of a single "Christian nationalism" enforced by a self-professed Christian state.

Under apartheid, the study of religion in South African universities displayed a specific division of labor, with Afrikaner theologians, biblical scholars, and missiologists claiming expertise not only in Christianity but also in "other" religions from a Christian perspective, while Afrikaner anthropologists, developing the science of *volkekunde,* claimed expertise in the "tribal" religions of indigenous Africans in South Africa.[14] Generally, Christianity was regarded as a dynamic force, capable of converting and transforming, but African indigenous religious life was depicted as static repetition of the past. Following the nonracial democratic elections of 1994, these highly politicized approaches to the study of religion—privileging Christianity, organizing religious diversity for Christian conversion, and denigrating African religious heritage—were rejected by the government of a postapartheid South Africa. New initiatives in affirming religious diversity, especially in education, and valuing African indigenous heritage as a basis for cultural renewal were also political strategies.[15] But they sought to engage religion in ways that might redress the religious divisions and Christian hegemony entrenched in South Africa under apartheid.

As a generic term for marking and enforcing religious boundaries, apartheid comparative religion highlights the role of power in the production of knowledge about religion and religions. Reflecting on the workings of hegemonic power, Talal Asad has observed that dominating regimes of knowledge are not necessarily based on dissolving differences into an overarching unity. They are not necessarily dependent upon achieving uniformity. Rather, in marking and enforcing boundaries, "dominant power has worked best through differentiating and classifying practices."[16] Clearly, in South Africa, apartheid comparative religion was a science of differentiating and classifying, producing knowledge about religion and religions that served a dominating political project. But the South African case drives us to ask: How have such practices registered in other colonial situations? How have imperial theorists of religion, even if they did not echo Max Müller's flamboyant motto "Classify and conquer," produced knowledge about religious diversity that underwrote European hegemony.[17] While colonial denials and containments, differences and classifications, have influenced knowledge about religion and religions all over the world, the imperial notion of separate and distinct "world religions" sometimes resembles the divisions of apartheid. Going beyond apartheid might be enabled by research that goes back through colonial and imperial histories to uncover enduring legacies of marking and enforcing boundaries in the study of religion.

Moving beyond apartheid also requires recovering what apartheid denied. In the name of purity, seeking to identify and maintain the purity of separate races, ethnic groups, languages, cultures, and religions, apartheid ideologues tried to prevent any mixtures. Religious mixtures, condemned as syncretism, were particularly decried when they appeared to weave together religious resources of indigenous and Christian traditions. Arguably, this apartheid obsession with purity was already subtly inscribed in European theories of "families" of world religions and ethnic religions. Such organic models, as Robert Young has observed, were "designed to deny the more obvious possibilities of mixture, fusion, and creolization."[18] Postapartheid possibilities in the study of religion have been opened by attention to indigenous religion as a dynamic, fluid, and contested set of resources that has been deployed in transcultural contact zones.[19] Certainly, this understanding of religion as resources and strategies could be extended more broadly to the analysis of any religious form of life. In the case of indigenous religions, however, such a situated and dynamic rendering is necessary to counteract colonial, imperial, or apartheid formulations of these resources and strategies as "religious systems" that can be contained or controlled.

A postapartheid study of religion, like recent initiatives in postcolonial anthropology, can be critical of the links between knowledge and power, analyzing the ways in which disciplinary knowledge might be "embedded in certain social, cultural and political dynamics that unfold in contexts which are differently and historically structured by changing power relations."[20] But such a project can also be creative in exploring the vitality of religious resources and the dynamics of religious strategies within the changing power relations of local, regional, and global contact zones.

PART III   Circulations

If the material dynamics of religion are dynamic, they must move, flow, and circulate. The following chapters highlight that mobility. They track circulations in three senses. First, they engage religion in motion, from the mobility of shamans to the crossing of oceans, in ways that require a shift from analyzing snapshots of religious institutions to analyzing motion pictures displaying religious contacts, encounters, and exchanges. Second, as an index of religious change, circulations are ongoing oscillations between persistence and innovation, continuity and discontinuity, in which the truism that there is nothing permanent but change is evident in the trajectories of religious formations in motion. Third, as characteristically religious motifs, patterns, and processes move in and through popular culture, circulation is evident in the diffusion of religion beyond specialized religious institutions. In the following chapters, these three aspects of religious circulation—mobility, change, and diffusion—are explored through case studies of religion in motion that require new ways of thinking about religion.

Chapter 11 considers shamans, religious specialists who have become archetypes for archaic techniques of ecstasy, in their circulations through colonial situations. As a characteristic feature of shamanism, mobility is evident in the shaman's capacity to move between worlds, material and spiritual, but also to move between central and marginal positions under the impact of various imperial impositions and colonial situations. Chinese and Russian empires, for example, dramatically altered shamanic geography, restricting freedom of movement in ways that directly affected spiritual mobility. As a result, shamans, unable to move around in a sacred territory, instead moved between the sky and the underworld. This change is just one impact of colonization on shamans. In competitions over sacred geography and sacred resources, Chinese and Russian empires altered the mediating roles of Siberian shamans. And while the term *shaman* circulated as a generic term for a religious specialist in other parts of the world, Europeans associated shamans with wild and dangerous spiritual forces. Under colonial conditions, features associated with shamanism, such as spiritual travel, healing, indigenous memory, and secrecy, changed into strategies of opposition to the incursions of alien political and religious forces. Mediating with a spiritual world, under those conditions, became a matter of survival.

Chapter 12 raises the important question of religious change. How do we explain change? Without giving a definitive answer to that question, this chapter recalls how one theorist and historian of theory in the study of religion, Walter H. Capps, wrestled with the problem of religious change. Professor of religious studies at the University of California, Santa Barbara, from 1963 to 1996, Capps focused his research on studying the dynamics of contemporary religious change against the background of changing narratives of the history of the study of religion. At a meeting of the International Association for the History of Religions in Finland in 1973, Capps delivered a paper in which he combined these interests by suggesting new ways to understand the "second-order tradition" of the study of religion and calling for new attention to dynamic processes of change in studying religion. Taking this presentation as a point of departure, this chapter examines how Walter Capps imagined new ways of narrating the history of the study of religion that were characterized by dynamism, multiplicity, and flexibility and how he developed a theory of change based on the oscillation of binary oppositions. These interrelated interests remain alive in the academic study of religion.

Chapter 13 explores the circulation of characteristically religious patterns and processes through popular culture. Although religious themes might appear in cultural media, popular culture, too, generates formations that seem to operate like religion. This chapter highlights three ways in which popular culture acts like religion in the formation of communities of sacred allegiance, the devotion to sacred objects, and the rituals of collective effervescence in sacred exchange. As a business enterprise and cultural formation that displays all three of these features, Tupperware can be analyzed as a popular cultural religion, a religion of plastic that demonstrates the plasticity of religion in the modern world.

Chapter 14 undertakes a tactile exploration of the sense of touch in modern American culture and religion. After briefly recalling the denigration of tactility in Western thought, the discussion considers the usefulness of the work of two theorists, Emmanuel Levinas and Walter Benjamin, in recovering the sense of touch—the intimate caress, the violent shock—as deep background for tracking basic modes of religious tactility. By paying attention to sensory media and metaphors, the chapter suggests some features of religious tactility that are not necessarily seen or heard but which nevertheless pervade contemporary religion and culture. Schematically, the chapter proceeds from cutaneous binding and burning, through kinesthetic moving, to haptic handling in order to enter this field of tactile meaning and power. Along the way, specific cases of tactility are quickly considered, including binding covenants, fire walking, flag burning, alien abduction, global capitalism, and cellular microbiology. By exploring the religious dynamics of the sense of touch, this chapter points to the presence of a tactile politics of perception circulating through personal subjectivities and social collectivities in the modern world.

Chapter 15 explores the circulations of religion across vast bodies of water. With special attention to the work of Charles H. Long, who has been a cartographer of oceans in the study of religion, this chapter highlights relations and mediations between land and sea. Returning to the fetish and the cargo, we can place these contested material objects within the worlds produced by oceans, situating the materiality of religion within changing relations between people of the land and people of the sea. Between the mercantile fetish and the virtual cargo, a third object, guano, which was sacred bird excrement in ancient Inca religion, signifying fertility and sovereignty, became, during the nineteenth century, the nexus of an industrial religion of fertilizer, explosives, and networked islands under

European and United States imperial control. Like the fetish and the cargo, guano emerged from an ocean world as a material focus for conflicting religious orientations.

Religion in motion, therefore, circulates through material networks as intimate as the body and as vast as the oceans. Moving, changing, and diffusing, religion registers in the following chapters as dynamic material circulations.

11 Shamans

According to the classic definition proposed by Äke Hultkrantz, a shaman is "a social functionary who, with the help of guardian spirits, attains ecstasy to create a rapport with the supernatural world on behalf of his [or her] group members."[1] As a social functionary, the shaman is defined not merely by the extraordinary personal ability to achieve ecstasy, communicate with spirits, or affect the healing of individuals but also by a public capacity to mediate between a transcendent reality and a particular social group. In many instances, the relevant social group for a shaman is constituted by kinship, since shamans often serve as hereditary ritual specialists for their clans. But the constitution of a community might also be determined by broader social relations within a territory. Operating as an inspirational mediator on behalf of a community, the shaman necessarily performs a range of political, social, and economic roles. Under colonial conditions, those roles are inevitably altered.

In simple terms, colonialism is the use of military and political power to create and maintain a situation in which colonizers gain economic benefits from the raw materials and cheap labor of the colonized.[2] Generally, colonizers come from outside a territory, arriving as alien intruders to dominate an indigenous people, although situations of internal colonialism have also established similar relations of domination.

Not only a system of military, political, and economic power, colonialism is also a cultural project advancing a cultural agenda and entailing intercultural contacts, relations, and exchanges. Often legitimated by explicitly invoking religion, colonialism inevitably affects indigenous religious life. Following the colonial disruption, dispossession, and displacement of an indigenous community, everything changes, including the religious roles of shamans. Characteristically, in response to colonizing forces, shamans are faced with the options of extinction, assimilation, or resistance. However, more complex, creative responses have also been evident in new strategies for weaving together alien and indigenous religious resources. Although colonization has always been destructive of indigenous religion, shamans have often played new, innovative roles as mediators not only between the supernatural and human beings but also between the religious worlds of the colonizers and colonized.

MOBILITY, GEOGRAPHY, AND RESOURCES

By providing the original source of the term *shaman,* Siberian shamans have often been regarded as the classic type of indigenous religious specialist. However, subject to two empires, Chinese and Russian, Siberian shamanism has been shaped by a long history of colonization. That history has witnessed both political fluctuations and religious changes in the mobility, spiritual geography, and spiritual resources of shamanism under colonial conditions.

Buryat shamanism illustrates religious persistence and change, surviving persecution but also adopting a new mobility under colonial conditions. In Buryat shamanism, ritual specialists mediated between humans and the supernatural in two ways: developing a hunter's shamanism, which negotiated access to game animals, and a cattle breeder's shamanism, which negotiated relations between the living and the dead, the ancestral masters of the mountains. Chinese imperial states, such as the Manchu Qing Dynasty (1644–1911), that supported Buddhism tended to force shamanism into a marginal position by asserting a centralized claim over material and spiritual resources. When those states collapsed, Buddhism retreated and shamanism resurged in Inner Asian states. In these imperial religious politics, the vitality of shamanism was clearly affected by the fate of empires.

Many indigenous people living in tribal arrangements during the nineteenth century, however, recalled an earlier history of imperial power, a time in which their shamans were at the center of political power. In relation to the Chinese empire, competing religious interests could operate in the same political economy of the sacred. Although the political status of shamanism depended on the historical rise and fall of empires, shamans, Buddhist clergy, and officials of imperial ancestor-veneration operated in the same field of religious references, making competing claims on access to the sky, for example, which represented the supreme symbol of political authority from all religious perspectives encompassed within the Chinese empire.[3] Accordingly, shamanic ascent, which represented the hallmark of a shaman's spiritual capacity, also registered as an explicitly political claim.

When subjected to the force of a dominant, colonizing Chinese empire, however, shamans were usually prevented from establishing access to centralized political power. Beginning in the nineteenth century, Buryat shamanism survived Buddhist persecutions because a kind of division of spiritual labor was worked out between shamans and lamas. Making no explicitly political claims, shamans assumed responsibility for healing. As the case of Buryat shamanism shows, shamans have generally been vulnerable to centralizing religious power. Although shamanism can be adapted, what often survives are the most portable aspects of shamanic practice, techniques of healing, for example, that are not necessarily anchored in the political economy of a community but are services that can be made available to clients wherever they might be. In colonial situations all over the world, this new mobility of shamanism has been made necessary not only by the expansion of imperial power but also by the disruption of local communities. In the process, religious mobility became a new requirement of indigenous survival.

Although marginalized under the centralized, hierarchical power of Chinese empires, Buryat shamans nevertheless survived, even if their sphere of political, social, and economic influence was circumscribed. Buryat shamans enclosed during the seventeenth century within the

Russian protectorate found that Russian colonization allowed much less room to maneuver. Although shamans were active in anti-Russian revolts, they were forced to retreat in the face of overwhelming military power. Legitimated by Orthodox Christianity, Russian colonization entailed a more pervasive project of converting indigenous people, land, and wealth to Russian ends.

As the Russian empire advanced, shamans were systematically persecuted. In response to the colonization of their religious life, indigenous people displayed a range of strategic positions, rejecting, accepting, or selectively appropriating the Christian mission that accompanied Russian colonization. For example, in nineteenth-century Siberia and Alaska, the Chuckchi disregarded the missionary message; the Dena'ina embraced Christianity; and the Altaians engaged in selective borrowing of Christian symbols.[4] Although different indigenous responses were possible, Russian colonialism inevitably altered the religious position of shamans. In addition to adopting a new colonial mobility, often demonstrated by fleeing to remote places, shamans developed new spiritual geographies and new spiritual resources for negotiating with the spiritual world on behalf of their fractured communities.

Among the Khanty and the Mansi, an indigenous political system of chiefdoms was destroyed by Russian colonization during the sixteenth century. Beginning in the eighteenth century, these Ob-Ugrian people were subjected to forced conversion to Christianity. Since they were closer to the imperial center of Russia, the Khanty and Mansi were exposed to the full range of colonizing measures developed by European states— alienation of land ownership, multiple forms of taxation, exactions by professional civil servants, and legal prohibitions on indigenous religion. Instead of adapting to these measures or inspiring revolts against Russian colonization, shamans retreated to the forests. Surviving in exile, they developed a new spiritual geography.

Like many indigenous people displaced by colonial incursions, these shamans found that the meaning of their territory, including their spiritual territory, had been fundamentally altered. In earlier practice, a shaman might have been adept at spiritual travel, but shamanic voyages generally moved on a horizontal plane from the ordinary world of the community to the places of extraordinary power associated with the forest or the sea. Under colonial conditions, horizontal movement within this spiritual geography of the world tended to be replaced by a vertical axis along which shamans ascended to the sky or descended to the under-world. Living in exile in the forest, shamans no longer traveled to the spir-itual forest but, instead, journeyed into heavenly realms and subterranean regions beyond the geography of this world. Since this world had come under the control of an alien colonizing power, shamans had to work out an alternative spiritual geography that transcended colonial conditions.[5]

New maps for the spiritual world, therefore, could be developed in colo-nial situations. Subjected to foreign domination, shamans all over the world found that they were suddenly in a world turned upside down, a world in which alien intruders from foreign places had become central and indigenous people were alienated from their own land. In the case of many Siberian communities, shamans assumed the responsibility for remapping the contours of a spiritual geography in such a distorted world. No longer able to draw upon spiritual meaning and power within the world, they looked to other worlds. Although the vertical axis of ascending and descending into spiritual worlds has often been regarded as a constant, universal feature of shamanism, in many cases this verticality, replacing earlier attention to the spiritual contours of a territory, represented an innovative religious response to the crisis of colonial domination.

While developing new spiritual geographies, shamans under colonial conditions also appropriated new religious resources of spiritual power from the Christian mission. In northern Siberia, Yakut shamanism, which had been subjugated by Russian colonization from the beginning of the seventeenth century, displayed this indigenous appropriation of alien sacred symbols. Although the Yakut people converted to Christianity for a variety of material reasons, whether avoiding persecution or gaining tax relief, the majority had been baptized by the end of the eighteenth cen-tury. Preserving the indigenous traditions of shamanism, Yakut ritual specialists modified those traditions by introducing aspects of Russian Orthodox Christianity, including God, the Virgin Mary, guardian angels, and the promise of spiritual rewards in a heavenly afterlife. By integrating these Christian features, Yakut shamans were not merely developing a syncretism of foreign Christianity and indigenous religion. They were drawing in new, transcendent, and powerful negotiating partners in their ongoing spiritual work of securing the health, prosperity, and survival of their community.

Shamanism is mediation but also negotiation with supernatural forces on behalf of a community. In the case of the indigenous Yakut religion, with its basis in hunting, shamans were particularly adept at negotiating with the masters of animals for the souls of wild game. Expert in techniques of ecstasy, they were also skilled in negotiating techniques—supplicating and imploring—as well as bartering, trading, and exchanging with the spiritual world. In rituals of healing, for example, shamans could negotiate with spirits by trading a sacrificial animal for the soul of a sick person. Such negotiations with spirits were central to shamanic sessions. Aided by a principal spirit, usually an ancestral spirit, Yakut shamans conducted ongoing negotiations with the forces of the spiritual world on behalf of their clans or communities.

Under colonialism, however, indigenous ritual specialists experienced a breakdown in negotiations, a shift from earlier relations of reciprocal exchange to new colonial relations based on the invasive, coercive, one-way flow of value from the colonized, who were dispossessed of their resources, displaced from their territory, and exploited for their labor, to the colonizers. By introducing new negotiating partners into the spiritual world—spiritual negotiating partners associated with the religion of the colonizers—shamans struggled to change the very terms of negotiation in ways that might restore reciprocity between indigenous people and the spiritual world.

As specialists in ritual techniques of trance, healing, and spiritual power, shamans continued to play a significant role in Siberian and Alaskan religious life, even under Russian domination and Christian conversion. Sent to Alaska in the 1820s, the Russian Orthodox missionary Ioann Veniaminov (later, Bishop Innocent [1797–1879]) found a Christian shaman among the Aleuts, an elderly man by the name of Ivan Smirennikov, who had been baptized into the Russian Orthodox Church but who was regarded by the local Aleutian people as a shaman because of his familiarity with spirits that enabled him to see the future, heal individuals, and locate food for the community. Based on his investigations, Veniaminov found that Ivan Smirennikov was a "shaman, not an ordinary person."

During his interview with the shaman, Veniaminov learned that shortly after Smirennikov's baptism in 1795, the latter had been visited by two spirits who said that they had been sent by God to instruct him in Christian teachings. Over the next thirty years, the spirits appeared to him almost daily, providing Christian instruction but warning him not to listen to the Russians or to confess his sins to their priests. Instead, he was to rely directly on the spirits and they would grant his requests and the requests made by others through him. To Veniaminov's surprise, he found that Smirennikov had become not only a noted shaman but also an informed Christian through the mysterious intervention of the two spirits. Although Veniaminov worried that these spirits were demons, he became convinced that the Aleut shaman's spirits provided confirmation rather than competition for his Christian gospel. The two spirits, according to Smirennikov, were even prepared to reveal themselves to the Russian priest, although they chastised him for his curiosity: "What does he want? Does he consider us demons?" Accepting the orthodoxy of Ivan Smirennikov, the Russian priest nevertheless insisted that he should not be regarded among the local people as a shaman. "I told the other Aleuts who were present not to call him a Shaman," Veniaminov reported, "not to ask him for favours, but to ask God." Apparently, the shaman agreed with this resolution, since he was also convinced that his spiritual negotiating partners were not demons but emissaries of the one true God of heaven and earth.[6]

MEMORY, CONCEALMENT, AND NOISE

In Christian representations of indigenous religion, we find a long history of demonizing local forms of religious life, from narrations of the expansion of Roman Catholic Christianity into Europe to descriptions of the explorations and conquests of the New World. From the earliest appearances of the term *shaman*, travelers' reports tended to demonize indigenous religious specialists. Having served at the court of Peter the Great and journeyed through imperial Russia, Nicolas Witsen (1640–1717) reported in his travel account, *Noord en Oost Tartaryen*, that a "Schaman" was nothing more nor less than a priest of the devil.[7] While allegedly serving the devil and his demons, shamans were also represented as fakes, frauds, or imposters, thus combining genuine evil with artifice and deception. This mixture of authenticity and fakery made the shaman a strange contradiction—full of real demonic power, but empty of legitimate religious power—in colonial representations of indigenous religions. Certainly, these accounts recycled classic features of superstition, which could be rendered as beliefs and practices based on ignorance, fear, and fraud, as the defining antithesis of authentic religion. Nevertheless, the depiction of shamans as authentic frauds represented a strange crisis for the ideology of Christian colonization well into the nineteenth century. Working in southern Africa during the 1830s, the missionary Robert Moffat dismissed the local ritual specialists, the Tswana *ngaka*, as nothing more than imposters, but demonized them—along with all other indigenous religious specialists, whether the "angekoks" of Greenland, the "pawpaws" of North America, or the "greegrees" of West Africa—by identifying them as the "pillars of Satan's kingdom."[8] In this formula, shamans, who supposedly were empty of any real power, allegedly were full of demonic power as the primary obstacles to the advance of a colonizing Christian empire.

Suggesting more than merely an alien incomprehension of indigenous religious specialists, this colonial representation of shamans as demonic obstacles, simultaneously immaterial and material, underwrote specific colonial policies of religious destruction. In the Americas, the "extirpation of idolatry" entailed both physical and spiritual warfare against shamans. According to Bishop Peña Montenegro in 1668, Indian shamans, who "since time immemorial had been worshiping the devil," formed "the principal obstacle to the spread of the Gospel." These sorcerers and magicians, charlatans and imposters, he argued, "resist with diabolical fervor" in order to avoid being exposed as frauds, "so that the light of truth shall not discredit their fabulous arts." To overcome these diabolical obstacles, Bishop Peña Montenegro advocated a campaign against what he regarded as fake material objects and real immaterial demons. Military action had to be taken to "destroy their drums, deerheads, and feathers," the bishop urged, "because these are the instruments of their evil and bring on the memory of paganism."[9] Destroying sacred objects, therefore, was part of a campaign against real spiritual forces of memory—the memory of ritual, the memory of ancestors, the memory of the land, or the memory of an indigenous way of life—that were identified by the alien logic of colonialism as an integral part of the evil, diabolical work of shamans.

In northern Siberia, shamanism was also reconfigured under colonial conditions as a work of memory. As reported by Martin Sauer, secretary to the expedition of Joseph Billings (ca. 1758–1806), which had been commissioned by Catherine the Great, the advance of colonization and Christianization had undermined the authority of once almost omnipotent shamans. Like the Roman Catholic campaign of extirpation of idolatry in the Americas, the Russian Orthodox campaign against indigenous religion attacked the material signs of shamanism: the masks, musical instruments, and other objects. In the process, Sauer observed, "all their old customs were abolished," but the shaman was recast as the guardian of indigenous memory. Weaving together threads of indigenous continuity that had been broken by colonization, the shaman assumed a new role that could be acquired through extraordinary acts of resistance or recalled in ordinary, everyday nostalgia for a lost heritage. Among the Yakuts, as Sauer reported, a man by the name of Aley had shown remarkable skill in avoiding the Russian conquerors and leading people to safety. By demonstrating this extraordinary power against the overwhelming power of the colonizers, Aley was regarded as a shaman and began to practice traditional divination.[10] As this case suggests, colonial situations could redefine the role of the shaman as defender of tribal survival, thereby creating new ways of becoming a shaman.

Under the weight of colonial oppression, however, many indigenous people could recall the power of shamans only as a lost legacy, a memory preserved but also distorted under colonial conditions. According to one of Sauer's Yakut informants, who had been forcibly converted to Christianity, shamans represented traces of a lost world that only survived in memory, even if the indigenous terms of memory had been Christianized. Indigenous shamans, Sauer's informant recalled, "were observers of omens, and warned us of approaching dangers, to avert which sacrifices were made to the demons." Betraying the influence of a pervasive Christian demonology, this Yakut account nevertheless located the shaman not as an obstacle to overcome but as the dividing line between current misery and a precolonial world in which the Yakuts had been "wealthy, contented, and free." Under colonial conditions, that lost world could only be re-created in memory, a memory so fragile, however, that Sauer's Yakut informant concluded that "our former religion was sort of a dream."[11]

In this new work of memory under colonial conditions, shamans concealed ritual objects from alien colonizers, adding another layer to the practice of concealment that was already part of the shaman's ritual repertoire. As the traveler Giuseppe Acerbi reported, Siberian shamans hid their ritual drums from Christian missionaries, in the process concealing their true religious identities from outsiders.[12] Accused in colonial accounts of being diabolic deceivers, shamans actually were forced to engage in deception to preserve themselves, their practices, and their ritual objects from destruction. Secrecy, therefore, assumed new meaning under colonial conditions.

Although shamanic practices were concealed from the colonial gaze, they often registered, to colonial ears, as incomprehensible noise. From a colonial perspective, the sound of the shaman's drum produced meaningless noise rather than coherent music. Songs, chants, and ritual performances were often described in colonial accounts as dissonant noise. As Acerbi reported, the song of the Siberian shaman, performed in secret in the mountains, was "the most hideous kind of yelling that can be conceived."[13] Likewise, in early reports from the Americas, shamans were said to produce the "most hideous Yellings and Shrieks," while accounts from southern Africa claimed that indigenous ritual experts "sang only ha, ho, HO, HO, until one almost lost hearing and sight because of the terrible noise."[14]

For colonial regimes relying upon visual surveillance, verbal command, and embodied discipline, the practices of shamans represented a kind of sensory disorganization. Inherently threatening to colonial rule, this alternative ordering of the senses was sometimes intentionally deployed by indigenous ritual specialists in opposition to colonial domination. In the Eastern Cape of southern Africa during the late 1830s and early 1840s, a Xhosa diviner by the name of Mngqatsi conducted regular rituals outside the British colonial settlement of Grahamstown, frightening the settlers with loud drumming and chanting. Often performed on Sundays, these rituals sought to disrupt the religious order of colonialism.[15] During the 1920s in central and southern Africa, anticolonial noise was transposed into a Christian idiom, under the influence of Pentecostal missions, in the practice of *chongo*, all-night sessions of loud drumming, singing, shouting, and speaking in strange tongues. Although *chongo* was nothing more than "gibbering, shivering, and generally mad fits," according to the colonial administrator Charles Draper, his attempt to suppress this religious activity suggests that the sounds of shamanic ecstasy could be perceived as threatening colonial authority and control.[16] Occasionally, shamans were involved in explicitly anticolonial movements and revolts.[17] Their mere existence, however, represented a wild space beyond colonial control.

WILDNESS

In colonial situations, shamanism can be located in struggles over the meaning and power of wildness. Drawing on a long history of literary and pictorial representations of the "wildman," European colonizers generally saw shamans as the wildest among wild people. As a hunting religion, requiring familiarity with wild animal spirits, shamanism has been perceived as essentially wild, but only from the perspective of people whose social order is based on animal husbandry and settled agriculture. For colonizers based in metropolitan centers of empire, shamanism represented the wild, dangerous, and disruptive antithesis of urban order.

As the opposite of domestication, wildness has often appeared as an indigenous category. Throughout southern Africa, for example, indigenous African religious life was organized by a structured opposition between the domestic space of the home, which was sanctified through relations with ancestors, and the wild space of the forest, bush, or desert, which harbored wild, dangerous, and evil forces. Operating between the domestic space and the wild space, African ritual specialists invoked ancestral spirits to protect the home against evil forces of the wild. Often, those evil forces were identified with witches, those antisocial agents who drew upon the dangerous power of the wild space. When colonial governments intervened to stop the detection and exposure of these agents of evil, indigenous ritual specialists could only conclude that the colonists were in league with the witches, colluding with these wild forces to disrupt the stable order of the ancestral home.[18]

In precolonial Andean religion too, shamans moved between domesticated order and the wild forces associated with the forests. Under the Inca empire, the shamans of the highland, who assumed religious responsibility for maintaining social order, stood in contrast to the lowland shamans of the forest, the wild, dangerous, and sometimes rebellious specialists in techniques of ecstasy.[19] In the highlands, *kubu* (priestly) shamans tended to comprise a small elite, the "owners of the chants," skilled in the regular rituals of the life cycle, social relations, and political stability. In the lowlands, *payés* (jaguar) shamans formed a more egalitarian, decentralized network of religious practitioners, gaining extraordinary power through rituals of trance and spirit possession, aided by hallucinogens, that could be used in healing, hunting, or warfare. The lowland shamans were conversant with *auca*, "the wild." Challenging the centralized political power of the highlands during the era of Inca sovereignty, these wild shamans of the forest were also at the forefront of religiously inspired rebellions against Spanish colonial authority. During the nineteenth century, shaman-prophets, identifying themselves with Christ as the "*payés* of the Cross," organized messianic movements in opposition to both foreign domination and indigenous shamans of the highlands.[20] As these religious rebellions suggest, anticolonial resistance can also address indigenous tensions between religiously sanctioned social order and the religious power of the wild.

In colonial engagements with wildness, indigenous and alien categories generated hybrid productions of meaning and power. Although wildness defied colonial control, many colonizers, entering what the novelist Joseph Conrad would call the "heart of darkness," were both repulsed and attracted by the "mysterious life of the wilderness that stirs in the forest, in the jungles, in the hearts of wild men."[21] As the wildest of the wild, the shaman was a focal point of colonial fear and fascination. Despite colonial policies of opposition, European settlers on colonial frontiers were known to consult indigenous shamans for healing or divination, although these intercultural exchanges have been largely neglected in the history of shamanism.

Today, they still consult. For many scholars in the academic study of religion, following Mircea Eliade's classic text *Shamanism*, the shaman exemplifies premodern religious experience, cultivated by "archaic techniques of ecstasy," a spirituality, however, that has been irrecoverably lost in modernity.[22] For enthusiasts of New Age spirituality, including self-proclaimed "white shamans" in the United States, the shaman exemplifies postmodern religious experience, available to anyone, anywhere.[23] By signing up for guided shamanic tours, which take spiritual tourists to meet with shamans in Siberia, Africa, or the Amazon, anyone can be initiated into the wild spirituality of the shaman. Between the premodern and the postmodern, the realities of colonialism anchored the religious practices of shamans within specific relations of meaning and power. Acting on behalf of a community, even when that community was displaced and dispossessed, shamans developed new religious strategies, not only for preserving archaic techniques of ecstasy, but also for exercising new capacities for memory, concealment, performance, translation, and transformation in negotiating indigenous religious survival under difficult colonial conditions.

12 Mobility

Our globalizing world has been characterized by the increased pace and scope of transnational flows of people, money, and technology but also by rapidly changing images of human possibility and by new ideals of human solidarity.[1] All of this mobility, speed, and transformation has certainly had an impact on religion, although theoretical resources are still being worked out to deal with globalizing effects on religious worlds.[2] Mobility requires mobile theory.

At a meeting of the International Association for the History of Religions held in Turku, Finland, August 1973, Walter H. Capps issued a challenge to develop mobile theory. Concluding his discussion of the history of the study of religion, which focused on what he called the "second-order tradition" of theoretical reflection, Capps called for a theoretical turn from trying to identify patterns of stability or permanence, what he called "arrested pictures," toward "processes of change, motion, movement, and spontaneity," making theory responsive to the dynamic, the kinetic, the catalytic. As Capps proposed, theory and method in the study of religion must be mobile enough to engage "the moving, inconstant, spontaneous, irregular, discontinuous, non-forensic, once-only, explosive, surprise element."[3]

That sentence, itself, was explosive, surprising. Nothing in the preceding discussion necessarily anticipated it. Capps's interest in recovering a second-order tradition might have seemed to be a conservative program that was designed to preserve a sense of continuity, whether discovered or invented, with earlier generations of scholarship on religion. But this sentence marked a radical break with the past. That breakthrough was both substantial and rhetorical—substantial in announcing a theoretical reorientation from recurring patterns to spontaneous change, and rhetorical not only in the implicit juxtaposition between still photographs and motion pictures but also in the rapid movement of adjectives, jump-cutting from one to another, evoking speed, picking up pace, as hints of theoretical possibilities fly by.

If we slow down this sentence, watch it develop in slow motion, we must be amazed by all of the possibilities on display. *Moving*, of course, is the point of departure. But look at what follows:

Inconstant: Changing frequently, unpredictably, without discernible pattern or reason, unstable, mercurial, capricious, fickle, and even faithless.

Spontaneous: Changing impulsively, without external constraints, voluntarily, instinctively, naturally.

Irregular: Changing idiosyncratically, like irregular verbs, with irregular rules of transformation.

Discontinuous: Changing radically, breaking totally and completely from a prior state or condition.

Nonforensic: Processes that cannot be policed or contained by any system of adjudication, whether through established judicial procedures or through conventional means of public argumentation.

Once-only: Events that cannot be repeated, cannot be replicated, even through formal attempts at retelling, remembering, or reenacting their singularity.

Explosive, surprising: Dramatic, perhaps even violent, breakthroughs, violating standard assumptions and conventional expectations about the nature of religion.

In reproducing this lexicon, I have added the brief elaborations for each term, although I do not know if I am even approximating what Walter

Capps had in mind when he included these words in his sentence. Certainly, all of these terms, all explosive and surprising, have wider resonance. Cumulatively, however, they are striking, startling in their speed and force. They seem to embody a mobile theory of religion. I want to review Capps's work of the early 1970s to examine the ways in which his dynamic understanding of religion and the study of religion, which one reviewer called "Capps' kinetic model for religious studies," anticipated the emergence of mobile theoretical resources for engaging dynamic religious change.[4]

SURPRISING

The International Association for the History of Religions study conference that convened August 27–31, 1973, in Turku, Finland, was designed to be a small gathering, with eighteen invited speakers and thirty-one respondents, in counterpoint to the larger quinquennial meetings of the association, positioned between the congresses of Stockholm 1970 and Lancaster 1975. Nevertheless, this meeting was important. As Eric J. Sharpe observed, out of all the conferences devoted to method, this one was "the most successful."[5] In a session on the phenomenology of religion devoted to "evaluation of previous methods," two responses were presented, one by C. J. Bleeker, the other by Walter Capps. Their evaluations were strikingly different. While Bleeker insisted on a return to core methods of history and philology, Capps called for a methodological revolution.

"The notion of previous methods which should be evaluated," Bleeker complained, "suggests that there exist novel methods, differing from the old ones and better than those previous methods." He doubted that was the case. Methods of the history of religions and the phenomenology of religion remained adequate, with philological and historical research uncovering religious "material" and phenomenological reflection developing "heuristic principles." Although he affirmed this basic reciprocity between history and phenomenology, Bleeker insisted that the "average" historian of religions should leave methodological speculation alone and stick to historical and philological methods. In addition to avoiding the risk of "dabbling" in questions that can only be solved by scholars with philosophical training, the "average" historian of religions "needs all his time and energy to increase his philological and historical capacities." In conclusion, Bleeker reinforced this fundamental core of history and philology by varying Rousseau's exhortation, "retournons à la nature," as a methodological imperative: "retournons à la philology et à l'histoire."[6]

While C. J. Bleeker concluded by urging fidelity to the "natural" methods of the history of religions, Walter Capps began his commentary by invoking Locke's metaphors of construction—the master builders, the underlaborers—in the introduction to his *Essay Concerning Human Understanding*. In an era dominated by intellectual "master builders," Locke proposed that it is "ambition enough to be employed as an underlaborer in clearing ground a little and removing some of the rubbish that lies in the way to knowledge."[7] Quickly, Capps assured his audience that he was not alleging that the study of religion was full of rubbish. He did not want to say, directly, that the study of religion "has been cluttered by the grand, all-encompassing, systematic thought patterns of the prominent master builders." Nevertheless, Capps maintained that some ground clearing was necessary. Pursuing the metaphor of building, he proposed that the study of religion cannot be advanced by piling theory upon theory, by revering grand theories, which might be obsolete but remain "monumental," or by indiscriminately invoking theoretical "master builders" from a variety of academic disciplines who "hardly ever enter the science of religion from the same standpoint or on the same grounds."[8]

Ground clearing, however, was not an end in itself. Capps wanted to clear a space for imagining new stories about the history of the study of religion, the second-order tradition. In a compelling phrase, he insisted that this intellectual enterprise "cannot pretend to find its way until it can relate to its past in narrative form." Not a single epic of the "apostolic succession" of master builders, the narratives Capps imagined would be multiple and mobile; they would be "disparate, disjointed, flexible, and accumulated or even created rather than discovered."[9]

According to Walter Capps, new narratives for the second-order tradition of the study of religion can be expected to bear two basic features: multiplicity and flexibility. First, these narratives will be multiple as they emerge out of different subject-positions. Researchers are necessarily situated. Location is crucial. Everyone stands somewhere. As Capps observed,

"What the scholar does within the subject-field depends upon where he is standing. Where he stands influences what he discovers. Furthermore, where he stands and what he discovers are implicit in what he is trying to do."[10] Scholarship, in this rendering, is pragmatic, trying to accomplish something, but it is also strategic and tactical in attempting to do something within a specific situation. Given the many different locations of academic inquiry, coming to terms with the past in narrative form will inevitably result in multiple narratives.

Second, narratives of the history of the study of religion will be flexible in accommodating diverse and even conflicting interests. "When the second-order tradition of the subject-field is conceived," Capps advised, "it must possess both sufficient dynamism and flexibility to sustain the following kinds of variability"—varieties of operational definitions; multiple methodological interests and intentions; and the "multiplicity of large controlling questions."[11]

Recasting the second-order tradition of the study of religion in narrative form cannot, according to Walter Capps, be a faithful retelling of a uniform or governing myth of origin and destiny. As he reflected two decades later on the power of narrative in *Religious Studies: The Making of a Discipline* (1995), Capps observed that any tradition, including the second-order tradition of religious studies, requires dynamic narratives, "stories that can be traced, stories that get retold, stories in whose retelling the traditions find ongoing shape, design, and purposes that may not have been recognized or anticipated by the founders."[12] Therefore, the founders, the master builders, have no privileged place in the stories that are told and retold within an ongoing tradition that is constantly reinventing itself in and through the process of formulating narratives.

Back in Finland in 1973, in his response to a session devoted to the evaluation of previous methods, Walter Capps did not evaluate previous methods. Instead, he sought to reevaluate the ways in which we think, talk, and tell stories about the cumulative tradition of the academic study of religion. Multiplicity and flexibility, he argued, must shape these stories of the past if the study of religion is going to find its way as a "dynamic subject-field." Fidelity to the past, he suggested, was not found in worshiping the "permanent" monuments of the master builders; it was demonstrated by including them critically, reflexively, in narratives shaped by new theoretical interests. As Capps observed in 1995, any tradition, including the second-order tradition of the study of religion, should be understood not as that which is handed down but as that which is taken up, as multiple and flexible, as "always in process, perennially susceptible to innovation and transformation."[13]

These observations about the study of religion as a dynamic subject-field might have prepared the audience in Turku for Capps's concluding remarks, in the final paragraphs of his presentation, about the dynamism of religion. But we should not underestimate the surprise. Suddenly, shifting focus, he jumped from past to future. Practitioners of past methods, unless they self-consciously recast those methods within new, dynamic narratives, were "doomed to maintain a rigid focus on permanence (norms, laws, structures, and recurrent patterns) within the science of religion." Stuck in the past, looking for enduring essences, stable structures, or recurring patterns, they could not engage the dynamic character of religion. "At some future point," Capps asserted, "the turn must be taken away from permanence to processes of change, motion, movement, and spontaneity."[14]

This turn from permanence to change was a methodological imperative that Walter Capps asserted at the Turku conference but did not develop through argumentation supported by evidence. Provocatively, but effectively, he evoked the "change factor" as the crucial focus for a study of religion, implicitly situating the subject-field in a world that was still undergoing the social, cultural, and religious changes associated with the 1960s. Although he made no direct reference to these changing times, Capps was attentive to his context. His reflections on the past and his imperatives for the future were deeply embedded in his struggles to make sense out of this shifting terrain of religious change.

At the same time, Capps's dichotomy of permanence and change, a thematic as old as Parmenides and Heraclitus, was invigorated by his juxtaposition of still photography and motion pictures, with his rejection of photographs, "arrested pictures" or "moments of stopped action," in favor of the dynamic, kinetic, and cinematic power of movies. However, this phrase, "arrested pictures," which Capps placed in quotation marks, without attribution, must have been familiar to his audience from the work of none other than the previous commentator, C. J. Bleeker. In his programmatic profile of the phenomenology of religion published in 1959 in *Numen*, the official journal of the International Association for the History of Religions, Bleeker had argued that "the significance of religious phenomena can be clarified to a great extent if they are examined, so to say, as arrested pictures."[15] Bleeker reinforced this point in his book *The Sacred Bridge*, published in 1963, by observing, "Generally the task of the phenomenology of religion is taken as a static one. It is certainly true that the significance of religious phenomena can be clarified to a great extent if they are examined, so to say, not as moving pictures but as arrested pictures."[16] While the history of religions must necessarily deal with historical change, the phenomenology of religion, according to Bleeker, focused on enduring patterns that could be discerned only by stopping the action, arresting the motion, and taking a still photograph.

Nevertheless, C. J. Bleeker also had an appreciation for the tension between arrested and moving pictures. While freezing the action, as a matter of method, in taking the phenomenologist's "arrested pictures," he argued that "it should not be forgotten that they are also moving pictures i.e. that they are subject to a certain dynamic." Although Bleeker's theory of religious dynamism, a kind of developmental essentialism that sought to trace the "course of events in which the essence is realized by its manifestations," might not seem very dynamic, he was aware that "arrested pictures" were what Capps called "moments of stopped action" taken out of the flow of moving pictures of dynamic change.[17]

As if he were anticipating the recent flourishing of research in religion and media, Capps might be misunderstood to be urging attention to religion in film. But he meant something more profound. He wanted scholars of religion to see that all religion, everywhere, is always in motion. Methods in the study of religion needed to respond to this mobility. Nevertheless, media studies might still provide a counterpoint to this injunction. For example, in his classic essay "The Work of Art in the Age of Mechanical Reproduction," the critical theorist Walter Benjamin argued that movies induced a "shock effect" in audiences. What Benjamin called the "shock effect of the film" had nothing to do with subject matter. Rather, the basic techniques used in the production and reproduction of film produced shocks by hitting, striking, engaging, and distracting the audience—through techniques of cutting, panning, zooming, and so on—

in ways that create a dynamic and variable aesthetic experience.[18] Moving pictures, therefore, have their own ways of moving people.

As he brought his commentary at the conference in Turku to a close, Walter Capps performed a cinematic sentence, with all of the "shock effect of film," striking and engaging, driven by jump-cutting and panoramic zooming, in urging the study of religion to "come to terms with the change factor." Once again, we return to this surprising sentence, having reviewed the context but also attuned to its cinematic "shock effect" in propelling us through a study of religion that attends to its "moving, inconstant, spontaneous, irregular, discontinuous, non-forensic, once-only, explosive, surprise element." As Capps argued, only mobile theorizing, which was informed by a multiple, flexible, and dynamic sense of theoretical tradition, could gain access to the dynamics of religion, its "catalytic and kinetic realities." However, in concluding his commentary for this session of the meeting, he observed that moving into mobile theory would "shift our topic to new ground." Accordingly, Capps ended where he began by concluding, "It is necessary to clear that ground a little."[19]

CHANGING

How did Walter Capps respond to his own challenge? Although he posed his challenge to an academic study of religion that had abandoned theology for historical and phenomenological methods, his own attempts to work out a theory of change were deeply embedded in theological reflection on the political, social, and cultural changes of the 1960s. While developing his arguments about a variable second-order tradition and religion in motion, Capps was also wrestling with the changes he was tracking in Christian theology, observing a pendulum shift from the social engagement of the theology of hope to the "positive disengagement" he found in the contemplative tradition, a change he explored in 1976 in *Hope against Hope: Moltmann to Merton in One Theological Decade.*

Set in the long decade of the 1960s, which in the U.S. political terrain explored by Walter Capps extended until the defeat of George McGovern in the presidential election of 1972, Christian theology underwent a "profound and shocking transition, a veritable revolution." This transition, this revolution, according to Capps, was not merely a change from one position to another, as if Christianity were working out its essence in a sequence of manifestations. Rather, this profound transition was a change into change, what Capps called "a decided shift to a dynamic, innovative, fluid and mobile, almost experimental orientation." Essential, enduring features of religious tradition dissolved in this tide of change. "In the process," Capps observed, "theologies of change have come to replace theologies of permanence."[20]

In trying to make sense of this radical shift into change, Capps engaged conversation partners—Robert Jay Lifton for his understanding of the protean style, Norman O. Brown for his celebration of erotic embodiment, and James Dittes for his analysis of the life-affirming possibilities in disengaging from an oppressive and alienating social world—who offered psychological perspectives on identity formation and fragmentation under changing social conditions.[21] In keeping with an abiding interest in the psychology of the "religious personality," especially as the personal intersected with the social in the psycho-historical analysis of Erik H. Erikson, these conversation partners helped Capps think about the disjuncture between personal subjectivity and any sense of a stable, enduring, or permanent social collectivity.[22]

However, for Walter Capps, the guiding intellectual agenda for wrestling with change was still set by the theology of hope, especially as it was informed by the work of Ernst Bloch. Returning to themes explored in his earlier book, *Time Invades the Cathedral,* Capps invoked Bloch's metaphors of the cathedral and the ship, with the cathedral standing for permanence and the ship moving in time. As Capps related, "Unlike the cathedral, the bastion of permanence, Bloch describes the ship, which, in learning how to move, was equipped to traverse change, process, and perpetual unrest." Now, Capps proposed, we are all on the ship, not only because of the dramatic social changes of the 1960s, but also because the ship is truer to life. In short, staccato, moving phrases, he observed, "Life moves. Reality is dynamic. Process rules."[23]

So, we are all in the same boat. The only thing permanent is change. All we know, in reality, is that we are moving. Sometimes, Walter Capps seems to celebrate change, for its own sake, as a dynamic life force. For example: "Change is rugged and powerful. It transforms everything it touches. It

rearranges boundaries. It upsets preestablished order. It modifies relationships. It alters contours. It reallocates and redistributes resources. It creates
new shapes and inserts qualifications into definitions. Not content with
simple composition, it decomposes, then recomposes. It modulates, trans-
poses, transfigures, and diversifies."[24] Change, in this rendering, which
again was delivered in a staccato, striking formulation, is a force in its own
right. Change changes everything: rearranging, upsetting, modifying, alter-
ing, reallocating, redistributing, reshaping, decomposing, recomposing,
transposing, modulating, transfiguring, and diversifying everything it
touches. Change, as Capps observed, is powerful.

Had he left the analysis at this point, we would have to conclude that
Capps was going around in a circle, stuck in the tautological assertion that
change produces change. However, having called attention to the dynamics of change, he pushed the analysis forward in two directions, one methodological, the other historical, in trying to work out a theory of change
that resonated with what he saw as the transition, even revolution, in contemporary Christianity.

At the midpoint of *Hope against Hope,* Walter Capps placed a chapter
on methodology, "Wisdom from the Analytical Fathers," which sketched
out a theory of change. Theologians and lay readers, who were part of his
intended audience, might skim or skip over this chapter, but it was a serious attempt, at the center of his book, to articulate his understanding of
change as ongoing alternations between binary oppositions.

The whole book, Capps revealed, had been about binary oppositions,
since he had "focused on tension, conflict, and the place and role of contrariness in contemporary religious consciousness." In all of his case studies, from Ernst Bloch's distinction between the cathedral of permanence
and the moving ship of change to Lifton's distinction between traditional
stability and protean transformations, Capps was interested in tracking
the "dynamic interaction between two poles of contrariness." As he noted,
"Contrariness is one of the most crucial facts about the way we design and
negotiate religious orientations." But contraries, binaries, and polar oppositions were also a matter of academic method in the study of religion. In
these methodological reflections, Capps wanted to make his theoretical
principles explicit, as an act of intellectual integrity, "because of an obligation to make our conceptual strategy self-conscious."[25]

Strategically, Walter Capps analyzed change as alternations between binary oppositions. Here, we must expect, he would make this conceptual strategy self-conscious by moving into the conceptual terrain charted by the structuralism of Claude Lévi-Strauss. Although this theoretical framing of binary oppositions received due mention, Lévi-Strauss did not guide the analysis. Capps started his reflections on method by returning to the problems of permanence and change that he raised at the International Association for the History of Religions meeting in Finland: "Ours has been an attempt to discern the dynamic of change. Most methodologies have turned their attention the other way. They have been designed to identify normative features—that is, the normative and repeatable law-like element, the pattern, standard, essence, nature, ontological, meta-physical, or conceptual core element, etc. But the approach used in this book is designed to mark and trace processes in motion. It is conceived to enunciate dynamic factors rather than permanent, inflexible, repeatable patterns." Some methods, Capps noted, have attended to change, such as statistical analysis or evolutionary theory, but they have failed to meet the challenge. Statistical methodologies, which are "designed to measure paths of deviation, alteration, variation, and change in religious attitudes and behavior," were inadequate because "additional intellectual work is required to explain and interpret." Evolutionary theory, with its sequence of progressive changes, was already overinterpreted, Capps argued, because no "simple straightline-forward evolutionary model" can account for the "skips and halts, movements back and forth, occurrences followed by their own dissolution, positive steps forward creating their own nega-tions, contrariness, conflict, opposition, antipathy, antagonism, contrari-ness, etc." Clearly, "contrariness," a term that was oddly repeated in this sentence, was crucial. But everything depended upon how we understand the dynamics of the contrary.[26]

As Capps asserted, contrariness was profoundly complex, signifying, simultaneously, a structural binary, in which the contrary stands in anti-thetical opposition, and a temporal sequence, in which the contrary dis-places and perhaps replaces its opposition. However, both of these relations of opposition, the structural and the temporal, depend upon the contrary retaining its opposite within the scope of its structural transposi-tions and temporal transformations. Therefore, he observed, contrariness is a modality that is both discontinuous and continuous with its opposition. Not a simple either-or proposition—as if the one was simply opposed to the other, as if one could simply replace two—contrariness entails complex mediations of continuity and discontinuity. "To deal with modes that are contrary is a different matter," he noted. "It requires a different strategy. For, in the case of contrariness, the relation of one to two is both continuous, sequential, and antithetical." Trying to clarify this complex relationship, Capps translated it into a mathematical formula, a simple calculus of contrariness. When dealing with contraries, he maintained, "it is not one plus two simply, but one plus two and one versus two simultaneously, like this: $(1 + 2) + (1 \text{ vs. } 2) = $ the structure of religious reality." In case we miss the complexity, Capps advised that "this is a complicated sequence."[27]

At this point, we might be longing for the simplicity of Hegel, with his progressive dialectics of thesis, antithesis, and synthesis, but Walter Capps argued that change followed no progression because it was "formed by a dialectic which oscillates back and forth, almost like a pendulum swinging." Moving back and forth, like a pendulum, might suggest that change is not actually going anywhere. But Capps insisted that this oscillation was the engine of change because contrariness, which simultaneously opposed, replaced, and retained its opposition, generated dynamic energy, created dynamic momentum, in social, cultural, and religious life. "Contrariness," he held, "has been formed by a specific dialectic, a logic which applies uniquely to the interrelationship between terms that are conceived to be both sequential and contrary, simultaneously and recurrently."[28] This contrariness, which Capps understood as a colliding and coinciding of oppositions, a *coincidentia oppositorum* with a difference, was both the logic and energetics of change.

All of this methodological reflection, however, was not an end in itself. Capps was primarily interested in using this dynamic model of change to understand the history of Christianity. Here he identified the contraries, the binaries, in Christian history as two religions, one oriented toward permanence, the other toward change, one preserving the past, the other imagining the future, one vertically aligned with timeless transcendence, the other horizontally engaging with the world. Clearly, Ernst Bloch's metaphors of the cathedral and the ship informed this understanding of two religions. Jürgen Moltmann's theology of hope suggested to Capps that

Christianity was moving out of the cathedral and into the sea of change. In Moltmann's *Religion, Revolution, and the Future* (1969), he saw the Christian pendulum swinging from the religion of permanence to the religion of change.[29] In an extended review, Capps argued that Moltmann's work marked a dramatic shift from Christianity's religion of stable permanence to its religion of dynamic change.

> Most fundamentally, I believe, *Religion, Revolution, and the Future* serves as a sketch of the rudiments and formative interests of the second of the two religions of Christianity. This is the religion which builds upon "dynamic" rather than "static" categories (to borrow the distinction from Henri Bergson) and which yields to horizontal rather than vertical structural depiction. It is oriented toward the future rather than toward the past or the present, and it locates transcendence in an anticipated temporal norm. It is regulated by change rather than by permanence, and its philosophical *Urvater* is Heraclitus rather than Parmenides.[30]

Only a few years later, however, Capps found the Christian pendulum swinging back "from change to permanence." He associated this retreat from an engaged political theology of transformation with the political defeats of liberal politicians and projects during the early 1970s. But he also argued that such a pendulum swing was intrinsic to the dynamics of religious change. "Our analysis discloses that binary relationships are intrinsic to religious orientations," Capps explained. "Because of this, one can expect a perpetual oscillation between binarial poles." Observing an oscillation from progressive change to conservative authority, he also held out hope that this return to the religion of permanence would retain aspects of its polar opposite, resulting in the emergence of a "new sort of permanence and a refined, updated, dynamic, and more resilient basis of authority."[31]

Walter Capps took this analysis of change forward beyond the 1960s. Having passed through an era of change, the enduring traditions of Christian mysticism and monasticism, he imagined, might be recovered as a new kind of religious authority, "positively disengaged" but still incorporating dynamic features of change.[32] Nevertheless, keeping hope alive required engaging a world of political struggle. Over the years, Capps engaged the unresolved legacy of Vietnam, the oppositional religious politics of the New Religious Right, and American electoral and rhetorical politics in running, successfully, for Congress in the United States.[33]

Clearly, Capps's kinetic model of religious studies was situated in a turbulent era of dramatic social, cultural, and religious change. But all models are situated in changing times. During the early 1970s, Capps tried to engage the contradictions of his time by developing a theory of change as the oscillations and energies created by shifting contraries, binaries, or polar oppositions. In *Hope against Hope*, struggling with religious change, he was not writing a methodological treatise, noting, "The intention of this book is not to concentrate on scholars' methodology. Important as that may be—especially to readers who have been professionalized into theology or religious studies—the real point concerns contrariness."[34] This real point helps us understand his contribution to the "evaluation of previous methods" at the 1973 meeting of the International Association for the History of Religions. While calling for dynamic, multiple, and flexible narratives of the history of the study of religion and attention to the dynamism of religion in motion, Walter Capps was also trying to think through the dynamics of religious change.

13 Popular

Religion is not an isolated activity in human life but is engaged with popular culture at every level—in work and in play, in regular rituals and in social relations. Although religion is conventionally regarded as a separate and distinct social institution dealing with the supernatural and anchored in the church, synagogue, mosque, or temple, it has assumed complex and ambivalent relations with the popular media as well as with other aspects of the culture industry. Religious themes are consistently represented in media such as radio, recordings, television, film, and the Internet, technologies that in turn have been adopted by religious groups. In this exchange, tensions often arise between religious interests and the popular cultural formations of the larger society. For example, on June 18, 1996, the Southern Baptist Convention passed a resolution to boycott the Walt Disney Company. Arguing that the company had abandoned its former commitment to providing healthy family entertainment, the convention accused Disney of promoting immorality, homosexuality, and adultery. In launching a crusade against Disney, the group argued that the company was a cultural force working against conservative Christian beliefs, values, and sexual ethics. In addition, they suggested that Disney was actually promoting an alternative religion, an earth-based, pagan, and pantheistic

166

religiosity celebrated in animated features such as *The Lion King* (1994) and *Pocahontas* (1995), films that, in the view of the Southern Baptist Convention, constituted a threat to Christianity.[1]

As this religious crusade against Disney suggests, popular culture can appear from different perspectives as religion. If religion refers to a symbolic system of beliefs and practices, experiences, and social relations revolving around a sacred focus, a focus of attention that is set apart from the ordinary, then many forms of popular culture seem to have a religious character. Disney animation invokes supernatural themes, and Disney theme parks—in Anaheim and Orlando, in Tokyo and outside Paris—have become both tourist destinations and pilgrimage sites in a popular cultural religion.[2] Many other sacred sites of religious pilgrimage in American popular culture could be identified: national parks maintain the "sacred ground" of American battlefields, for example; the shrine of Graceland in Memphis, Tennessee, preserves the sacred memory of Elvis Presley; the Baseball Hall of Fame in Cooperstown, New York, stands as the "Mecca of Baseball" and has been described by Hall of Fame pitcher Don Sutton as a "sacred place" that holds the "Holy Grail of baseball"; the World of Coca-Cola in Atlanta, Georgia, is a "temple to the great American soft drink" that celebrates the Coca-Cola religion of a world in perfect harmony; and even McDonald's fast-food restaurants, with their ordinary efficiency but extraordinary golden arches, advertising imagery, and popular appeal, have been identified by sociologist George Ritzer as an American "sacred institution."[3] In all of these locations of popular culture, religious symbols, myths, and rituals seem to be at work; indeed, a kind of religious work seems to be taking place in and through popular culture.

POPULAR CULTURE AND RELIGION

According to a quantitative definition, popular culture is popular because it is mass-produced, widely distributed, and regularly consumed by large numbers of people. Demographically, the popular might be simply understood as a measure of popularity. A cultural form is popular, in this sense, because many people like it. Implicit in this quantitative definition of the

popular is a distinction between "high" culture, maintained by a numeri-
cally small social elite, and the "low" culture of the majority of people in a
society. As a result, the popular, whether in popular culture or popular
religion, has tended to be located among the laity rather than the clergy,
among rural folk rather than city dwellers, and among urban lower classes
rather than urban elites.[4] In cultural studies, however, the popular has
come to refer to a much more complex range of social positions within the
production, circulation, and consumption of culture. As people actively
decode cultural content through interpretation, they also participate in
rituals of consumption, rituals of exchange, ownership, and care through
which the arts and artifacts of popular culture are personalized.[5]

Three basic relationships have been established between religion and
popular culture: religion appears in popular culture; popular culture is
integrated into religion; and religion is sometimes in conflict with the production and consumption of popular culture.

First, representations of religion and religions are expressed in the productions of popular culture. During the twentieth century, the explosion
of electronic media expanded the scope of religious representations
through radio, film, television, and the Internet. On December 24, 1906,
the first wireless radio broadcast in the United States consisted of a religious program of devotional music and Bible reading. Although electronic
media have certainly been exploited by religious groups for their own
interests, the culture industry has also been actively involved in representing religious themes. In American popular culture, the secular and commercial productions of Hollywood films have played a powerful role in
shaping public perceptions of religion and religions. On the one hand,
representations of religion can be explicit. Popular films depict recognizable religious characters—priests and nuns, evangelists and rabbis, gurus
and lamas—in their narratives. They draw story lines from religious traditions, especially from the Bible, in producing popular films. On the other
hand, according to many cultural analysts, representations of religion in
film are often implicit. Basic religious motifs of sin, sacrifice, and redemption, for example, can structure the plots of ostensibly secular films.[6]

Second, the practices of conventional religions incorporate aspects of
popular culture. Successful religious groups generally adopt the material
culture, the visual media, the musical styles, and other features of popular

culture. In American culture, the prominence of religious broadcasting on television has demonstrated the success of Christian evangelicals in appropriating an advanced communications technology in the service of the "great mandate" to preach their gospel to all nations. More recently, religious groups have established their presence on the Internet, exploring the potential of cyberspace for religious mobilization. Drawn into the service of transmitting religion, the media of popular culture present both new possibilities and new limits for the practice of religion. In the entire range of electronic media, the transmission of religion is exclusively visual and auditory, offering new forms of visual piety and new styles of preaching, praying, and singing. But the religion of electronic media is devoid of all the smells, tastes, and physical contacts that feature in conventional religious ritual and religious life. While converting popular culture to religious purposes, religious groups are also converted by the pervasive culture of consumerism in American society. As a prominent if not defining feature of American popular culture, consumerism has resulted in "selling God," transforming religious holy days into "consumer rites," and even fostering "religio-economic corporations," such as Amway, Herbalife, and Mary Kay Cosmetics, that merge business, family, and a Christian gospel of prosperity into a "charismatic capitalism."[7]

Third, tensions often develop between religious groups and the productions of popular culture. Frequently, conservative Christians complain about the moral relativism and spiritual corruption of American popular culture in general. With particular intensity, they single out rock 'n' roll, rap, and other forms of popular recorded music as being dangerously immoral, antisocial, and antireligious. Like the Baptist boycott of the Walt Disney Company, religious campaigns to censor, label, or influence popular music are periodically waged by conservative Christian activists and organizations. Going beyond the music and lyrics, these critics attack the imagery, values, and lifestyles associated with these popular art forms. In this cultural conflict over popular music, evangelical Christians have created a successful commercial industry in Christian rock music—or contemporary Christian music—that is unified less by musical style, rhythm, or performance than by the explicitly religious content of the lyrics. As a result of conflict between a particular religious grouping and the productions of popular culture, therefore, alternative cultural movements can emerge and even establish a place within the culture industry.

As conventional religious groups interact with popular culture in these ways—by being represented in its media, by adopting its techniques, or by rejecting its productions—the dividing line between religion and popular culture blurs. While popular media are telling religious stories and religious groups are appropriating popular media, culture wars engage intense religious interests. The very term *religion* becomes part of the contested terrain of popular culture. Although representatives of conventional religious groups tend to reserve the term for themselves, relegating popular culture to the realm of the secular, they occasionally designate the production or consumption of popular culture as "religion" in order to intensify the cultural contest. As noted, the Southern Baptist Convention boycotted Disney not only because it was a secular alternative to religion but also because the corporation was allegedly advancing an alternative religion in competition with Christianity. Likewise, religious critics occasionally attack rock music for promoting the alternative religions of Satanism or pantheism. In these exchanges, it is hard to tell where religion leaves off and popular culture begins. Participants in popular culture often report that religious interests are at stake. Does it make sense, however, to say that popular culture can operate as religion?

POPULAR CULTURE AS RELIGION

In any analysis of popular culture as religion, everything depends, of course, on what one means by "religion." The academic study of religion draws upon an intellectual legacy of competing definitions. For example, E. B. Tylor, the founder of the anthropology of religion, defined religion as beliefs and practices relating to the supernatural; Emile Durkheim, the founder of the sociology of religion, defined it as beliefs and practices relating to a sacred focus that unify people as a community. These academic definitions share a common interest in setting religion apart from ordinary, everyday, or mundane aspects of human life. Religion is cast as superhuman and sacred, as transcendent and ultimate, as highly charged and extraordinary. Looking at popular culture, however, we find ordinary, everyday cultural production and consumption. How could such ordinary activity be regarded as extraordinary?

Participants in popular culture make claims about its religious character. Reflecting on baseball after a lifetime devoted to the sport, Buck
O'Neil asserted, "It is a religion." On behalf of the Coca-Cola Company,
advertising director Delony Sledge declared, "Our work is a religion rather
than a business." Responding to the extraordinary popularity of his rock 'n'
roll band, John Lennon observed that popular music seemed to be replacing Christianity in the field of religion because the Beatles were "more
popular than Jesus." Many participants in the popular culture of rock 'n'
roll would probably subscribe to rock critic Dan Graham's statement of
faith professed in his book and video titled *Rock, My Religion*.[8] Still, the
problem remains: What do people mean when they use the term *religion?*
Although all of these participants in popular culture use the term, they are
using it in different ways.

Baseball is a religion because it defines a community of allegiance, the
"Church of Baseball." Uniform in the present and continuous with the past,
baseball operates like a religious tradition in preserving the symbols,
myths, and rituals of a sacred collectivity. Certainly, other sports provide a
similar basis for sacred allegiance. As one wrestling journalist observed, a
television exposé of the alleged fakery in the World Wrestling Federation
was contemptible because it tried to reveal "the 'secrets' of our sacred
'sport.'"[9] Although this journalist put the term *sport* within quotation
marks, he did not similarly bracket the term *sacred*. Although staged, con-
trived, and faked as if it were a sport, federation wrestling might still be
regarded as sacred because it enacts a popular American contest of good
against evil. As ritual rather than sport, federation wrestling can be
regarded as religion because it reinforces a certain kind of sacred solidarity
in American popular culture.

Like sports fans, the fans of Hollywood films, television shows, and popular music can participate in similar kinds of sacred solidarity, especially
when that community of allegiance is focused upon the extraordinary personality of a celebrity.[10] Elvis, the King, of course, has emerged as the
preeminent superhuman in American popular culture. He is celebrated
posthumously throughout America, at sites ranging from the official sanctuary of Graceland to the unofficial website of the First Presleyterian Church
of Elvis the Divine on the Internet, as an extraordinary being. Devotees
of Elvis Presley, who collect, arrange, and display Elvis memorabilia,

participate in the annual rituals of Elvis week, and go on pilgrimage to his shrine at Graceland, find in the King not only a religious focus of attention but also a focal point for mobilizing an ongoing community of sacred allegiance. Similarly, fans of the *Star Trek* television series and movies have created a community of sacred solidarity with its own myths and rituals, its own special language, and regular pilgrimages. The series has thus assumed the proportions of a popular religion. In all of these cases, the term *religion* seems appropriate because it evokes a sacred solidarity.

Coca-Cola is a religion because it revolves around a sacred object, the fetish of Coca-Cola. As a consumer product that no one needs but everyone desires, Coca-Cola is also an icon of the American way of life. Although that way of life is celebrated at the pilgrimage site World of Coca-Cola in Atlanta, Georgia, it has also been diffused throughout the world. Coca-Cola is a sacred object at the center of a cultural religion that is both American and global, within arm's reach of desire, all over the world, according to former Coca-Cola president Robert Guizueta. In its materiality, the religion of Coca-Cola recalls the importance of icons, relics, and other sacred objects in the history of religions. Certainly, American popular culture enjoys a rich diversity of sacred icons, such as Disney's mouse, McDonald's arches, and Nike's swoosh. As many cultural analysts have observed, these icons have been established by an advertising industry that has functioned like a religion, a religious enterprise that one critic has called Adcult U.S.A.[11] The sacred materiality of these icons, however, reflects the importance of material culture in religion. In the production and consumption of popular culture, even ordinary, everyday objects can be transformed into icons, extraordinary magnets of meaning with a religious cast. For these objects of popular culture, the term *religion* seems appropriate because it captures a certain quality of attention, desire, and even reverence for sacred materiality.

Rock 'n' roll is a religion because it enacts an intense, ritualized performance, the "collective effervescence," as Durkheim put it, which is generated by the interaction between ritual specialists and congregants or, in this case, between artists and audiences. Recent research on religious ritual has focused on the dynamics of performance. From this perspective, ritual is sacred drama. In performance, ritual is also an interactive exchange, a dynamic process of giving and receiving. According to rock critic Dave Marsh, rock 'n' roll is religious because it is precisely such a sacred ritual of exchange, a ritual of giving and receiving perhaps best exemplified by the break in the archetypal rock song "Louie, Louie," when the singer screeches, "Let's give it to 'em, right now!"[12] This gift, as a pure gift, transcends the prevailing American value system that is based on maximizing profits and minimizing losses within an overarching system of capitalist market relations. American popular culture valorizes gift giving—at birthdays, weddings, and other ritual occasions—in ways that the market cannot value. In such rituals of giving and receiving, where value in the exchange is not determined solely by the market, popular culture preserves important aspects of traditional religious life. For these ritualized occasions of gift giving, the term *religion* seems appropriate to identify performances, practices, or events of sacred exchange.

A POPULAR CULTURAL RELIGION

In practice, all of these aspects of religion—the mobilization of a community of sacred allegiance, the focus on a sacred object, and the ritualization of sacred exchange—might come together in the same cultural formation within American popular culture. Around 1942, Earl Silas Tupper took the black industrial waste product of polyethylene slag and transformed it into what he called "Poly-T: Material of the Future," the basic material for a range of household products he created as Tupperware. "Through an act of genius and alchemy," according to historian Alison J. Clarke, "Earl Tupper summoned forth a divine creation to benefit humanity."[13] Envisioning the total Tupperization of the American home, Earl Tupper was frustrated by the lack of popular interest in his products. In department stores, catalogs, and direct marketing, Tupperware did not sell. Although he was the originator of a "divine creation," Earl Tupper found no devotees for the products of Tupperization. In the early 1950s, however, an unemployed, divorced housewife, Brownie Wise, initiated the Tupperware party, an invention more important than the production of Poly-T in the history of Tupperware because it created a community of sacred allegiance. The Tupperware party was a radical innovation in direct marketing. In contrast to the traveling salesman, who was generally distrusted, as Clarke observed, because of "his dislocation from the most sacred of all American institutions—the home," the housewife who hosted a Tupperware party was able to reinforce the sanctity of the home.[14] In this domestic ritual, chairs were arranged so "guests face the product as if on an altar." Hosts presented the product with "religious zeal," trying to "invest their bowls with qualities demanding 'reverence,' 'awe,' and 'respect.'" Accordingly, the Tupperware party created small-scale, local communities of sacred allegiance through these "religious-like rituals."[15]

Once those "religious-like" communities had been formed, the sacred object, Poly-T, could become a focal point for religious attention. As the mediologist Régis Debray has observed, the material organization of a community always precedes the organization of the matter that enables the transmission of its culture.[16] Following the formation of a social network for Tupperware, Brownie Wise reported in 1954 that she had preserved the original black polyethylene slag, which she affectionately referred to as Poly, and insured it for fifty thousand dollars. Taking this black lump of plastic to Tupperware sales rallies, Brownie Wise invited dealers "to shut their eyes, rub their hands on Poly, wish, and work like the devil, then they're bound to succeed."[17] In this promise, Wise echoed the widespread belief in the power of positive thinking, especially as exemplified by Norman Vincent Peale's maxim "Faith Made Them Champions," which pervaded the worldview of American popular culture. Self-realization, however, demanded being of service to others. Focusing on Poly as a sacred object, Tupperware dealers could imagine that they were engaged in both personal fulfillment and public service. As one journalist reported, "Seeing every day the results of their work in other people's happiness, they find in their activity a kind of religion."[18]

Like any religion, Tupperware had to locate itself within a broader religious sense of territory, identifying its sacred center. Built in 1954 on a thousand acres in Orlando, Florida, that sacred center, the Tupperware Mecca, became a pilgrimage site for Tupperware dealers. Reinforcing the importance of the sacred object, Wise sanctified Poly Pond by throwing a handful of polyethylene pellets into the water. Dealers came to be baptized by touching the water of "sacred Poly Pond" at Tupperware headquarters. As Wise declared in 1955: "The very ground here is consecrated to a program of furthering the interests of you in the Tupperware family."[19] By casting plastic upon the waters, Wise had ceremoniously consecrated that sacred ground in Orlando through the ritual deployment of a sacred object.

Of course, Tupperware was a commercial enterprise, a business venture committed to maximizing profit and minimizing loss. Clearly committed to making money, the Tupperware organization also incorporated traditional forms of gift giving. Although the Tupperware party in private homes regularly featured gifts, the small tokens of appreciation given to guests, the hosts of those parties, the Tupperware dealers, could go on pilgrimage once a year to Tupperware headquarters to participate in a gift-giving ritual. At the Tupperware Mecca in 1954, for example, Brownie Wise gathered her dealers to "dig for gold." With symbols of wealth buried in the consecrated grounds, she urged the dealers to dig for their gifts. As a journalist reported, "Six hundred erect shovels, set in the sacred Tupperware grounds, awaited the eager gold diggers."[20] In such ritualized display and extravagant expenditure, Wise reinforced the power of Tupperware, not according to conventional economic indicators, but through symbols, myths, and rituals of religion. As Alison Clarke observed, Tupperware developed a corporate culture "which bolstered concepts of religiosity, ritual, love, kinship, and informal economy," relying "on systems of barter, reciprocity, and displays of ritual, mysticism, and gift giving."[21] A crucial ingredient in Tupperware's success, therefore, was the company's incorporation of rituals of sacred exchange into its business practice.

AMERICAN POPULAR CULTURE

"Tupperware—Everywhere!" was Brownie Wise's slogan for her network of home parties. By the end of the 1950s, however, the inventor Earl Tupper had forced Tupperware's organizational, cultural, inspirational, and religious mobilizer out of the business, reportedly because he was outraged by her proposal that the company should open up a new product line by producing a Tupperware dog dish. Regarding this suggestion as a heresy, a blasphemous denigration of his gift to humanity, Tupper effectively excommunicated Wise, only to sell the Tupperware enterprise a few months later to the Rexall Drug Company. In these transactions, from the universal claims of Tupperware executives to their local conflicts, Tupperware operated exactly like a religion.

By the end of the twentieth century, American popular culture was global. In the case of Tupperware, for example, a company that has been described as "all-American as the stars and stripes," 85 percent of its sales came from outside of the United States. Similarly, major transnational corporations— Coca-Cola, McDonald's, Disney, and others—carried American popular culture around the globe. As Arjun Appadurai has proposed, *globalization* is a term in the intellectual armory that might advance ongoing struggles to analyze the shifting terrains of a changing world. At the very least, *globalization* signals a growing awareness that things have changed in the world's landscapes of human, technological, financial, ideological, and media geography. This new global geography, without fixed borders, calls attention to global fluidity, fluctuations, circulations, and dispersions of people, machinery, capital, ideas, and images, the global flows that Appadurai has identified as the fluid movement of people through new ethnoscapes, of machinery through new technoscapes, of capital through new financescapes, of ideas of political solidarity through new ideoscapes, and of mass media–generated images of human possibility through new mediascapes.[22] All of this global fluidity, of course, seems entirely too fluid, divorced from any political economy, but also divorced from the intractable problems posed by the translation, rationalization, and imagination of matter. Materiality might flow, but it might not flow quite so fluidly.

Looking back at the twentieth century, historians in the future could very well find that the entire world was living in the Age of Plastic. In the early decades of the century, plastic was still a metaphor, a figure of speech that signified the opposite of the fixed, the permanent, or the rigid. In the academic work of the pioneering American sociologist Edward Alsworth Ross, for example, everything in human society could be classified as either rigid or plastic. Every social institution—religious, scientific, legal, and so on—had its rigid and plastic sides. As Ross maintained in his classic text *Social Psychology*, originally published in 1908, the rigid aspects of a society are always at risk, only waiting for destruction, because the rigid "admits only of the replacement of the old by the new." By contrast, the plastic features of social institutions are able to survive change. "Advance on the plastic side," Ross explained, "is much easier than on the rigid side."

Instead of risking the fate of being entirely replaced by the new, the plastic side of any social institution "admits of accumulation by the union of the new with the old."[23] While this American sociologist was calculating the stress relations between the rigid and the plastic, the French philosopher Henri Bergson undertook an investigation of laughter, which he also conducted as a sociological study. He was interested in the ways in which laughter worked "to readapt the individual into the whole" and employed a similar structural opposition between the rigid and the plastic in finding that the function of laughter "is to convert rigidity into plasticity."[24]

During the Age of Plastic, plasticity might have remained a mere metaphor, a figurative, rhetorical opposition to rigidity in cultural analysis, if not for the dramatic transformations in the imagination of matter that attended the chemical engineering of polyethylene. Through this breakthrough in scientific imagination, intervention, and ingenuity, plasticity was transformed into plastic, the polyethylene substance of material plasticity. In the Age of Plastic, one must forgive any historian the rhetorical extravagance of invoking divinity or alchemy when talking about a development in plasticity as important as Tupperware. During the Age of Plastic, one of the leading scholars of signs, the semiologist Roland Barthes, realized that plasticity signified everything important in the imagination of matter in the twentieth century. According to Barthes, the production of plastic was an alchemical transformation that mediated exchanges not only between base matter and gold but also between human beings and God. As Barthes described these alchemical transactions: "At one end, raw, telluric matter, at the other, the finished human object; and between these two extremes, nothing; nothing but a transit, hardly watched over by an attendant in a cloth cap, half-god, half-robot."[25] Half God, half robot; part divine, part machine; something superhuman, but also something subhuman—the scientist overseeing the alchemical transformation of earth into plastic was positioned, Barthes noted, at the intersection of these supreme, absolute extremes—divinity above, machines below—that framed the meaning and power of the modern world.

In this way of imagining matter, therefore, plastic seemed to represent a midpoint, a nexus, or an *axis mundi* in creative exchanges, in the sudden, unobserved, and perhaps imperceptible transitions conducted among the more than human, the human, and the less than human. In a plastic age celebrating its alchemy, plasticity seemed to define the contours of a religious world. Plasticity, however, was not only fluid. Plastic signified the alchemical transactions between different levels of reality, but also a basic, underlying uniformity. Plastic signified a substantial uniformity of materiality. After all, however it might be produced, plastic was always plastic. Recognizing that homogeneity of plastic, Barthes declared, "The hierarchy of substances is abolished: a single one replaces them all: the whole world *can* be plasticized, and even life itself since, we are told, they are beginning to make plastic aortas."[26] Replaced, in principle, by plastic, human life and all other values became equivalent. In this plastic imagination of matter, with the abolition of any differentiation of material substances, everything is plastic, even life itself.

Between the same and the different, all over the world, religious groupings seek to mold the plasticity of American popular culture in the service of their own religious interests. At the same time, in those negotiations local cultural formations are also molded, American-style, but not necessarily in ways that are controlled by corporate headquarters in the United States. Within the United States, as well, new forces and discourses have shaped cultural formations on frontiers, in the borderlands, or through processes of creolization that are beyond any centralized control, while much of what is regarded as distinctively "American" culture can be traced to Africa, Asia, Europe, or elsewhere. In all of these cultural exchanges, the term *religion* identifies a layer, dimension, strand, or thread of culture that bestows a certain degree of urgency upon questions of human identity, location, and media. In the constellation of discourses and forces shaping American religion in the twenty-first century, popular culture operates at the intersection of new technologies of cultural production, new modes of cultural consumption, and new strategies for imagining human possibility. These innovations have made a dramatic difference in the ways in which religion intersects with popular cultural formations not only in the United States but also in the rest of the world.

14 Touching

Like other disciplines devoted to the study of culture, the study of religion has discovered the body as a crucial location for analysis. Displacing earlier concerns with religious beliefs and doctrines, with inner experience and spirituality, this academic interest in the body signals a new engagement with materiality—perhaps a new materialism—in the study of religion. However, a certain mystification persists in thinking about religion that risks eliding its embodied, material dynamics. Introducing a series of essays titled *About Religion,* Mark C. Taylor observes that it is "impossible to grasp what religion is about—unless, perhaps, what we grasp is the impossibility of grasping." Neither quite there nor exactly not there, religion is "always slipping away."[1] However, even this slippage that signals the impossibility of touching, holding, or grasping religion forces us back to the body, to its sensory media and metaphors and the kinds of knowledge that can be gained only by the body.

We can explore the sense of touch as an avenue for entering the embodied, visceral, and material field of religion. By paying attention to sensory media and metaphors, and particularly to tactile practices, postures, and pressures, we may recognize some basic features of religious tactility that are not necessarily seen or heard but which nevertheless pervade contemporary religion and culture. Schematically, I proceed from cutaneous binding and burning, through kinesthetic moving, to haptic handling in order to enter this field of tactile meaning and power. I draw examples and illustrations primarily from the United States. However, the centrality of tactility in religious discourse and practice has wider resonance. Although this chapter replicates a tactile experience by renouncing visual mapping and verbal argumentation, it points to the presence of a tactile politics of perception that might help us understand one of the most vexed questions of critical theory: How do we account for the intersections between human subjectivity and the social collectivity?

CARESS AND SHOCK

A long tradition of Western philosophical reflection on the senses has identified touch as the lowest sense, the most animal, servile, and unconscious of the resources of the human sensorium. At the same time touch was conceptualized as the most fundamental sense and the basis of all sensory perception.[2] In the formation of Christian religious discourse, this underlying tactility of perception was never explicitly thematized. Certainly, the New Testament displayed an ambivalence about touch. As the patron saint of Christian tactility, the apostle Thomas is presented in the Gospel of John as demonstrating that touching is believing, while Mary, the patron saint of a kind of antitactility, is told, "Do not touch" (John 20:24–29, 20:17). More than a contradiction, this calculus of touching and not touching has been central to the practice of Christianity. Laying on hands, anointing with oils, washing feet, holy kissing, swearing oaths on the Bible, taking up snakes, and so on, are all forms of religious tactility that both signify and enact a direct, powerful, and even intimate contact with the sacred. At the same time, the sacred is inevitably surrounded by prohibitions on illicit contact, with those restrictions implicitly or explicitly backed up by force or the threat of force, as in the case of the Israelites before Mount Sinai who were warned that "whosoever touches the mount shall surely be put to death" (Exod. 19:12). For early Christian theorists, this dialectic of touch was generally submerged under the transcendent demands of sight and hearing. Augustine of Hippo, for example, was clear that "the objects that we touch, taste, and smell are less like truth than the things we see and hear."[3] By paying attention to the sense of touch, however, religious discourse and practice can be situated in this dialectic of contact and concussion, embracing and striking, that defines the basic character of religious tactility.

During the twentieth century, two theorists of tactility, Emmanuel Levinas and Walter Benjamin, expanded our understanding of contact and concussion—the intimate caress, the violent shock—in the perceptual dynamics of the sense of touch. Both explicitly addressed the tactility of religion. On the one hand, Emmanuel Levinas was a theorist of the embrace, finding in the sense of touch the basic engagement of the self with the world and the underlying unity of the senses. Levinas proposed that the flesh implicated the self in a world of contact, proximity, and intimacy.[4] In this approach, the world is experienced because it is intimately touched, rendering tactility, in the process, more than merely a sense. As a metaphor for embracing the world of experience as a whole, touch represented for Levinas the basis for all sensory experience. According to Levinas, "One sees and hears like one touches."[5]

On the other hand, Walter Benjamin was a theorist of the shock, finding in tactile concussion both the underlying unity of the senses and the basic organization of art, religion, and politics in modernity. Benjamin stated in "The Work of Art in the Age of Mechanical Reproduction" that the sense of touch had been reorganized by recent technological developments creating what Benjamin called "shock effects." In subjects ranging from Dada to cinema, Benjamin found that aesthetics had become "an instrument of ballistics," with images and words, styles and techniques, deployed in ways that "hit the spectator like a bullet[,] . . . thus acquiring a tactile quality."[6] By identifying the characteristically modern aesthetic experience as tactile, Benjamin developed a basic analytical opposition between visual concentration and tactile distraction: "The tasks which face the human apparatus at the turning points of history cannot be solved by optical means, that is, by contemplation alone. They are mastered gradually by habit, under the guidance of tactile appropriation. . . . The distracted person, too, can form habits."[7] As the "polar opposite" of visual attention, habitual distraction represented the characteristically tactile mode of human sense perception that had come to prominence under the historical conditions of modernity.

With the historical shift from visual attention to the tactile distractions of the arts of mechanical reproduction, the work of art had been alienated from its traditional location. Tradition, as that which is "handed down," anchored objects in place, signifying precisely where and when they might be touched, thereby certifying the "aura" of their originality and authenticity. Under the impact of mechanical reproduction, however, art underwent "a tremendous shattering of tradition." "Instead of being based on ritual," Benjamin observed, "it begins to be based on another practice—politics."[8] What kind of a politics of perception, we might ask, operates in the tactility—the intimate caresses, the violent shocks—of contemporary American religion? Furthermore, to what extent does this tactile politics operate not only in mainstream American religion but also on the fringes of American popular culture?

BINDING

If we gave credence to etymology—and if we accepted that *religio* has its root in *religare*, "to bind"—then we would have a tactile basis for the very notion of religion. From its ancient origins, according to this rendering, religion has been about binding relations, either among humans or between humans and gods, that have constituted the fabrics and textures, the links and connections, the contracts and covenants of religion. In this respect, although religious discourse might very well point beyond all that can be seen, heard, smelled, tasted, or touched, it points with a hand that is religiously bound. Tactility, therefore, is the fundamental bond of religion.

For the history of religion in America, however, we need to pay attention to a more contingent and complex sense of the religious dynamics of "binding" in contact zones, in the bondage of slavery, or in the binding terms and conditions of a new covenant. Rhetorically, the seventeenth-century Puritan settlers in North America proceeded hand-in-hand with their God. Invoking the paradigmatic biblical narrative of oppression and resistance, in all its symbolic tactility, John Winthrop insisted that his Puritans had been liberated from the "spiritual bondage of Egypt," led across the sea by God's "own immediate good hand," to undertake in America the "great work in hand."[9]

While this tactile imagery culminated in the central symbol of covenant, the sacred bond between God and a "peculiar people," it carried certain implications that are worth noting. The tactile bond of the covenant was a bondage not only of pleasure but also of pain. As Increase Mather put it, the covenant entailed "sanctified afflictions," the painful suffering that Mather understood to be both punitive and purifying.[10]

The bond of the covenant furthermore entailed violence against the indigenous inhabitants of America, a violence represented in explicitly tactile terms by the Puritan poet Michael Wigglesworth, who celebrated God's "fury's flaile" and "fatall broom" that had been deployed against Native Americans "to make my people elbow room."[11] In these potently tactile terms, the covenant disclosed the inherent violence of tactility as concussion, as the blow that was struck by the violent hand of God in the forceful extension of body space—the "elbow room"—over a territory.

The covenant community was also consolidated by economic relations that were represented (and mystified) as a process of gift giving, from hand to hand, that fulfilled the religious bond with God precisely because of the inherent inequalities of wealth, status, and power upon which those covenantal relations depended. As John Winthrop declared in his sermon on charity, God was glorified more "in dispensing his gifts to man by man, than if he did it by his own immediate hand."[12] In the Puritan covenant, God's gifts had to be handled by an elite class of middlemen in the exchange relations between God and the world.

During the first half of the 1990s, U.S. president Bill Clinton invoked the powerful imagery of the covenant—the "New Covenant"—as his central political slogan. Although we have probably forgotten this initiative, distracted by subsequent preoccupations with a different register of tactility that was found in the insistent investigation into precisely when and where the president might have touched a White House intern, it was enshrined in 1992 in the very title of the national platform of the Democratic Party, "A New Covenant with the American People," a covenant that promised to repair "the damaged bond" between Americans and their government. In his acceptance speech, Clinton countered the vision of his political opponent, explicitly deriding "the vision thing" of George H. W. Bush, with the tactile symbolism of the covenant, stressing in particular the relations of giving and receiving. "I call this approach a New

Covenant," Clinton proclaimed, "a solemn agreement between the people and the government, based not simply on what each of us can take, but on what all of us must give to our nation."[13]

As the defining terms of this covenant, Clinton declared, "opportunity and responsibility go hand-in-hand." Opening and enclosing, empowering and constraining, liberating and binding—the terms and conditions of the new covenant were certainly vague yet somehow compelling in their inherent tactility. By invoking the bond of the gift, the new opportunities for receiving and the new responsibilities for giving, "hand-in-hand," this new covenant rhetorically configured an America bound together by a compact in which, as Clinton declared in his 1992 acceptance speech, "there is no them; there is only us."

After 1995, perhaps partly in response to the vigorous publicity attending the Republican "Contract with America," Clinton dropped the slogan "New Covenant" as a representation of the bond that unified America. Increasingly, he began to use the phrase "a bridge to the twenty-first century," to capture the common interests that should be shared by Americans in embracing a global future. Toward the end of his administration, however, Clinton was also distracted by impeachment, a term that, incidentally, is derived not from an etymology of verbal accusation but from the tactile root of *impedicare* ("to fetter, to snare, to tie the feet together"—in other words, "to bind") which suggests, at the very least, that not all bonds create an "us" in which there is no "them" to be excluded.

BURNING

While tactile metaphors can configure religious bonds, indicating the adhesive character of religion as a "unified system of beliefs and practices," following the classic Durkheimian formula, "which unite into one single moral community . . . all those who adhere to them," such binding social adhesion is only one feature of religious tactility. In addition to the apparently stable terms of religious adherence, a different range of tactility, its thermal register, its "collective effervescence," generates heat. As an important dimension of Rudolf Otto's classical formulation of the *mysterium tremendum*, heat is found in the religious energy or urgency of "vitality, passion, emotional temper, will, force, movement, excitement, activity, impetus," culminating in the "consuming fire" of mystical experience.[14]

As a register of religious temperature, religious discourse often has had recourse to a fire that gives off much more heat than light. In his classic formula, the founder of Methodism, John Wesley, characterized his conversion of 1738 as an experience of the "heart strangely warmed."[15] In American history, an acutely developed tactile understanding of sacred energy has often been invoked as a defining feature of religion and politics. This tactile understanding is sensitive both to the transgressive and punitive qualities of heat—burning lusts and hellish fires—and to its vitalizing properties. During the revolutionary era, for example, Thomas Jefferson reported that a national holiday of humiliation, fasting, and prayer could produce a tangible effect "like a shock of electricity."[16] During the era of the Civil War, to cite another example at random, Horace Bushnell could characterize Americans in his Yale graduation address of 1865 as "souls alive all through in fires of high devotion."[17] Accordingly, religion has been a matter not only of binding relations but also of burning energy—the warmth, the electricity, the sacred fires—that could only be perceived through and engaged by a spiritual sense of touch.

Among the many evocations of "sacred fire" found in American culture, one seemingly marginal ritual, fire walking, gained a considerable following. Some organizations developed an explicitly religious understanding of fire walking. The "Fire Tribe" of "Sundoor," for example, pointed to the universal religious significance of fire. "Because of its integral role in the survival of the human species," Sundoor declared, "fire has had aspects of religious significance to all the peoples of the Earth." Similarly, an organization known as "Wings of Fire" proclaimed that "firewalking, next to prayer, is one of the oldest transformational tools the world has ever known," a religious method used for "ritual purification, healing and worship." In the United States, however, the ritual of fire walking has been primarily employed as a method of empowerment. Wings of Fire, for example, promised that "a whole New World of opportunities and possibilities become reality, because, we say to ourselves, 'I WALK ON FIRE, I CAN DO ANYTHING I CHOOSE.'"[18]

According to the fortuitously named firewalk guide Heather Ash, the fire "teaches you to overcome your fears and do what you thought was impossible," thus expanding personal opportunities for love, health, success, wealth, and prosperity. Furthermore, the ritual of fire walking, "an ancient practice in many cultures," has been democratized in the United States. "Historically," Heather Ash said, "this opportunity was given only to medicine men, priests, and shamans."[19] As practiced in the United States, however, the ritual was no longer the preserve of a ritual elite, but was available to anyone: fire walking had effectively democratized access to spiritual power. The basic principles of the firewalk as practiced in the United States might, therefore, be glossed as opportunity and democracy.

Skeptical observers, of course, could provide scientific explanations, noting that hardwood, charcoal, and even volcanic rock are poor conductors of heat, while the soles of human feet, especially sweaty soles, are good insulators.[20] Nevertheless, even the science editor of *National Geographic*, Rick Gore, found his own experience of fire walking to be liberating and empowering. As promised, he experienced fire walking as a technique for overcoming fear. "Whenever fears surge up," he reported, "I recall the fire walk." According to Gore, the teachings of the fire generated "an energy that seemed almost religious." By walking on fire, therefore, anyone could achieve what Otto called "vitality, passion, emotional temper, will, force, movement, excitement, activity, impetus." Before taking his twelve steps across the burning coals, Gore was given one last instruction. "Always respect the fire," he was told. "Otherwise, you're going to get burned." Concluding his account, Gore testified, "I have learned now to embrace the fire."[21]

The ritual of fire walking must certainly appear to be a fringe phenomenon in American religion, a marginal, New Age, self-help, human-potential, or quasi-religious enterprise that mixes a tactile spirituality with promises of tangible prosperity, attracting, as the Sundoor reported, both "individuals seeking to deepen their spiritual connection and empower themselves" and "corporate executives wanting to give their companies the leading edge." As a teacher, however, the fire conveyed lessons—democracy, opportunity, and respect—that were central to an American imaginary, an imagined sense of America that came to be most tangibly signified by the flag of the United States. The supreme act of disrespect to the flag—burning—became the focus of legal controversy, state legislation, and proposed amendments to the U.S. Constitution.

A visit to the Flag Burning website, especially the "Flag Flames page," demonstrates that Americans can have a tactile, tangible, and visceral identification with the flag. For example, one correspondent, identified as "Pissed Off American," experienced flag desecration as a personal assault, as a kind of ordeal by fire that touched him directly. "When people burn the flag, it's like touching my ass with a lit match," he reported. "I don't like people touching my ass." In another testimony to the visceral connection between flag and body, Craig Preston asserted that "you can burn my flag when you rip it off of my smoldering rotting corpse." Ultimately, the flag symbolized, as a tangible sign, all the dead bodies sacrificed for America. According to another correspondent, identified as "someone.who.cares," burning a flag was an act "desecrating the symbol of our nation, the one that my fellow servicemen have given their lives for in the past," a sentiment echoed by many speeches in the *Congressional Record* in support of legislation against flag burning, confirming Jean Bethke Elshtain's observation, in another context, that the modern nation has been built on mounds of bodies, a corporeal mound, we might add, with a flag at its summit.[22] Like the lessons of the fire, therefore, the lessons of the flag, especially when desecrated by burning, highlighted issues of democracy, opportunity, and respect in the visceral engagement with embodied limits and their transcendence.

Beyond the geographical boundaries of the United States, the meaning of America has been produced in ways that dramatically suggest the importance of its thermal register. For example, during the 1920s, throughout central and southern Africa, religious movements adopted "America" as a symbol of the promise of liberation from colonial oppression. In apocalyptic expectation, these "American" movements anticipated the imminent arrival of black Americans in the most modern aircraft, armed with the most modern automatic weapons, to destroy the colonial oppressors and liberate the indigenous people by "raining fire from the skies."[23] At the end of the twentieth century, Americans were still hot in southern Africa, especially in Cape Town's impoverished Coloured township of Manenberg, which was called "America" by the criminal gang that named itself the "Americans." The Americans had appropriated the U.S. flag as its central symbol for the secret, sacred truth of blood and money. Adopting the motto "In God We Trust, in Money We Believe," the Americans interpreted the white stripes of the U.S. flag as signifying the

organized criminal activity required to make money and the red stripes as
the violence that was required to sustain it.[24] For better or worse, therefore, the tactile "collective effervescence" of opportunity, money, blood,
and fire has been an American reality that has flourished outside of the
United States of America.

MOVING AND HANDLING

In the kinesthetic movements of the body, tactile information is acquired. In the study of religion, kinesthesia calls attention to embodied
movements—kneeling, standing, prostrating, walking, climbing, dancing,
and so on—not only as types of ritual performance but also as instruments
of knowledge. As a significant feature of the American imaginary, mobility
has been a distinctively tactile way of knowing the world, especially as the
moving body has been mediated by machines, from the bicycle to the
space shuttle, that have extended the speed, rhythm, and scope of embodied motion. The religious aura carried by machines of mobility is striking.
The Model T automobile, according to Henry Ford, was "more than a car;
it was a calling," a mission to extend to every American "the blessings of
hours of pleasure in God's great open spaces." According to historian
James J. Flink, the American "cult of the automobile" promised that every
American could achieve the blessings of "mass personal automobility." In
even more extravagant terms, historian Joseph J. Corn has argued that the
"winged gospel" of air travel was embraced by Americans as "an instrument of reform, regeneration, and salvation, a substitute for politics, revolution, or even religion." More recently, space travel, whether undertaken
by NASA astronauts or by alien abductees, has assumed a religious aura in
transcending spatial limits through the extraordinary movement of the
body out of this world.[25]

What sort of tactile knowledge is gained through all this mobility? In a
discussion of "democratic social space," literary critic Philip Fisher has
outlined the basic features of an American imagination of space that is
uniform, open, and familiar. According to Fisher, "It is this feeling of familiarity that lets us move from point to point without much effort," engaging
even new places on familiar terms as if their "novelty has no strangeness."

In the uniformity, openness, and familiarity of democratic social space, "it feels 'like' home everywhere." As a result, Fisher has argued, democratic social space allows for no outsiders, no critical observers, no oppositional positions external to the fabric of society.[26] In democratic social space, to recall Clinton's campaign promise, "there is no them; there is only us.".

Someone, however, must be watching this American space. In American popular culture, such alien observers can be found not only in foreign nations but also in outer space. According to Joseph Firmage, the former "Silicon Valley mogul" who became purveyor of "the Truth," aliens from outer space have long adopted that "observer position," watching the earth from a distance. Firmage has promised that these alien observers will soon "touch down." In response to this contact, he advises, all we need to do is "have the wisdom and courage to warrant an opportunity to touch heaven."[27] By anticipating this tactile exchange—touching down, touching heaven—Firmage has joined many enthusiasts of the extraterrestrial, not only those who report visual sightings of UFOs, but also those who claim tangible contact, the "close encounters of the fourth kind," including cases of physical abduction by aliens from outer space. As an extraordinary kind of embodied mobility, alien abduction has been defined as the "forced removal of a person from his or her physical location to another place. It may include an altered state of awareness for the purpose of physical, surgical, or psychological procedures performed by non-humans. After the abduction, the person is returned to his or her physical location and frequently has little or no recollection of the experience."[28] Since most abductees have no memory of the experience, a website, the Official Alien Abduction Test-Site, provides a helpful questionnaire with fifty-two indicators that will answer the question "Are you an alien abductee?" One of the indicators, of course, is that you do not remember. But those who pass the test are entitled to send in $4.95 for an "official alien abduction certificate" that will prove to their families, friends, and coworkers that they have been moved by aliens.[29]

Turning from kinesthetic movement to haptic manipulation, the sense of touch is engaged in handling the environment, in acquiring sensory information by moving and manipulating objects. As in the case of alien abduction, however, Americans often have imagined that they are moved and manipulated by hidden hands—the "invisible hand" of the market, the unseen touch of contagion—that put at risk their most basic goals of health, wealth, and prosperity. In the tactile imagery of an economic reasoning that has become common sense, reality is moved and manipulated by tactile forces that cannot be seen. According to the website Guide to Economic Reasoning, "Economic reality is controlled by three invisible forces—the invisible hand (the price mechanism), the invisible handshake (social and historical forces), and the invisible foot (political and legal forces)." Although these three invisible forces—the hand, the handshake, and the foot—are supposedly responsible for the "smooth" allocation of capital, they often send the economy on a "rough" ride.[30]

Like the capitalist economy, the microscopic realm of the body is also imagined to be driven by invisible tactile forces, by invisible contacts at the cellular level. "Cells interact by touch," as Mary Catherine Bateson and Richard Goldsby have observed, "you might even say embrace."[31] Invisible to the naked eye, healthy cellular embraces maintain the immune system, which ensures the safety and security of the body, guaranteeing the body's sanctity as, in Jacques Derrida's terms, the "safe and sound."[32] In violating that sanctity, the invading cells of a virus enter into illicit embraces, grasping and bonding with the cells of the immune system. As cultural analyst Marita Sturken has noted, this religious imagery of illicit contact is frequently evoked in popular scientific literature depicting HIV and AIDS. "HIV is seen to enter the immune system's most sacred space and to rescript its genetic memory," Sturken has observed. "HIV is constantly described as entering the 'innermost sanctum' of the cell and the 'sacrosanct environment' of the body."[33] In these highly charged religious terms, the body is configured as a sacred space at constant risk of desecration by the unseen contact, the secret touch, the illicit embrace of intruders that enter its "innermost sanctum" only to violate.

How do people handle living in such a world—from the global economy to the physical body—that is driven by invisible tactile forces? With respect to the physical body that has come to be dominated by the "gaze" of modern scientific medical practice, alternative forms of healing often make use of touch, from the techniques of chiropractic, literally healing "done by the hands," to dramatic rituals of faith healing by "laying on hands," to recent innovations in pastoral counseling that employ what one advocate has called "healing touch, the church's forgotten language."[34] In all of these instances, the hands touch not only the physical body but also the unseen forces—chiropractic's innate intelligence of the body, faith healing's Holy Spirit, pastoral counseling's faith, hope, and love—that are imagined to be responsible for health and well-being. Although these forms of "body work" usually depend upon establishing direct physical contact, the haptic manipulation of unseen forces can also be accomplished at a distance, as demonstrated by the charismatic faith healer Ernest Angley, who used to end his televised faith-healing services by putting his open palm up to the camera, thus projecting the image of an enormous hand into American living rooms, so that his viewers could bring whatever parts of their bodies that might be afflicted into contact with the screen. In the hands of Ernest Angley, television truly became a tactile medium, a medium for establishing a kind of physical contact that manipulated unseen powers of healing.

During the golden age of television evangelism, television also became a religious medium for economic exchange, as incessant appeals for funds to support the television ministries became an integral part of the evangelical message, often motivated by promises of miraculous financial returns for the donor. In a characteristic sermon of the 1980s, for example, the Reverend Jerry Falwell could identify four kinds of giving—systematic, spontaneous, sacrificial, and spiritual giving—with the ultimate form of giving, the spiritual, defined as the act of pledging money to the ministry of Christ that you do not presently have, based on the faith that Jesus would provide. Of course, all major credit cards were accepted. In this haptic manipulation of money, with its implicitly tactile reference to the hand-to-hand exchange of giving and receiving, spiritual gifts could be explicitly identified as material.

In the ministry of Reverend Ike, who preached a distinctive gospel of prosperity on television, this equation of the spiritual and material was the whole point. "I am telling you, get out of the ghetto and get into the get-mo. Get some money, honey. You and me, we are not interested in a harp tomorrow, we are interested in a dollar today. We want it NOW. We want it in a big sack or a box or a railroad car but we WANT it. Stick with me. Nothing for free. Want to shake that money tree."[35] Clearly, the rhetoric of Reverend Ike's gospel of money sent potently tactile signals—the binding promise of "stick with me," the burning desire to "get-mo," the kinesthetic movement out of the ghetto, and the haptic shaking of the "money tree"—which we have considered here as basic features of religious tactility. In practical terms, all Reverend Ike asked was that people tithe 10 percent of their monthly income to him. In return, they could expect a miraculous tenfold increase in their wealth, a dollar in the hand that was far better than any promise of a harp in the future. "I say LACK OF money is the root of all evil," Reverend Ike declared. "The best thing you can do for poor folks is not be one of them."[36] By handling the invisible forces that produce wealth—by shaking hands with the "invisible hand"—poor people could hope to eradicate the root of all evil in their own lives. As an occult economy, this gospel of prosperity provided religious techniques of haptic manipulation for handling the world.

RELIGION UNDER PRESSURE

As Walter Benjamin proposed, the challenges faced by human beings at the turning points of history cannot be solved solely by visual contemplation. Guided by what Benjamin called "tactile appropriation," people gradually and perhaps unconsciously adjust to new situations by habit. In adjusting to the new era of sensory challenges presented by electronic media—the shocks to sensibility, the bombardment of sensory stimuli, the risk of sensory overload, and so on—they have developed new strategies of engagement to deal with what Benjamin identified as the most characteristic sensory condition of modernity: distraction. The discovery of a new and apparently pervasive medical condition characterized by habitual distraction, attention deficit disorder, seems to confirm this insight. Apparently, one of the diagnostic signs of attention deficit disorder is a lack of awareness of being distracted. In this respect, the disease is like alien abduction, a disturbance, dislocation, or disorientation that touches people unawares.

In religious ritual, where attention to detail is required, distraction poses a serious problem. According to the catechism of the Catholic Church, for example, "the habitual difficulty in prayer is distraction." Not only disrupting the flow of words in verbal prayer or deflecting the focus of inner vision in contemplative prayer, distraction "can concern, more profoundly, him to whom we are praying." From God's perspective, "a distraction reveals to us what we are attached to," suggesting that a distracted person in prayer is touching the world rather than engaging with God.[37] The medical diagnosis of a disease of distraction, therefore, strangely recalls a long history of religious valorization of strict, single-minded, and pure attention.

Distracted, we also struggle with the invisible hands, the secret embraces, the shocking disclosures, and what Jean Baudrillard has called the "strike of events."[38] The classic study of American "civil religion" produced by the sociologist Robert Bellah and his colleagues is titled *Habits of the Heart*.[39] In the midst of so many distractions, however, how can individuals form habits that are not shaped under pressure? Risking a broad generalization, we can conclude that the habits of the heart formed under the conditions of modernity are a haptics of the heart: strategies for handling distraction, pressure, and stress. A quick trip through any bookstore, even by a distracted observer, reveals the wealth of advice for handling stress. Selecting at random, we could read any number of the following titles: *Dealing with Stress, a Biblical Approach; Heavenly Ways to Handle Stress; Healthy and Holy under Stress; Too Blessed to Be Stressed; How to Make Work, Stress, and Drudgery a Means to Your Sanctity; Prayerstarters to Help You Handle Stress; What Would Jesus Do to Rise above Stress?;* or, if we really wanted to gain a perspective on life that might reverse the pressures of stress, we could read the book *Stressed Is Desserts Spelled Backwards*. Without reading any of these religious texts, however, we can only conclude that they are positioned in a world under pressure, stressed out, struggling to cope with the tactile conditions of a modernity that Benjamin called distraction.

The modern world is supposedly a domain of visibility, constituted by the hegemony of the gaze, governed by panoptic surveillance, and ruled by the "scopic regimes of modernity."[40] Under the predominance of vision, all modern individuals are required to pay attention. But modernity is also tactility, distraction, and pressure. By paying so much attention to the dominance of sight in Western culture, we forget that our principal theorists of modernity, Marx and Freud, were theorists of tactility—capitalist oppression, psychological repression—in touch with resistance. Marx proposed that "the forming of the five senses is a labour of the entire history of the world down to the present."[41] In the Marxist inversion of the senses, with its anticipation of a materialist apocalyptic inversion of the senses in which the first would finally be last and the last would be first, the eyes and ears could never compete for authenticity with eating, tasting, smelling, or touching, or, above all, with working in the sensory economy of knowledge and power. Pulling in another direction, Freud's discovery of the unconscious, with its multiple repressions, developed an entirely different hermeneutics, energetics, and economy of the senses that nevertheless also wrestled with the problem of motion. How can we possibly move forward when we are bound—by completely unconscious primal repression, by the semiconscious repression that Freud called "after-pressure," by the driving fixations of cathexis that bind desire to objects, or even by the "uncanny" (often religiously rendered as the holy, the sacred, or supernatural power) that Freud analyzed casually as "something repressed which recurs," as "something which is familiar and old-established in the mind and which has become alienated from it only through the process of repression."[42] If modernity is about freedom of movement, its mobility is clearly negotiated in relation to powerful forces of resistance, repression, and oppression.

Religious tactility is ultimately the capacity to handle the challenges of living in the world, especially the challenges posed by what cannot be seen or heard. Under pressure, religious resources are deployed under difficult conditions. Adapting the distinction between strategies and tactics proposed by Michel de Certeau, we might understand religious strategies to be exercises within the domain of power, as transparent uses of religion for the legitimation or reinforcement of a political order that is "bound by its very visibility," while we might regard religious tactics as oppositional maneuvers, as tactile maneuvers in the dark, so to speak, that defy, subvert, or otherwise interfere with an established domain of visibility by engaging in "the very transformation of touch into response, a 're-turning' of the surprise expected without being foreseen."[43] In trying to make sense out of the intersections between the individual and the collective, this distinction between strategies and tactics, between the strategic domain of visibility and the tactical terrain of touch, response, twists, turns, and surprises that defy any hegemony of vision, further reinforces the importance of the senses in the material dynamics of religion.

15 Oceans

If Charles H. Long had not become a historian of religions, he would have been a mapmaker. As a cartographer, Long certainly would have developed new ways to represent territory, but I suspect that his maps would have been particularly remarkable for what they revealed about oceans. Somehow, his maps would have shown that while human beings might live on land, their most significant geographical formation is defined by large bodies of water. Accordingly, his maps would have illuminated how human beings actually live in a watery world—a Mediterranean world, an Atlantic world, a Pacific world, or an Indian Ocean world—that defines the relevant contours of a human geography. Charles Long, mapmaker, would have been a cartographer of oceans.

In the study of religion, Charles Long has been a cartographer of oceans, mapping the relations of human contact and exchange, conquest and colonization, representation and signification, materiality and opacity, double consciousness and popular resistance, and many other features of modernity that have all been mediated by bodies of water. As Long has insisted, something of crucial significance happens when people get onto a boat and get into the water. Long follows Michel Foucault's account in *Madness and Civilization* by observing that when a group of mad people get onto the medieval European "ship of fools," the "water adds to this dark mass its own values; it carries off, but it does more, it purifies." Getting into the water, therefore, signals both a separation and a transformation; it is "at once a rigorous division and an absolute passage."[1] In the Atlantic world that emerged during the era of European exploration, conquest, and colonization, getting on a boat certainly marked profound separations and transformations. "When the Europeans landed on the shores of the West Indies, and later of South America," Alexis de Tocqueville observed, "for the first time the extraordinary transparency of the water disclosed the ocean's depths to the navigators."[2] This "extraordinary transparency," however, was achieved at the expense of others who were forced onto the boat—as slaves, as prisoners of war, as convict laborers, as kidnapped translators—and forced into an extraordinary opacity. Transparency and opacity, therefore, were born out of the same sea changes of colonialism.

The opposition between colonizer and colonized has often been rendered as a dualism. "The colonial world is a Manichaean world," Frantz Fanon held.[3] Recent research on religion and colonialism, however, has explored the complex ways in which religion has been fashioned and refashioned in the asymmetrical power relations of colonial contact zones. Long has emphasized the complexity of colonial contact zones, transcultural exchanges, and reorientations. Although people all over the world were submerged under European conquest, enslavement, and oppression, they found new ways to discern and articulate human meaning, as Charles Long has observed, "through traces of memory of a forgotten past, through reinterpretations of the meanings of their oppressors, through the latent possibilities of language, through a forced and new orientation to the land."[4]

For the study of religion and colonialism, the ocean is a crucial unit of analysis. Mediated by "water and watery passages," colonialism generated new meanings for both sea and land out of contacts, relations, and exchanges.[5] In mapping oceans for the study of religion, a morphology is not sufficient, although Long has attended to the primordial importance of water in Mircea Eliade's imagination of matter. Rather, the watery passages of the colonial era require attention to the zones and temporalities in which "*homo religiosus, homo faber,* and *homo aeconomicus* converge," situating the religious, technological, and economic formations of the human in oceanic circulations.[6] Profiling the potential for mapping oceans in the study of religion, I will review some of the recurring features of colonial relations between sea and land and recall the crucial role of two generative nodes of materiality, the fetish in the Atlantic world and the cargo in the Pacific world, which have been the twin polestars in Long's mapping of new religious orientations across oceans. As a small contribution to this work of mapping, I add a third term, *guano,* which during the nineteenth century was the matrix for opening the Pacific world to industrial exploitation. During what has been called the "Age of Guano," the sacred excrement that had been integrated into religious practices of fertility and sovereignty within the Inca empire was at the center of new transactions across oceans and new orientations to the land. If we include guano in our mapping, we might find that religious meanings fluctuated from the time of mercantile fetish through the time of industrial guano to the time of virtual cargo in a history of religions that is situated in the colonial contacts, relations, and exchanges of oceans.

LAND AND SEA

The origin of religion can be relocated in modernity, not only in the emergence of the modern category of "religion" out of Enlightenment reflections on the natural, the exotic, and the primitive, but also in the violent oppositions and complex chains of reference that were established during the modern era of European conquest and colonization. As Charles Long has advised, we should look for the new *arche* of religion—as a category of human discourse, practice, experience, and association—in the colonial contact zones of sea and land. From that beginning, religion was a matter of fluid relations, negotiations, and exchanges, which were simultaneously symbolic and material, between people of sea and land.

To recall a familiar but foundational illustration: During the era of Spanish conquests in the Americas, the conquistadores were armed with a theological formula, known as the Requirement, that they brought across the Atlantic to read before a gathering of natives in order to enact what historian Patricia Seed has called a "ceremony of possession" that certified Spanish claims on new land. The terms of the Requirement carefully constructed a chain of references that stretched from the New World back across the water to powerful and sacred centers in the Old. In reciting this formula, the Spanish conqueror asserted that he represented the authority of the king of Spain in Castile, who represented the authority of the pope in Rome, who represented the authority of the apostle Saint Peter in Jerusalem, who represented the ultimate authority of the supreme God who had created the heavens and the earth. This chain of references, therefore, brought God to the New World. Inviting the natives to freely submit, the Requirement warned that those who refused to be bound by this chain of references that spanned the Atlantic Ocean would experience the force of total warfare, dispossession, and destruction. "I solemnly declare," the text of the Requirement concluded, "that the deaths and damages received from such will be your fault."[7] From the Spanish conquests of the sixteenth century to the foreign policy of neo-imperialism, religion in the Americas has often registered as a sacralized chain of references from sea to land that establishes ultimate authority, delivers ultimatums, and ultimately transfers guilt for alien aggression to the local victims of that aggression.

But religion has also registered as indigenous initiatives in reappropriating, reversing, or breaking those chains of reference. To cite only one striking example: The Andean nobleman Felipe Guaman Poma de Ayala, who had lived through the Spanish conquest of the Inca empire, the subjugation of Andean people, and the dispossession of native lands, in 1621 published his illustrated book—*Nueva corónica y buen gobierno* (New history and good government)—in part as an effort to reverse the chains of reference that linked sea and land in the colonial world system. Drawing upon both indigenous and Christian religious resources, Guaman Poma intervened in that new world of colonial relations. "The world is upside down," Guaman Poma observed. "It is a sign that there is no God and no king."[8]

To restore the proper order of the world, he proposed, the chain of references established by Spanish colonization had to be reversed. According to the Spanish conquerors, the God of heaven and earth was represented by Saint Peter, who was represented by the pope in Rome, who was represented by the king in Castile, who was represented by the local Spanish colonial agents in Peru that had deposed the Inca emperor, imposed Christian conversion, and forced Indians to labor in the silver mines.

According to Guaman Poma, however, the work of turning the world right-side-up again depended upon restoring the Inca emperor. That renewal of indigenous sovereignty would reveal the order of a new world in which the mineral wealth of Peru supported Spain, which supported the church, which supported the Christian faith in the supreme God of heaven and earth. In his caption to an illustration of the mining capital of Peru, Guaman Poma observed, "Thanks to this mine exists Castile, Rome is Rome, the pope is pope and the king is monarch of the world, and holy mother church is defended and our holy faith is preserved by the four kings of the Indies and by the Inca emperor."[9] Therefore, in Guaman Poma's rendering, Peru was not subject to Spain, the Roman Catholic Church, and the Christian God; instead, the very existence of Castile, Rome, and the "holy faith" depended upon Peru. The restoration of indigenous political sovereignty, however, was crucial to establishing that new chain of references. In the meantime, reciting a traditional Andean prayer, Guaman Poma asked, "Where is God?"[10]

Certainly, these examples do not exhaust the scope, meaning, or power of religion in colonial situations. They do, however, represent extreme positions of foreign aggression and indigenous resistance that suggest the contours of religion in the modern world. In between these extremes of aggression and resistance a complex range of contacts, relations, and exchanges have given specific and detailed content to religion in the Atlantic and Pacific worlds. If we were to map the oceans rather than the land, Charles Long has proposed, we would find that two crucial symbols— the fetish in the Atlantic, the cargo in the Pacific—are the twin polestars that provide the most reliable orientation for navigating the strange waters of religion in modernity.[11]

FETISH AND CARGO

As William Pietz has shown in a remarkable series of articles, the fetish emerged as a term of contact in West Africa with the convergence of Portuguese, Dutch, and English Christians, African Christians, African Muslims, and African adherents of an indigenous religious heritage who were all involved in an expanding mercantile zone.[12] Essentially, the fetish was originally identified by Europeans in that context of exchange as material evidence that Africans were unable to assess the value of trade goods. While they supposedly undervalued European goods that were offered in exchange, Africans allegedly overvalued apparently trifling objects, whether found or made, in ways that thoroughly baffled European traders. As a result, Europeans in that West African trading zone concluded that African fetishism represented the fundamental absence of any indigenous religious system for rationalizing or regulating relations of exchange. By asserting fetishism as the defining absence of religion, these European merchants advanced an implicit definition of religion that would eventually dominate the Atlantic world. Religion was implicitly defined as beliefs, practices, and institutions that rationalized and regulated the value of material objects in relations of exchange. In the Atlantic world, therefore, the very definition of *religion* in European usage emerged in relation to the uncertain meaning and unstable value represented by the West African fetish.

In the Pacific world, the cargo has played a similar role in defining the nature of religion. As Melanesian islanders developed complex beliefs and practices in relation to the material goods brought by white merchants, missionaries, and colonial administrators, the cargo emerged as a new location for negotiating meaning, value, and power. What was the secret of the cargo? Long refers us to the testimony of a Christian convert in New Guinea: "The white men hide the secret of the Cargo."[13] But the secret seems to be most hidden from those who possess the material signs of the cargo. In recalling two different accounts collected by Kenelm Burridge about Mambu, the leader of a cargo movement in the 1930s, Long asks us to confront the difference between reality as history and reality as myth-dream. In the first account, provided by the Reverend Father Georg Höltker, Mambu had been a Roman Catholic convert who assisted in the rituals of the church, but who left to form a strange, subversive, and dangerous cult that mixed ancestral and Christian practices. In the second account, however, which was provided by an indigenous informant, no mention is made of Mambu's involvement in the church. According to this version, Mambu stowed away on a ship to Australia, survived attempts by the ship's captain to throw him overboard, learned the secret of the white man's cargo, and returned to New Guinea to raise money, perform miracles, and mobilize people to "be strong and throw the white men out of New Guinea and into the sea."[14] Therefore, the relevant fact of Mambu's life was not that he had been in the church but that he had been on the boat. These two accounts cannot be easily divided into history and myth. Rather, they are fragments of the same colonial story about sea and land.

Clearly, the fetish has emerged as one of the polestars of modernity. Marx, Freud, and their intellectual descendants have found that the fetish—the desired object, the objectification of desire—has been integral to the making of modern subjectivities and social relations. The fetish is at the heart of the making and masking of all the imagined communities, invented traditions, political mythologies, and state fetishisms that are obviously artificial constructions but which nevertheless produce real effects in the world. The cargo, however, awaits further analysis if it is to develop as the second polestar for navigating the modern world. As a key term in the study of religion, the cargo evokes imitation, simulation, and mimetic desire in a modern or postmodern political economy of the sacred.

In the cargo movements of Melanesia, mimetic desire has assumed many forms: as magical imitation, as narratives of desire, as indigenous ethnography, and as cultural critique. The classical anthropological accounts by Kenelm Burridge, Peter Lawrence, and Peter Worsley documented how the islanders imitated Europeans by building piers, erecting flagpoles, and sitting on verandas waiting for the imminent arrival of the cargo.[15] This imitative behavior, which was economically irrational, anticipated the advent of extraordinary wealth signified by European manufactured goods. While cargo movements attracted the participation of islanders, they also allured Westerners, as Lamont Lindstrom has argued, into narratives about exotic others that mirrored their own desires for commodities. As a recurring feature in the "shopping list" of cargo movements, the refrigerator was also an important feature in Western desires for a modern home. Stories about cargo cults, therefore, are "parables about our desire."[16] In recent research, returning to the indigenous perspective, cargo movements have been rendered as a kind of indigenous ethnography, reading the West by means of what Nils Bubandt has called the "mimicry of the cargoism of modernity."[17] Like the anthropologists Franz Boas and Frank Hamilton Cushing, who imitated the gestures, postures, and artifacts of Native Americans in their ethnographies,[18] participants in cargo movements might be cultivating a kind of embodied knowledge of an alien culture through active imitation. Imitating the cargoism of modernity, however, might also entail an implicit critique, a mimicry that exposes what Karl-Heinz Kohl has called "a 'money cult' issuing from the very heart of a modern capitalist society."[19] Like the cargo cult, the money cult of capitalism is a failed prophecy that nevertheless continues to attract enthusiastic adherents by its promise of extraordinary wealth.

HOLY SHIT

In between the fetish and the cargo, I would like to introduce a third term, *guano,* into the mapping of oceans for the study of religion. Here we return to Peru, not to the colonized Andes of Guaman Poma that looked across the Atlantic Ocean to Spain, but to the offshore islands that held vast reservoirs of guano, nitrates, and phosphates that opened up the Pacific world. For the ancient Inca, this bird excrement, identified as *huanu* in Quecha, was at the nexus of the sacred. Any sacred person, object, or place—*huaca*—bore associations with procreation and death, with fertility and kinship, which could be symbolized by birds and guano. Following its discovery by Alexander von Humboldt in 1802, guano was exploited for fertilizers and explosives, ushering in the Guano Age, in which, George Burges observed in 1848, "God's gift Guano spread."[20] Guano also became the matrix for a new guano imperialism exemplified by the United States Guano Islands Act of 1856, which asserted U.S. claims on this natural resource and authorized the seizure of ninety-four islands, rocks, and keys as American possessions in the oceans. Competition over access to guano, which resulted in the War of the Pacific (1879–1883), was attended by large-scale migrations of workers from Asia to South America. Although I cannot develop this suggestion fully here, I propose that guano was a material nexus for generating new meanings of fertility and sovereignty—fertilizing industrial agriculture, producing explosives, and inspiring the guano imperialism of networked islands—that bore traces of new religious orientations to the sea and land during the nineteenth century.

In 1877 the British travel writer, translator of *Don Quixote,* and mining chemist Alexander James Duffield used religious imagery to represent the intersection of industrialized nations, migrant labor, and resource extraction on the Chincha Islands of Peru. This island world had been turned upside down: the site of deposits from the "sacred frigatebirds," it had been transformed into a hell for the laborers digging the guano to be put on ships and transported for the benefit of nations across the seas.[21] According to Duffield, "No hell has ever been conceived by the Hebrew, the Irish, the Italian, or even the Scotch mind for appeasing the anger and satisfying the vengeance of their awful gods, that can be equalled in the fierceness of its heat, the horror of its stink, and the damnation of those compelled to labour there, to a deposit of Peruvian guano when being shovelled into ships."

Recalling Michael Taussig's analysis of mining in Colombia as entering the realm of the devil,[22] Duffield's deployment of religious imagery was clearly in an ironic mode. But that mode seemed appropriate to the irony of the Age of Guano in which labor, resources, and value were extracted by distant nations. The laborers in this island hell, Duffield proposed, might have had a better religion than the capitalists across the seas. He observed, "The Chinese who have gone through it, and had the delightful opportunity of helping themselves to a sufficiency of opium to carry them back to their homes, as some believed, or to heaven, as fondly hoped others, must have had a superior idea of the Almighty, than have any of the money-making nations mentioned above, who still cling to an immortality of fire and brimstone."[23] In this remarkable passage, Duffield implied that the Age of Guano had placed everyone in hell, although the laborer's opium provided a better promise of salvation than the capitalist's immortality. Between heaven and hell, the world had been turned into shit, a cataclysm of biblical proportions. "One passage of the Hebrew Scriptures, and this the only passage in the whole range of sacred or profane literature, supplies an adequate epitaph for the Chincha islands." Duffield concluded. "But it is too indecent, however amusing it may be, to quote."[24] Religious meanings in the Age of Guano were accordingly filtered through irony, disconnection, and the displacement of value into the sea.

In his reading of the imagination of matter in the work of Mircea Eliade, Charles Long highlighted the importance of agriculture. Long explained, "The new time and space revealed in the hierophanies of agriculture and the ability of the human community to make use of and control these processes establishes a new possibility for human relationships with matter and the meaning of totalization of a form of nature thus symbolizing a total form of human existence. Agriculture is the point at which *homo religiosus*, *homo faber*, and *homo aeconomicus* converge."[25] But the agriculture ushered in by the Age of Guano was industrial agriculture, linking fertilizers to explosives, capitalist exploitation, and eventually the production of synthetic substitutions for the sacred bird excrement. This convergence of agriculture and industry, therefore, generated new religious meanings. In compensation for its loss of guano, the Republic of Peru was to gain a railway, which Duffield again represented in religious terms deployed in the ironic mode. "The railway fever has had its virulent type in all parts of the world where railways have appeared," he declared. "In Peru from 1868 to 1871–2 this fever was perhaps more active and deadly than anywhere; than in Canada, even, which is saying much, for there it took the form of a religious delirium. The Peruvians believed that if they offered a great and wonderful railway to the deities of industry, great and happy commercial times would follow. Just as they believe that give a priest a pyx, a spoon, some wine, and wheaten bread, he can make the body and blood of God; so they believed that give a great American the required elements, he could by some equally mysterious power make Peru one of the great nations of the earth."[26] Engineers from the United States were the high priests, led by the "Messiah of railways," who promised to enact this new doctrine of transubstantiation. Foreign agents of this messianic priesthood, Duffield concluded, would be the only ones to benefit from this new religion.

MAPPING OCEANS

By mapping oceans, we see how religion emerges in the Mediterranean, Atlantic, Pacific, and Indian Ocean worlds. Mapping oceans calls attention to religious meanings and orientations that circulate around material objects in different historical modes of exchange. At the risk of being too schematic, we might find changing orientations in space and time by recovering the role of the fetish in a mercantile age, guano in an industrial age, and the cargo in a virtual age of simulations, imitations, and mimetic desire. Raising in different ways the general problem of "the nature and origin of the social value of material objects," these objects of the ocean were also material nodes of religious orientation.[27] By taking oceans as basic units of analysis, we can see how these potent objects surface as key terms in the history of religions.

As our cartographer of oceans in the history of religions, Charles Long has consistently shown us that there are many ways to cross the seas. In his essay "Perspectives for a Study of Afro-American Religion in the United States," for example, Long points to a hero of African American folklore, High John the Conqueror. "It is stated explicitly in the folklore," Long recalls, "that High John came dancing over the waves from Africa, or that he was in the hold of the slave ship." Obviously, those are two very different ways of crossing the seas. You either come dancing freely over the waves or you come bound in slavery. Isn't that the case? In High John's case, however, that is not the case. Whether he came dancing over the waves or bound in chains, as Long reports, "High John is a flamboyant character. He possesses great physical strength and conquers more by an audacious display of his power than through any subtlety or cunning. He is the folkloric side of a conquering Christ," Long concludes, "though with less definite goals."[28] The conquering Christ of colonialism, of course, had definite goals of gaining profit, expropriating resources, and exploiting labor for economic interests across the seas. As the folkloric other side of this conquering Christ, conquering John seems to work by indirection, with no plan but a powerful presence, flamboyant and audacious, emblematic of alternative mobilizations of language, memory, and meaning between sea and land.

Conclusion

DYNAMIC MATERIALITY

In this book we have moved through religious materiality, exploring striking and illuminating cases, guided by attention to material categories, formations, and circulations. We have considered different meanings of materiality. People engage objects; objects engage people; and both people and objects are interwoven in material conditions and consequences that can rise to the level of materiality. Following the usage of the term in the practices of law and accounting, materiality is less a question of metaphysics than a matter of political economy. In this respect, materiality is a matter of force and effect, a configuration of discourse and power that makes a difference in the world. As a result, our exploration of the material dynamics of religion has been as much about dynamics—power, energy, force, and motion—as it has been about material objects.

Our thinking about objects is conditioned by the proliferation of perceptual metaphors in any language we use to think about anything. Believing is seeing, understanding is hearing, and making connections, whether through caressing or striking, is tactile. Sensory metaphors pervade religious discourse. In the beginning was the word, and the word said, "Let there be light."[1] Although we have encountered many objects in this book, from feathers to refrigerators, material objects do not stand alone. They are engaged in practice, entangled in relations, and embedded in discourse. In the sensory register of religious discourse, embodied metaphors are an integral part of the stuff of material religion. Although seeing and hearing have been privileged senses, we have learned that tactility, perhaps underlying our entire sensory repertoire, informs religious discourse, practice, and association.

Crucial religious objects, such as the fetish or the cargo, have been discursive objects, since there is no single bedrock object at stake but rather an argument about the meaning and value of all objects. As boundary objects, the fetish and the cargo, the relic and the icon, have been flash points around which competing communities of interpretation contend. Generally, the dynamic materiality of such objects has been generated by the contestation. The fight, as we have seen, is not only over matters of meaning but also over material ownership. In the political economy of the sacred, ownership is everything, whether it is underwritten by timeless entitlement or justified by rectification through theft.

In these engagements with objects, the being of human being is at stake. What is a human being? In the material dynamics of religion, we have seen the human positioned between the superhuman and the subhuman, between the more than human—animistic spirits, ancestors, gods, the British Empire, the American flag, Coca-Cola, and Tupperware—and the less than human, which might include animals, vegetables, and minerals. We have seen the plasticity of the human negotiated between gods and machines. But we have also seen colonizing and missionizing humans, acting mechanically like machines, generating laughter, and we have seen colonized humans dehumanized. In all of these cases, the dynamic materiality of religion rises to the level of materiality in negotiations over the classification of persons in a contested field of material relations.[2]

Orientations in space and time, as we recall, are also negotiated and navigated in material terms. Embodied space, from up to down, from left to right, intersects with temporal regularities and regulations. These material orientations in space and time are integrated into the material dynamics of religion. Embodied practices, such as fasting or feasting, intersect with temporal regularities; embodied practices, even including the sacrificial destruction of resources and collective suicide, might engage temporal ruptures. Operating within time and space, the material dynamics of religion makes time and makes space through intensive interpretation, regular ritualization, and inevitable contestation over the religiously legitimated regulation of temporality and the ownership of territory.[3]

Certainly, these generalizations about classifications and orientations in the dynamic materiality of religion are painted broadly, with a very wide brush. The specific cases we have engaged in this book, dwelling in detail, have suggested some ways in which the brushstrokes might be refined. However, in the art or science of studying religion, we all benefit from critical and creative reflection on the categories we employ for thinking about religion. Animism and the sacred, religious space and time, are categories undergoing constant reappraisal. The material dynamics of these categories, including their incongruity, should be essential to our thinking about categories in the study of religion.

Our thinking is inevitably positioned within power relations and social locations. We have used the term *formations* to designate configurations of meaning and power, not as contexts, frameworks, or structures, but as force fields of constraints and possibilities. Limiting and enabling, formations include fields of economic scarcity and surplus, colonial impositions, imperial ambitions, and all of the forms and forces in which the dynamic materiality of religion operates. Some readers might feel that we have neglected the importance of religious institutions, but institutions, as the material organization of social allegiance, can be seen as arising within broader configurations of meaning and power that we have been calling formations.

In colonial formations, the dynamic materiality of religion appears in starkly oppositional terms, with religious strategies deployed in appropriating the lives, land, and labor of the colonized but also redeployed to resist colonial dispossession and displacement.[4] In imperial formations, the ambition for territorial expansion, transcending limits by establishing new relations between imperial centers and colonized peripheries, orchestrates materiality, including the dynamic materiality of religion, around political, social, and economic forces asserting universal presence and power.[5] Colonial and imperial formations, as we have seen, have profoundly shaped the material dynamics of religion.

Circulating in mobility, change, and diffusion, the dynamic materiality of religion has been investigated in this book with special attention to two apparently extreme positions, the local religion of indigenous religion and the global religion appearing in popular culture. Intimately attached to place, cultivating traditional relations with land, natural resources, and material objects, indigenous religion seems, at first glance, to be the opposite of the fluid, mobile beliefs, practices, and associations invested in the products and productions of popular culture. However, attention to the dynamic materiality of religion enables us to appreciate the ways in which indigenous religions have moved through mobilizing circuits of environmentalism, human-rights activism, and New Age shamanism. Indigenous religion can also be fluid and mobile in transacting with a changing world.[6] At the same time, the diffusion of religious impulses through popular culture, which animate personal subjectivities, can form communities of sacred solidarity, direct desire toward sacred objects, and facilitate relations of sacred exchange that replicate features associated with indigenous religion. In this respect, popular culture, media, and consumerism have operated as the dynamic materiality of the "indigenous" religion of the contemporary world, the religion that people are born into, grow up in, live within, and take for granted.[7]

In conclusion, we might reflect on the scope of material religion. What is included? Everything. What is excluded? Nothing. Everything is material, including beliefs that arise within material conditions and texts that have material consequences in the world. Nothing, not even the emptiness of a vacuum in space or a zero point in time, is outside of materiality. If everything is in and nothing is out, the question is: What do we do with all this stuff? Here, I think, our linking of materiality with dynamics is crucial for the study of material religion. If everything is material, in some metaphysical sense, then the study of religion, however it might be pursued, is inevitably the study of material religion. But everything rides on how we pursue the material dynamics and the dynamic materiality of religion. We can focus on relations between people and objects; we can attend to the social lives of things; we can track the assemblages and entanglements of human-object networks; and we can imagine the vibrancy and agency of things in the world. All of these options are possible pursuits in the study of material religion. In this book, however, we have pursued material religion through political economy—the political economy of categories, such as animism or the sacred, emerging under material conditions; the political economy of formations, such as colonialism and imperialism, creating material conditions; and the political economy of circulations, such as the diffusions of indigenous religion and popular culture, generating material consequences. In the study of material religion, this focus on the material dynamics of conditions and consequences retains the matter of materiality while uncovering the ways in which things rise to the level of materiality by making a material difference in the world. That is the dynamic materiality of religion.

Notes

PREFACE

1. William James, *The Varieties of Religious Experience*, introduction by Reinhold Niebuhr (1902; New York: Collier Books, 1961), 393.

2. Peter Pomerantsev, *Nothing Is True and Everything Is Possible: The Surreal Heart of the New Russia* (New York: Public Affairs, 2014), 187.

3. Dave Asprey, *Moldy*, directed by Kee Kee Buckley and Eric Troyer (Bulletproof Films, 2015).

4. Jeremy Carrette and Richard King, *Selling Spirituality: The Silent Takeover of Religion* (London: Routledge, 2005).

INTRODUCTION

1. David Chidester, *Empire of Religion: Imperialism and Comparative Religion* (Chicago: University of Chicago Press, 2014).

2. Matthew Engelke, "Material Religion," in *The Cambridge Companion to Religious Studies*, ed. Robert A. Orsi (Cambridge: Cambridge University Press, 2012), 209–29; Sonia Hazard, "The Material Turn in the Study of Religion," *Religion and Society: Advances in Research* 4 (2013): 58–78; Paul Christopher Johnson, "Toward an Atlantic Genealogy of 'Spirit Possession,'" in *Spirited Things: The Work of "Possession" in Afro-Atlantic Religions*, ed. Paul Christopher

Johnson (Chicago: University of Chicago Press, 2014), 23–45; Birgit Meyer and Dick Houtman, "Introduction: Material Religion—How Things Matter," in *Things: Religion and the Question of Materiality,* ed. Dick Houtman and Birgit Meyer (New York: Fordham University Press, 2012), 1–23; David Morgan, "Introduction: The Matter of Belief," in *Religion and Material Culture: The Matter of Belief,* ed. David Morgan (London: Routledge, 2010), 1–17; Tracy Pintchman, introduction to *Sacred Matters: Material Religion in South Asia,* ed. Tracy Pintchman and Corinne G. Dempsey (Albany: State University of New York Press, 2015), 1–14; S. Brent Plate, "Material Religion: An Introduction," in *Key Terms in Material Religion,* ed. S. Brent Plate (London: Bloomsbury, 2015), 1–8; Sally M. Promey, "Religion, Sensation, and Materiality: An Introduction," in *Sensational Religion: Sensory Cultures in Material Practice,* ed. Sally M. Promey (New Haven, CT: Yale University Press, 2014), 1–19; Manuel A. Vásquez, *More Than Belief: A Materialist Theory of Religion* (Oxford: Oxford University Press, 2010).

3. David Morgan, *The Embodied Eye: Religious Visual Culture and the Social Life of Feeling* (Berkeley: University of California Press, 2012), 163–68.

4. Nicolas Howe, *Landscapes of the Secular: Law, Religion, and American Sacred Space* (Chicago: University of Chicago Press, 2016), 37–43.

5. E. B. Tylor, *Primitive Culture,* 2 vols. (London: John Murray, 1871), 1:383.

6. Harry Garuba, "Explorations of Animist Materialism: Notes on Reading/ Writing African Literature, Culture, and Society," *Public Culture* 15, no. 2 (2003): 267.

7. On the social life of things, see Arjun Appadurai, ed., *The Social Life of Things: Commodities in Cultural Perspective* (Cambridge: Cambridge University Press, 1986); Crispin Paine, *Religious Objects in Museums: Private Lives and Public Duties* (London: Bloomsbury, 2013). On assemblages, networks, and entanglements, see Manuel DeLanda, *A New Philosophy of Society: Assemblage Theory and Social Complexity* (London: Continuum, 2006); Bruno Latour, *Reassembling the Social: An Introduction to Actor-Network Theory* (New York: Oxford University Press, 2005); Ian Hodder, *Entangled: An Archaeology of the Relationships between Humans and Things* (Malden, MA: Wiley-Blackwell, 2012). On vibrant materiality, see Jane Bennett, *Vibrant Matter: A Political Ecology of Things* (Durham, NC: Duke University Press, 2010); Diana Coole and Samantha Frost, eds., *New Materialisms: Ontology, Agency, and Politics* (Durham, NC: Duke University Press, 2010).

8. Emile Durkheim, *The Elementary Forms of Religious Life,* trans. Karen E. Fields (1912; New York: Free Press, 1995), 36.

9. David Chidester, *Authentic Fakes: Religion and American Popular Culture* (Berkeley: University of California Press, 2005), 19; *Wild Religion: Tracking the Sacred in South Africa* (Berkeley: University of California Press, 2012), 43–50.

10. Robert Hertz, "The Pre-eminence of the Right Hand: A Study of Religious Polarity," in *Right and Left: Essays on Dual Symbolic Classification,* ed. Rodney Needham (1909; Chicago: University of Chicago Press, 1973), 3–31. See Kim Knott, *The Location of Religion: A Spatial Analysis* (London: Equinox, 2005), 133–228.

11. Jonathan Z. Smith, *Imagining Religion: From Babylon to Jonestown* (Chicago: University of Chicago Press, 1982), 90, 62–63.

12. Michael Allaby, *A Dictionary of Ecology* (Oxford: Oxford University Press, 1998), 143.

13. Pierre Bourdieu, *Outline of a Theory of Practice,* trans. Richard Nice (Cambridge: Cambridge University Press, 1977), 183.

14. Pierre Bourdieu, *In Other Words: Essays Towards a Reflexive Sociology* (Stanford, CA: Stanford University Press, 1990), 36.

15. Walter Benjamin, "Capitalism as Religion," in *Walter Benjamin: Selected Writings,* vol. 1: *1913–1926,* ed. Marcus Bullock and Michael W. Jennings (1921; Cambridge, MA: Harvard University Press, 1996), 288–91; Richard Foltz, "The Religion of the Market: Reflections on a Decade of Discussions," *Worldviews* 11, no. 2 (2007): 135–54; Chidester, *Authentic Fakes,* 112.

16. Sylvester A. Johnson, *African American Religions, 1500–2000: Colonialism, Democracy, and Freedom* (Cambridge: Cambridge University Press, 2015), 1.

17. Lisa Lowe, *The Intimacies of Four Continents* (Durham, NC: Duke University Press, 2015), 102.

18. Tony Ballantyne, *Entanglements of Empire: Missionaries, Maoris, and the Question of the Body* (Durham, NC: Duke University Press, 2014).

19. Johnson, *African American Religions,* 1.

20. See, for example, Jeremy M. Schott, *Christianity, Empire, and the Making of Religion in Late Antiquity* (Philadelphia: University of Pennsylvania Press, 2008).

21. Nilüfer Göle, "Manifestations of the Religious-Secular Divide: Self, State, and the Public Sphere," in *Comparative Secularisms in a Global Age,* ed. Linell E. Cady and Elizabeth Shakman Hurd (New York: Palgrave Macmillan, 2010), 47.

22. Thomas A. Tweed, *Crossing and Dwelling: A Theory of Religion* (Cambridge, MA: Harvard University Press, 2006), 54.

23. Curt Sachs, *Rhythm and Tempo: A Study in Music History* (New York: W. W. Norton, 1953), 13.

24. Thomas Karl Alberts, *Shamanism, Discourse, Modernity* (Surrey, U.K.: Ashgate, 2015).

25. Walter H. Capps, "Commentary," in *Science of Religion: Studies in Methodology,* ed. Lauri Honko (The Hague: Mouton, 1979), 185.

26. David Morgan, *The Sacred Gaze: Religious Visual Culture in Theory and Practice* (Berkeley: University of California Press, 2005); Charles Hirschkind, *The Ethical Soundscape: Cassette-Sermons and Islamic Counterpublics* (New York: Columbia University Press, 2006); Birgit Meyer, *Sensational Movies:*

Video, Vision, and Christianity in Ghana (Berkeley: University of California Press, 2015); Jeremy Stolow, ed., *Deus in Machina: Religion, Technology, and the Things in Between* (New York: Fordham University Press, 2012).

27. Thomas Luckmann, *The Invisible Religion: The Problem of Religion in Modern Society* (London: Macmillan, 1967). See Bruce David Forbes and Jeffrey H. Mahan, eds., *Religion and Popular Culture in America*, rev. ed. (Berkeley: University of California Press, 2005); Eric Michael Mazur and Kate McCarthy, eds., *God in the Details: American Religion in Popular Culture*, 2nd ed. (New York: Routledge, 2011); John C. Lyden and Eric Michael Mazur, eds., *The Routledge Companion to Religion and Popular Culture* (London: Routledge, 2015).

28. Chidester, *Authentic Fakes*, 71–90.

29. Jean Comaroff and John L. Comaroff, "Occult Economies and the Violence of Abstraction: Notes from the South African Postcolony," *American Ethnologist* 26, no. 3 (1999): 279–301.

30. Karl Marx and Friedrich Engels, *On Religion*, introduction by Reinhold Niebuhr (New York: Schocken, 1964), 7.

31. David Chidester, *Savage Systems: Colonialism and Comparative Religion in Southern Africa* (Charlottesville: University Press of Virginia, 1996).

32. Chidester, *Empire of Religion*, 41. See W.J.T. Mitchell, *What Do Pictures Want? The Lives and Loves of Images* (Chicago: University of Chicago Press, 2005), 163.

33. Robert D. Baird, *Category Formation and the History of Religions* (The Hague: Mouton, 1974).

34. David Chidester, *Christianity: A Global History* (London: Penguin, 2000), 495–503.

35. Kwame Nkrumah, *Ghana: The Autobiography of Kwame Nkrumah* (1957; London: Panaf Books, 2002), 164.

36. Elizabeth Shakman Hurd, *Beyond Religious Freedom: The New Global Politics of Religion* (Princeton, NJ: Princeton University Press, 2015).

37. On fabrication, see Bruno Latour, *On the Modern Cult of the Factish Gods* (Durham, NC: Duke University Press, 2010).

38. David Morgan, "Materiality," in *Oxford Handbook of the Study of Religion*, ed. Michael Stausberg and Steven Engler (Oxford: Oxford University Press, 2016), 276.

39. Susan Leigh Star and James R. Griesemer, "Institutional Ecology, 'Translations,' and Boundary Objects: Amateurs and Professionals in Berkeley's Museum of Vertebrate Zoology, 1907–39," *Social Studies of Science* 19 (1989): 393.

40. Star and Griesemer, "Institutional Ecology," 393.

41. James Boswell, *Boswell's Life of Johnson*, ed. George Birkbeck Hill and L. F. Powell, 6 vols. (1791; Oxford: Clarendon Press, 1934–1950), 1:471.

42. Michael Flynn, "The Hermeneutics of Perry Mason," *TOF Spot* (June 21, 2013), http://tofspot.blogspot.co.za/2013/06/the-hermeneutics-of-perry-mason.html.

43. Scott J. Burnham, *Contract Law for Dummies* (Hoboken, NJ: Wiley, 2012), 221–22.

44. Mary Poovey, *A History of the Modern Fact: Problems of Knowledge in the Sciences of Wealth and Society* (Chicago: University of Chicago Press, 1998).

45. Maire Loughran, *Auditing for Dummies* (Indianapolis, IN: Wiley, 2010), 80–86.

1. ANIMISM

1. E. B. Tylor, *Primitive Culture*, 2 vols. (London: John Murray, 1871), 1:383.

2. Gailyn Van Rheenen, *Communicating Christ among Folk Religionists: Kingdom Ministry in Satan's Nest* (2003), http://missiology.org/old/folkreligion/. This estimate was derived from Stephen C. Neill, *Christian Faith and Other Faiths: The Christian Dialogue with Other Religions*, 2nd ed. (Oxford: Oxford University Press, 1970), 125.

3. William Pietz, "The Problem of the Fetish I," *Res: Anthropology and Aesthetics* 9 (Spring 1985): 5–17.

4. John Ferguson McLennan, "The Worship of Animals and Plants," *Fortnightly Review* 6 (1869): 407–27, 562–82; 7 (1870): 194–216.

5. John Lubbock, *The Origin of Civilization and the Primitive Condition of Man*, 5th ed. (1870; London: Longmans, Green, 1889), 287.

6. Charles R. Darwin, *The Descent of Man, and Selection in Relation to Sex*, 2 vols. (London: John Murray, 1871), 1:65–68.

7. Tylor, *Primitive Culture*, 1:22–23.

8. Henry Callaway, *The Religious System of the Amazulu* (1868–70; Cape Town: Struik, 1970).

9. Tylor, *Primitive Culture*, 1:380.

10. Tylor, *Primitive Culture*, 1:430; Callaway, *Religious System*, 91, 126.

11. Callaway, *Religious System*, 228, 260, 316.

12. Tylor, *Primitive Culture*, 1:443.

13. Tylor, *Primitive Culture*, 1:104.

14. Tylor, *Primitive Culture*, 1:98; 2:367; see Callaway, *Religious System*, 64, 222–25, 263.

15. Tylor, *Primitive Culture*, 1:104.

16. Tylor, *Primitive Culture*, 2:387.

17. E. B. Tylor, "On the Limits of Savage Religion," *Journal of the Anthropological Institute* 21 (1892): 283.

18. Tylor, "On the Limits of Savage Religion," 298.

19. Tomoko Masuzawa, "Troubles with Materiality: The Ghost of Fetishism in the Nineteenth Century," *Comparative Studies in Society and History* 42, no. 2 (2000): 242–67.

20. Karl Marx, *Capital,* trans. Samuel Moore and Edward Aveling, 2 vols. (1867; London: Lawrence and Wishart, 1974), 1:81.

21. Stewart Elliott Guthrie, *Faces in the Clouds: A New Theory of Religion* (New York: Oxford University Press, 1993); Nurit Bird-David, "'Animism' Revisited: Personhood, Environment, and Relational Epistemology," *Current Anthropology* 40 (Supplement) (1999): 67–92.

22. Harry Garuba, "Explorations of Animist Materialism: Notes on Reading/ Writing African Literature, Culture, and Society," *Public Culture* 15, no. 2 (2003): 261–85; Graham Harvey, *Animism: Respecting the Living World* (New York: Columbia University Press, 2005).

2. SACRED

1. Anthony Synnott, "Shame and Glory: A Sociology of Hair," *British Journal of Sociology* 38, no. 3 (1987): 384. See Edmund R. Leach, "Magical Hair," *Journal of the Royal Anthropological Institute* 88, no. 2 (1958): 147–64; C. R. Hallpike, "Social Hair," *Man,* n.s., 4, no. 2 (1969): 256–64; Raymond Firth, "Hair as Private Asset and Public Symbol," in *Symbols: Public and Private* (London: Allen and Unwin, 1973), 262–98; Paul Hershman, "Hair, Sex and Dirt," *Man,* n.s., 9, no. 2 (1974): 274–98; Gananath Obeyesekere, *Medusa's Hair: An Essay on Personal Symbols and Religious Experience* (Chicago: University of Chicago Press, 1981), 13–46.

2. Chris Rock, *Good Hair,* directed by Jeff Stilson (Chris Rock Productions and HBO Films, 2009).

3. Synnott, "Shame and Glory," 390.

4. Britta Sandberg, "Hindu Locks Keep Human Hair Trade Humming," *Spiegel Online International,* February 19, 2008, www.spiegel.de/international /business/0,1518,536349-2,00.html.

5. Saritha Rai, "A Religious Tangle over the Hair of Pious Hindus," *New York Times,* July 14, 2004, www.nytimes.com/2004/07/14/world/a-religious-tangle-over-the-hair-of-pious-hindus.html?pagewanted=all.

6. Jonathan Z. Smith, *Imagining Religion: From Babylon to Jonestown* (Chicago: University of Chicago Press, 1982), 53–65.

7. Leach, "Magical Hair," 154. See David Chidester, *Wild Religion: Tracking the Sacred in South Africa* (Berkeley: University of California Press, 2012), 132–51.

8. Jean Comaroff and John L. Comaroff. "Millennial Capitalism: First Thoughts on a Second Coming," *Public Culture* 12, no. 2 (2000): 291–343.

9. Georges Bataille, "The Notion of Expenditure," in *Visions of Excess: Selected Writings, 1927-1939*, ed. Allan Stoekl, trans. Allan Stoekl, Carl R. Lovitt, and Donald M. Leslie Jr. (1933; Minneapolis: University of Minnesota Press, 1985), 116–29.

10. Access Hollywood, "Bad Day: Chris Rock Is Sued over 'Good Hair,'" *MSNBC Entertainment*, October 7, 2009, www.msnbc.msn.com/id/33200833 /ns/entertainment-access_hollywood/.

11. Leach, "Magical Hair," 162–63.

3. SPACE

1. Mircea Eliade, *Patterns in Comparative Religion*, trans. Rosemary Sheed (New York: Harper and Row, 1958), 367–85; *The Sacred and the Profane: The Nature of Religion*, trans. Willard R. Trask (New York: Harcourt, Brace and World, 1959), 20–65.

2. Jonathan Z. Smith, *Map Is Not Territory: Studies in the History of Religions* (Leiden: E.J. Brill, 1978), 88–103; *To Take Place: Toward Theory in Ritual* (Chicago: University of Chicago Press, 1987).

3. Gerardus van der Leeuw, *Religion in Essence and Manifestation*, trans. J.E. Turner, foreword by Ninian Smart (1933; Princeton, NJ: Princeton University Press, 1986), 210.

4. Kim Knott, *The Location of Religion: A Spatial Analysis* (London: Equinox, 2005). See Henri Lefebvre, *The Production of Space*, trans. Donald Nicholson-Smith (Oxford: Blackwell, 1991).

5. Thomas A. Tweed, *Crossing and Dwelling: A Theory of Religion* (Cambridge, MA: Harvard University Press, 2006), 54.

6. Manuel A. Vásquez, *More Than Belief: A Materialist Theory of Religion* (Oxford: Oxford University Press, 2010), 260–319.

7. W. D. Hammond-Tooke, "The Symbolic Structure of Cape Nguni Cosmology," in *Religion and Social Change in Southern Africa*, ed. M.G. Whisson and M. West (Cape Town: David Philip, 1975), 15–33; David Chidester, *Religions of South Africa* (London: Routledge, 1992), 9–13.

8. Jean Comaroff, "Healing and Cultural Transformation: The Case of the Tswana of Southern Africa," *Social Science and Medicine* 15, no. 2 (1981): 367–78.

9. Wyatt MacGaffey, "Dialogues of the Deaf: Europeans on the Atlantic Coast of Africa," in *Implicit Understandings: Observing, Reporting, and Reflecting on the Encounters between Europeans and Other Peoples in the Early Modern Era*, ed. Stuart B. Schwartz (Cambridge: Cambridge University Press, 1994), 257.

10. John Campbell, *Travels in South Africa* (1815; Cape Town: Struik, 1974), 526.

11. Jeffrey B. Peires, "Nxele, Ntsikana, and the Origins of the Xhosa Religious Reaction," *Journal of African History* 20, no. 1 (1979): 51–61.

12. Wilhelm H. I. Bleek, *Zulu Legends*, ed. J. A. Engelbrecht (1857; Pretoria: Van Schaik, 1952), 3–4.

13. David Coplan, "Land from the Ancestors: Popular Religious Reappropriations along the Lesotho-South African Border," *Journal of Southern African Studies* 29, no. 4 (2003): 977–93.

14. See, for example, Anna Bigelow, *Sharing the Sacred: Practicing Pluralism in Muslim North India* (Oxford: Oxford University Press, 2010); Margaret Cormack, ed., *Muslims and Others in Sacred Space* (Oxford: Oxford University Press, 2013).

15. David Chidester, *Christianity: A Global History* (London: Penguin, 2000), 114–15.

16. Chidester, *Christianity*, 490–92.

17. Peter van der Veer, *Religious Nationalism: Hindus and Muslims in India* (Berkeley: University of California Press, 1994), 153.

18. Diana L. Eck, *India: A Sacred Geography* (New York: Random House, 2012).

19. See Smith, *Map Is Not Territory*, 100–103; *Drudgery Divine: On the Comparison of Early Christianities and the Religions of Late Antiquity* (Chicago: University of Chicago Press, 1990), 121–42.

20. Roger Friedland and Richard D. Hecht, "The Bodies of Nations: A Comparative Study of Religious Violence in Jerusalem and Ayodhya," *History of Religions* 38, no. 2 (1998): 101–49.

21. Ernest Renan, "What Is a Nation?" in *Nation and Narration*, ed. Homi Bhabha (1882; London: Routledge, 1990), 19; Max Weber, "Politics as a Vocation," in *From Max Weber: Essays in Sociology*, ed. and trans. H. H. Gerth and C. Wright Mills (1918; London: Routledge and Kegan Paul, 1948), 78.

22. Karen McCarthy Brown, "Staying Grounded in a High-Rise Building: Ecological Dissonance and Ritual Accommodation in Haitian Vodou," in *Gods of the City: Religion and the American Urban Landscape*, ed. Robert A. Orsi (Bloomington: Indiana University Press, 1999), 79–102.

23. Steven Vertovec, *The Hindu Diaspora: Comparative Patterns* (London: Routledge, 2000).

24. Robert Hertz, "The Pre-eminence of the Right Hand: A Study of Religious Polarity," in *Right and Left: Essays on Dual Symbolic Classification*, ed. Rodney Needham (1909; Chicago: University of Chicago Press, 1973), 3–31. See Knott, *Location of Religion*, 133–228.

25. See Paul Christopher Johnson, *Diaspora Conversions: Black Carib Religion and the Recovery of Africa* (Berkeley: University of California Press, 2007).

4. TIME

1. John Locke, *An Essay Concerning Human Understanding*, 2 vols., ed. Alexander Campbell Fraser (1690; New York: Dover, 1959), 1:466–68.

2. Henri Bergson, *Time and Free Will: An Essay on the Immediate Data of Consciousness*, trans. Frank Lubecki Pogson (1889; London: S. Sonnenschein, 1910).

3. Henri Hubert, *Essay on Time: A Brief Study of the Representation of Time in Religion and Magic*, trans. Robert Parkin and Jacqueline Redding (1905; Oxford: Durkheim Press, 1999), 50. See William Watts Miller, "Durkheimian Time," *Time & Society* 9, no. 1 (2000): 5–20.

4. Mircea Eliade, *The Sacred and the Profane: The Nature of Religion*, trans. Willard R. Trask (New York: Harcourt, Brace and World, 1959), 91.

5. Mircea Eliade, *The Myth of the Eternal Return*, trans. Willard R. Trask (New York: Pantheon, 1954), 139–62.

6. Mircea Eliade, *Myth and Reality*, trans. Willard R. Trask (New York: Harper and Row, 1963), 75–91.

7. Eliade, *Myth and Reality*, 71.

8. Mircea Eliade, *The Forge and the Crucible*, trans. Stephen Corrin (Chicago: University of Chicago Press, 1978), 178.

9. See Alfred Gell, *The Anthropology of Time: Cultural Constructions of Temporal Maps and Images* (Oxford: Berg, 1992); Nancy Munn, "The Cultural Anthropology of Time: A Critical Essay," *Annual Review of Anthropology* 21 (1992): 93–123.

10. E. E. Evans-Pritchard, "Nuer Time Reckoning," *Africa* 12 (1939): 201; *The Nuer: A Description of the Modes of Livelihood and Political Institutions of a Nilotic People* (Oxford: Clarendon Press, 1940), 95–108.

11. Claude Lévi-Strauss, "Social Structure," in *Anthropology Today: An Encyclopedic Inventory*, ed. A. L. Kroeber (Chicago: University of Chicago Press, 1953), 530.

12. Clifford Geertz, *The Interpretation of Cultures* (New York: Basic Books, 1973), 393.

13. Maurice Bloch, "The Past and the Present in the Present," *Man*, n.s., 12, no. 2 (1977): 278–92.

14. Edmund R. Leach, *Rethinking Anthropology* (London: Athlone Press, 1961), 125.

15. See Roy A. Rappaport, *Ritual and Religion in the Making of Humanity* (Cambridge: Cambridge University Press, 1999), 169–276.

16. Arnold van Gennep, *The Rites of Passage*, trans. Monika B. Vizedom and Gabrielle L. Caffee, with an introduction by Solon T. Kimball (1909; Chicago: University of Chicago Press, 1960).

17. Anthony F. Aveni, *Empires of Time: Calendars, Clocks, and Cultures* (New York: Kodansha America, 1994).

18. David Landes, *Revolution in Time: Clocks and the Making of the Modern World* (Cambridge, MA: Harvard University Press, 1983); Gerhard Dohrn-van Rossum, *History of the Hour: Clocks and Modern Temporal Orders*, trans. Thomas Dunlap (Chicago: University of Chicago Press, 1996).

19. E. P. Thompson, "Time, Work-Discipline, and Industrial Capitalism," *Past and Present* 38 (December 1967): 56–97.

20. Edward G. Richards, *Mapping Time: The Calendar and Its History* (Oxford: Oxford University Press, 1999); Eviatar Zerubavel, *The Seven Day Circle: The History and Meaning of the Week* (New York: Free Press, 1985).

21. Endel Tulving, *Elements of Episodic Memory* (New York: Oxford University Press, 1983), 184–85.

22. Harvey Whitehouse, *Inside the Cult: Religious Innovation and Transmission in Papua New Guinea* (Oxford: Oxford University Press, 1995); *Arguments and Icons: Divergent Modes of Religiosity* (Oxford: Oxford University Press, 2000); *Modes of Religiosity: A Cognitive Theory of Religious Transmission* (Walnut Creek, CA: AltaMira Press, 2004).

23. David M. Knipe, "*Sapiṇḍīkaraṇa:* The Hindu Rite of Entry into Heaven," in *Religious Encounters with Death: Insights from the History and Anthropology of Religions,* ed. Frank E. Reynolds and Earle H. Waugh (University Park: Pennsylvania State University Press, 1977), 111–24.

24. H. I. E. Dhlomo, "Nature and Variety of Tribal Drama," *English in Africa* 4, no. 2 ([1939] 1977): 30.

25. Manu, *The Laws of Manu,* trans. Georg Bühler (Oxford: Clarendon Press, 1886), 22.

26. Thomas R. Trautmann, "Indian Time, European Time," in *Time: Histories and Ethnologies,* ed. Diane O. Hughes and Thomas R. Trautmann (Ann Arbor: University of Michigan Press, 1995), 186–90.

27. Augustine of Hippo, *The City of God* (New York: Modern Library, 1950), 390–92.

28. Evans-Pritchard, *The Nuer,* 125–26; Bruce Lincoln, *Priests, Warriors, and Cattle: A Study in the Ecology of Religions* (Berkeley: University of California Press, 1981), 13–48; *Discourse and the Construction of Society: Comparative Studies of Myth, Ritual, and Classification* (New York: Oxford University Press, 1989), 21–22.

29. Henry Callaway, *The Religious System of the Amazulu* (1868–70; Cape Town: Struik, 1970), 77.

30. Callaway, *Religious System,* 79–80.

31. Jeffrey B. Peires, *The Dead Will Arise: Nongqawuse and the Great Xhosa Cattle-Killing Movement of 1856-7* (Johannesburg: Ravan Press, 1989); Richard Landes, "Suicidal Millennialism: Xhosa Cattle-Slaying (1856–1857 CE)," in

Heaven on Earth: The Varieties of the Millennial Experience (Oxford: Oxford University Press, 2011), 91–122.

32. David Chidester, *Authentic Fakes: Religion and American Popular Culture* (Berkeley: University of California Press, 2005), 112. See Geertz, *Interpretation of Cultures*, 87–125.

33. David Graeber, *Debt: The First 5,000 Years* (New York: Melville House, 2011), 59–60, 248–50.

5. INCONGRUITY

1. William James, *The Varieties of Religious Experience*, ed. Martin E. Marty (1902; London: Penguin, 1982), 37–38.

2. See, for example, Hans Gaybels and Walter Van Herck, eds., *Humour and Religion: Challenges and Ambiguities* (New York: Bloomsbury, 2011); Ingvild Saelid Gilhus, *Laughing Gods, Weeping Virgins: Laughter in the History of Religions* (London: Routledge, 1997); Selva J. Raj and Corinne G. Dempsey, eds., *Sacred Play: Ritual Levity and Humor in South Asian Religions* (Albany: State University of New York Press, 2010).

3. Ninian Smart, *The Philosophy of Religion* (London: Sheldon Press, 1979), 42.

4. François Le Vaillant, *Travels into the Interior Parts of Africa, by Way of the Cape of Good Hope in the Years 1780–5*, 2 vols. (Edinburgh: W. Laine, 1791), 1:82.

5. Robert Moffat, *Missionary Labours and Scenes in Southern Africa* (London: John Snow, 1842), 268.

6. Robert Moffat, *The Matabele Journals of Robert Moffat, 1829–1860*, 2 vols. (London: Chatto and Windus, 1945), 1:16, 27.

7. Moffat, *Missionary Labours*, 252.

8. Moffat, *Missionary Labours*, 248.

9. Moffat, *Missionary Labours*, 269.

10. James Chapman, *Travels in the Interior of South Africa, 1849–1863*, ed. Edward C. Tabler, 2 vols. (1868; Cape Town: A.A. Balkema, 1971), 1:117.

11. John Mackenzie, *Ten Years North of the Orange River: A Story of Everyday Life and Work among the South African Tribes from 1859 to 1869* (Edinburgh: Edmonston and Douglas, 1871), 337.

12. Thomas Hodgson, *The Journal of the Reverend T.L. Hodgson, Missionary to the Seleka-Rolong and the Griqua, 1821–31*, ed. Richard L. Cope (Johannesburg: Witwatersrand University Press, 1977), 357.

13. Martin K.H. Lichtenstein, *Foundation of the Cape 1811; About the Bechuanas 1807*, ed. and trans. Otto Hartung Spohr (Cape Town: A.A. Balkema, 1973), 72.

14. Herbert Spencer, "The Physiology of Laughter," *Macmillan's Magazine* 1 (1860): 395–402; see William McDougall, *An Outline of Psychology*, 11th ed. (1923; London: Methuen, 1947), 165–70.

15. Henri Bergson, *Laughter: An Essay on the Meaning of the Comic*, trans. Claudesley Brereton and Fred Rothwell (New York: Macmillan, 1911).

16. John Campbell, *Travels in South Africa* (1815; Cape Town: Struik, 1974), 124.

17. Moffat, *Missionary Labours*, 247.

18. Fred D. Ellenberger and J. C. MacGregor, *History of the Basuto: Ancient and Modern* (London: Caxton, 1912), 241–42; Winifred Agnes Hoernlé, "Social Organization," in *Bantu Speaking Tribes of South Africa: An Ethnological Survey*, ed. Isaac Schapera (London: Routledge and Sons, 1937), 91; Isaac Schapera, *The Tswana* (London: International Institute, 1952), 35.

19. Mackenzie, *Ten Years North of the Orange River*, 135n1; John Mackenzie, *Day-Dawn in Dark Places: A Study of Wanderings and Work in Bechuanaland* (London: Cassell, 1883), 65–68.

20. Edwin W. Smith, *Robert Moffat: One of God's Gardeners* (London: Church Missionary Society, 1925), 147.

21. Moffat, *Missionary Labours*, 134.

22. James Beattie, "Essay on Laughter and Ludicrous Composition," in *Essays* (Edinburgh: William Creech, 1776), 321–455; cited in Christopher P. Wilson, *Jokes: Form, Content, Use, and Function* (New York: Academic Press, 1979), 11.

23. James Kern Feibleman, *In Praise of Comedy* (New York: Macmillan, 1939); John M. Willmann, "An Analysis of Humour and Laughter," *American Journal of Psychology* 53, no. 1 (1940): 72; Jerry M. Suls, "A Two-Stage Model for the Appreciation of Jokes and Cartoons," in *The Psychology of Humor*, ed. Jeffrey H. Goldstein and Paul E. McGhee (New York: Academic Press, 1972), 82.

24. Sigmund Freud, *Jokes and Their Relation to the Unconscious*, trans. James Strachey (1905; London: Hogarth Press, 1960).

25. Edmund R. Leach, "Anthropological Aspects of Language: Animal Categories and Verbal Abuse," in *New Directions in the Study of Language*, ed. Eric. H. Lenneberg (Amherst: Massachusetts University Press, 1963), 23–63.

26. Jonathan Z. Smith, *Imagining Religion: From Babylon to Jonestown* (Chicago: University of Chicago Press, 1982), 90.

27. Smith, *Imagining Religion*, 62–63.

28. A. R. Radcliffe-Brown, "On Joking Relationships," *Africa* 13, no. 3 (1940): 195–210; *Structure and Function in Primitive Society* (Glencoe, IL: Free Press, 1952), 91.

29. Andrew Apter, "In Dispraise of the King: Rituals 'Against' Rebellion in South-East Africa," *Man*, n.s., 18, no. 3 (1983): 521–34.

30. Jean Comaroff and John L. Comaroff, *Of Revelation and Revolution*, vol. 1: *Christianity, Colonialism, and Consciousness in South Africa* (Chicago: University of Chicago Press, 1991).

31. Norbert Elias, *The Civilizing Process: The Development of Manners, Changes in the Code of Conduct and Feeling in Early Modern Times* (New York: Urizen Books, 1978).

32. Mikhail Bakhtin, *Rabelais and His World*, trans. Hélene Iswolsky (Bloomington: Indiana University Press, 1984).

33. Lucien Lévy-Bruhl, *Primitive Mentality*, trans. Lilian A. Clare (1910; London: George Allen, 1923), 22.

34. John Philip, *Researches in South Africa*, 2 vols. (London: James Duncan, 1828), 2:116–17; Lévy-Bruhl, *Primitive Mentality*, 36.

35. Thomas Arbousset, "Station de Morija—Rapport de M. Arbousset sus la date du 26 Juin 1838," *Le Journal des missions évangéliques* 14 (1839): 57.

36. Lévy-Bruhl, *Primitive Mentality*, 23.

37. William John Burchell, *Travels into the Interior of South Africa*, 2 vols. (1822; London: Batchworth Press, 1953), 2:295; Lévy-Bruhl, *Primitive Mentality*, 24.

38. Henri-Alexandre Junod, *Life of a South African Tribe*, 2 vols. (Neuchâtel, Switzerland: Attinger, 1912–13), 2:152; Lévy-Bruhl, *Primitive Mentality*, 26.

39. Friedrich Nietzsche, *The Will to Power*, trans. Walter Kaufmann and R. J. Hollingdale (1883–88; New York: Vintage, 1968), 56.

40. Ninian Smart, *Buddhism and Christianity: Rivals and Allies* (London: Macmillan, 1993), 138.

41. Smart, *Philosophy of Religion*, 42.

42. Mary Douglas, "The Social Control of Cognition: Some Factors in Joke Perception," *Man*, n.s., 3, no. 3 (1968): 361–76.

43. Ninian Smart, "The Criteria of Religious Identity," *Philosophical Quarterly* 8 (1958): 328.

44. Elaine Scarry, *The Body in Pain: The Making and Unmaking of the World* (Oxford: Oxford University Press, 1985).

6. CULTURE

1. Ludwig Feuerbach, *The Essence of Christianity*, trans. George Elliot (1841; New York: Harper and Brothers, 1957), 4.

2. Charles H. Long, *Significations: Signs, Symbols, and Images in the Interpretation of Religion* (1986; Aurora, CO: Davies Group, 1999).

3. Régis Debray, *Media Manifestos*, trans. Eric Rauth (London: Verso, 1996).

4. Birgit Meyer, David Morgan, Crispin Paine, and S. Brent Plate, "The Origin and Mission of *Material Religion*," *Religion* 40, no. 3 (2010): 207–11.

5. John Kieschnick, *The Impact of Buddhism on Chinese Material Culture* (Princeton, NJ: Princeton University Press, 2003).

6. Patrick J. Geary, *Furta Sacra: Thefts of Relics in the Central Middle Ages* (Princeton, NJ: Princeton University Press, 1978).

7. Daniel J. Sahas, *Icon and Logos: Sources in Eighth-Century Iconoclasm* (Toronto: University of Toronto Press, 1986).

8. William Pietz, "The Problem of the Fetish I," *Res: Anthropology and Aesthetics* 9 (Spring 1985): 5–17; "The Problem of the Fetish II: The Origin of the Fetish," *Res: Anthropology and Aesthetics* 13 (Spring 1987): 23–45; "The Problem of the Fetish IIIa: Bosman's Guinea and the Enlightenment Theory of Fetishism," *Res: Anthropology and Aesthetics* 16 (Autumn 1988): 105–24.

9. Peter Lawrence, *Road Belong Cargo: A Study of the Cargo Movement in the Southern Madang District, New Guinea* (Manchester, U.K.: Manchester University Press, 1964).

10. Lindsay Jones, *The Hermeneutics of Sacred Architecture: Experience, Interpretation, Comparison*, 2 vols. (Cambridge, MA: Harvard University Press, 2000).

11. Debray, *Media Manifestos*, 171. See Régis Debray, *Transmitting Culture*, trans. Eric Rauth (New York: Columbia University Press, 2000).

7. ECONOMY

1. Laurence R. Iannaccone, "Rational Choice: Framework for the Scientific Study of Religion," in *Rational Choice Theory and Religion: Summary and Assessment*, ed. Lawrence A. Young (New York: Routledge, 1997), 25–45.

2. Pierre Bourdieu, *Outline of a Theory of Practice*, trans. Richard Nice (Cambridge: Cambridge University Press, 1977), 183. See Hugh B. Urban, "Sacred Capital: Pierre Bourdieu and the Study of Religion," *Method and Theory in the Study of Religion* 15, no. 4 (2003): 354–89.

3. Pierre Bourdieu, *In Other Words: Essays Towards a Reflexive Sociology* (Stanford, CA: Stanford University Press, 1990), 36.

4. Adam Smith, *An Inquiry into the Nature and Causes of the Wealth of Nations* (London: W. Strahan and T. Cadell, 1776), 161.

5. C. A. Gregory, *Gifts and Commodities* (London: Academic Press, 1982).

6. Marcel Mauss, *The Gift: Forms and Functions of Exchange in Archaic Societies*, trans. Ian Cunnison, with an introduction by E. E. Evans-Pritchard (1924; London: W. W. Norton, 1966).

7. Georges Bataille, "The Notion of Expenditure," in *Visions of Excess: Selected Writings, 1927–1939*, ed. Allan Stoekl, trans. Allan Stoekl, Carl R. Lovitt, and Donald M. Leslie Jr. (1933; Minneapolis: University of Minnesota Press, 1985), 116–29.

8. Jean-François Lyotard, *The Libidinal Economy*, trans. Iain Hamilton Grant (Bloomington: Indiana University Press, 1993).

9. Jean-Joseph Goux, *Symbolic Economies: After Marx and Freud* (Ithaca, NY: Cornell University Press, 1990).

10. Jean Baudrillard, *For a Critique of the Political Economy of the Sign*, trans. Charles Levin (St. Louis, MO: Telos, 1981); *Simulacra and Simulation*, trans. Sheila Faria Glaser (Ann Arbor: University of Michigan Press, 1994).

11. Scott Lash and John Urry, *Economies of Signs and Space* (London: Sage, 1994), 5.

12. Theodor W. Adorno, *The Culture Industry*, ed. J. M. Bernstein (London: Routledge, 2001).

13. Ernst Bloch, Theodor W. Adorno, and Georg Lukacs, *Aesthetics and Politics*, ed. and trans. Ronald Taylor (London: NLB, 1977), 123.

14. Max Horkheimer and Theodor W. Adorno, *The Dialectic of Enlightenment*, trans. John Cumming (1944; London: Verso, 1973), 137–38.

15. Walter Benjamin, *The Work of Art in the Age of Its Technological Reproducibility, and Other Writings on Media*, ed. Michael W. Jennings, Brigid Doherty, and Thomas Y. Levin (rev. ed. 1939; Cambridge, MA: Harvard University Press, 2008), 38; Miriam Hansen, "Of Mice and Ducks: Benjamin and Adorno on Disney," *South Atlantic Quarterly* 92, no. 1 (1993): 31.

16. Walter Benjamin, "Experience and Poverty," in *Walter Benjamin: Selected Writings*, vol. 2, pt. 2: *1931–1934*, ed. Michael W. Jennings, Howard Eiland, and Gary Smith (1933; Cambridge, MA: Harvard University Press, 1996), 735; Hansen, "Of Mice and Ducks," 41–42.

17. Stuart Hall, "Encoding/Decoding," in *Culture, Media, and Language*, ed. Stuart Hall, Dorothy Hobson, Andrew Lowe, and Paul Willis (London: Hutchinson, 1980), 128–38; "Notes on Deconstructing 'the Popular,'" in *People's History and Socialist Theory*, ed. Raphael Samuel (London: Routledge, 1981), 221–40.

18. Max Weber, *The Protestant Ethic and the Spirit of Capitalism*, trans. Talcott Parsons (1905; New York: Scribner's, 1958).

19. Walter Benjamin, "Capitalism as Religion," in *Walter Benjamin: Selected Writings*, vol. 1: *1913–1926*, ed. Marcus Bullock and Michael W. Jennings (1921; Cambridge, MA: Harvard University Press, 1996), 288–91; David R. Loy, "The Religion of the Market," *Journal of the American Academy of Religion* 65, no. 2 (1997): 275–90; Richard Foltz, "The Religion of the Market: Reflections on a Decade of Discussions," *Worldviews* 11, no. 2 (2007): 135–54.

20. John Sutherland, *Destination Earth* (New York: Sutherland Productions, 1956), www.archive.org/details/Destinat1956.

21. Jonathan Z. Smith, *Relating Religion: Essays in the Study of Religion* (Chicago: University of Chicago Press, 2004), 375–89.

22. Emile Durkheim, *The Elementary Forms of Religious Life*, trans. Karen E. Fields (1912; New York: Free Press, 1995), 44.

23. John Sutherland, *Make Mine Freedom* (New York: Sutherland Productions, 1948), www.archive.org/details/MakeMine1948.

24. Charles T. Mathewes, ed., "Special Issue: Religion and Secrecy," *Journal of the American Academy of Religion* 74, no. 2 (2006): 273–482.

25. Karl Marx, *Capital*, trans. Samuel Moore and Edward Aveling, 2 vols. (1867; London: Lawrence and Wishart, 1974), 1:81.

26. E. E. Evans-Pritchard, introduction to *The Gift: Forms and Functions of Exchange in Archaic Societies,* by Marcel Mauss, trans. Ian Cunnison (1924; London: W. W. Norton, 1966), ix.

27. Bataille, "Notion of Expenditure."

28. David Chidester, *Authentic Fakes: Religion and American Popular Culture* (Berkeley: University of California Press, 2005), 112.

29. William Pietz, "The Problem of the Fetish I," *Res: Anthropology and Aesthetics* 9 (Spring 1985): 5–17.

30. David Chidester, *Patterns of Transcendence: Religion, Death, and Dying,* 2nd ed. (Belmont, CA: Wadsworth, 2002), 141–42, 214.

31. Jean Comaroff and John L. Comaroff, "Occult Economies and the Violence of Abstraction: Notes from the South African Postcolony," *American Ethnologist* 26, no. 3 (1999): 279–301; "Millennial Capitalism: First Thoughts on a Second Coming," *Public Culture* 12, no. 2 (2000): 291–343.

32. Grant McCracken, *Culture and Consumption: New Approaches to the Symbolic Character of Consumer Goods and Activities* (Bloomington: Indiana University Press, 1988), 84–88.

33. David Chidester, *Christianity: A Global History* (London: Penguin, 2000), 515–16.

34. James Bonnet, *Stealing Fire from the Gods: A Dynamic New Story Model for Writers and Filmmakers,* 2nd ed. (Studio City, CA: Michael Wiese Productions, 2006).

35. Kenneth Burke, *Attitudes toward History* (1937; Boston: Beacon Press, 1961), 328.

8. COLONIALISM

1. David Lewis-Williams, *The Mind in the Cave* (London: Thames and Hudson, 2002).

2. Eduardo Mondlane, *The Struggle for Mozambique* (Harmondsworth, U.K.: Penguin, 1969), 23.

3. Patricia Seed, *Ceremonies of Possession in Europe's Conquest of the New World 1492–1640* (Cambridge: Cambridge University Press, 1995).

4. Mondlane, *Struggle for Mozambique,* 25.

5. Mondlane, *Struggle for Mozambique,* 26–27.

6. Mondlane, *Struggle for Mozambique,* 29.

7. Frantz Fanon, *The Wretched of the Earth,* trans. Constance Farrington (London: Penguin, 1967), 29–32, 48.

8. Richard King, *Orientalism and Religion: Postcolonial Theory, India, and the "Mystic East"* (London: Routledge, 1999), 134–35.

9. Mondlane, *Struggle for Mozambique,* 69.

10. Mondlane, *Struggle for Mozambique*, 71.

11. Mondlane, *Struggle for Mozambique*, 60.

12. Jean Comaroff and John L. Comaroff, *Of Revelation and Revolution*, vol. 1: *Christianity, Colonialism, and Consciousness in South Africa* (Chicago: University of Chicago Press, 1991); *Of Revelation and Revolution*, vol. 2: *The Dialectics of Modernity on a South African Frontier* (Chicago: University of Chicago Press, 1997).

13. Webb Keane, *Christian Moderns: Freedom and Fetish in the Mission Encounter* (Berkeley: University of California Press, 2007).

14. Mondlane, *Struggle for Mozambique*, 101.

15. Mondlane, *Struggle for Mozambique*, 104.

16. Fanon, *Wretched of the Earth*, 43.

17. Muhammad Sani Umar, *Islam and Colonialism: Intellectual Responses of Muslims of Northern Nigeria* (Leiden: Brill, 2005).

18. Bruno Latour, *We Have Never Been Modern*, trans. Catherine Porter (Cambridge, MA: Harvard University Press, 1993), 23–25.

19. Mondlane, *Struggle for Mozambique*, 107.

20. Mondlane, *Struggle for Mozambique*, 130–31.

21. David Chidester, *Savage Systems: Colonialism and Comparative Religion in Southern Africa* (Charlottesville: University Press of Virginia, 1996), 104–10.

22. Chidester, *Savage Systems*, 223–25.

23. Thomas David DuBois, ed., *Casting Faiths: Imperialism and the Transformation of Religion in East and Southeast Asia* (London: Palgrave, 2009).

9. IMPERIALISM

1. John G. A. Pocock, *Barbarism and Religion*, vol. 4: *Barbarians, Savages, and Empires* (Cambridge: Cambridge University Press, 2005); Collin G. Calloway, *White People, Indians, and Highlanders: Tribal Peoples and Colonial Encounters in Scotland and America* (Oxford: Oxford University Press, 2008), 77; Karuna Mantena, *Alibis of Empire: Henry Maine and the Ends of Liberal Imperialism* (Princeton, NJ: Princeton University Press, 2010), 59.

2. International Olympic Committee, "Opening Ceremony—London 2012 Olympic Games," *Official Olympic Channel by the IOC*, www.youtube.com /watch?v=4AsOe4de-rI.

3. Peter Hulme, *Colonial Encounters: Europe and the Native Caribbean, 1492–1797* (London: Methuen, 1986), 123.

4. Octave Mannoni, *Prospero and Caliban: The Psychology of Colonization*, trans. Pamela Powesland (1950; London: Methuen, 1956).

5. Barbara Bush, *Imperialism and Postcolonialism* (London: Pearson, 2006), 144.

6. International Olympic Committee, "Closing Ceremony—London 2012 Olympic Games," *Official Olympic Channel by the IOC,* www.youtube.com/watch ?v=ij3sgRG5sPY&feature=relmfu.

7. Pierre de Coubertin, *Olympism: Selected Writings,* ed. Norbert Müller (Lausanne, Switzerland: International Olympic Committee, 2000), 580; Thomas Alkemeyer, *Körper, Kult, und Politik: Von der "Muskelreligion" Pierre de Coubertins zur Inszenierung von Macht in den Olympischen Spielen von 1936* (Frankfurt am Main, Ger.: Campus, 1996).

8. Andrew Wernick, *Auguste Comte and the Religion of Humanity: The Post-theistic Program of French Social Theory* (Cambridge: Cambridge University Press, 2004).

9. Linda C. Raeder, *John Stuart Mill and the Religion of Humanity* (Columbia: University of Missouri Press, 2002), 253.

10. David N. Livingstone, "Evolution and Religion," in *Evolution: The First Four Billion Years,* ed. Michael Ruse and Joseph Travis (Cambridge, MA: Harvard University Press, 2009), 351; James A. Herrick, *Scientific Mythologies: How Science and Science Fiction Forge New Religious Beliefs* (Downers Grove, IL: InterVarsity Press, 2008), 103–5.

11. Bill Schwarz, *The White Man's World: Memories of Empire* (Oxford: Oxford University Press, 2011), 93; Alan Sandison, *The Wheel of Empire* (New York: St. Martin's Press, 1967), 25–45.

12. Terence Ranger, "The Invention of Tradition in Colonial Africa," in *The Invention of Tradition,* ed. Eric Hobsbawm and Terence Ranger (Cambridge: Cambridge University Press, 1983), 212.

13. Edward W. Said, *Culture and Imperialism* (London: Chatto and Windus, 1993), 9.

14. Eduardo Mondlane, *The Struggle for Mozambique* (Harmondsworth, U.K.: Penguin, 1969), 23; Vincent A. Wimbush, *White Men's Magic: Scripturalization as Slavery* (Oxford: Oxford University Press, 2012).

15. Frantz Fanon, *The Wretched of the Earth,* trans. Constance Farrington (London: Penguin, 1967), 41.

16. Paul S. Landau, *Popular Politics in the History of South Africa, 1400–1948* (Cambridge: Cambridge University Press, 2010), 235.

17. John D. Y. Peel, *Religious Encounter and the Making of the Yoruba* (Bloomington: Indiana University Press, 2000).

18. Jennifer Cole, *Forget Colonialism? Sacrifice and the Art of Memory in Madagascar* (Berkeley: University of California Press, 2001), 11.

19. G. Wilson Knight, *The Crown of Life* (1947; New York: Barnes and Noble, 1966), 255.

20. Roberto Fernández Retamar, "Caliban: Notes toward a Discussion of Culture in our America," in *Caliban and Other Essays,* trans. and ed. Edward Baker (1971; Minneapolis: University of Minnesota Press, 1989), 3–45.

21. Aimé Césaire, *A Tempest*, trans. Richard Miller (1969; New York: Theater Communications Group, 1985).

22. Souhayr Belhassen, "Aimé Césaire's *A Tempest*," in *Radical Perspectives in the Arts*, ed. Lee Baxandall (Harmondsworth, U.K.: Penguin, 1972), 176.

23. Césaire, *A Tempest*, 68.

24. David Chidester, *Empire of Religion: Imperialism and Comparative Religion* (Chicago: University of Chicago Press, 2014), 204–6. See Paul Christopher Johnson, *Diaspora Conversions: Black Carib Religion and the Recovery of Africa* (Berkeley: University of California Press, 2007).

25. Sugata Bose, *A Hundred Horizons: The Indian Ocean in the Age of Global Empire* (Cambridge, MA: Harvard University Press, 2006).

26. Partha Chatterjee, *The Nation and Its Fragments: Colonial and Postcolonial Histories* (Princeton, NJ: Princeton University Press, 1993), 6; Gauri Viswanathan, "Coping with Civil Death: The Christian Convert's Rights of Passage in Colonial India," in *After Colonialism: Imperial Histories and Postcolonial Displacements*, ed. Gyan Prakash (Princeton, NJ: Princeton University Press, 1995), 185–86.

27. Bose, *A Hundred Horizons*, 270.

28. Raymond Williams, *Keywords: A Vocabulary of Culture and Society*, rev. ed. (Oxford: Oxford University Press, 1985), 87.

29. Jean Comaroff and John L. Comaroff, *Of Revelation and Revolution*, vol. 1: *Christianity, Colonialism, and Consciousness in South Africa* (Chicago: University of Chicago Press, 1991); Webb Keane, *Christian Moderns: Freedom and Fetish in the Mission Encounter* (Berkeley: University of California Press, 2007); Dipesh Chakrabarty, *Provincializing Europe: Postcolonial Thought and Historical Difference* (2000; Princeton, NJ: Princeton University Press, 2007), 12–16.

30. David Chidester, *Savage Systems: Colonialism and Comparative Religion in Southern Africa* (Charlottesville: University Press of Virginia, 1996); Richard King, *Orientalism and Religion: Postcolonial Theory, India, and the "Mystic East"* (London: Routledge, 1999); Tomoko Masuzawa, *The Invention of World Religions: Or, How European Universalism Was Preserved in the Language of Pluralism* (Chicago: University of Chicago Press, 2005).

31. David Chidester, "Thinking Black: Circulations of Africana Religion in Imperial Comparative Religion," *Journal of Africana Religions* 1, no. 1 (2013): 1–27.

10. APARTHEID

1. Hermann Giliomee, "The Making of the Apartheid Plan, 1929–1948," *Journal of Southern African Studies* 29, no. 2 (2003): 373–92.

2. David Chidester, *Savage Systems: Colonialism and Comparative Religion in Southern Africa* (Charlottesville: University Press of Virginia, 1996).

3. David Chidester, "'Classify and Conquer': Friedrich Max Müller, Indigenous Religious Traditions, and Imperial Comparative Religion," in *Beyond Primitivism: Indigenous Religious Traditions and Modernity*, ed. Jacob K. Olupona (New York: Routledge, 2004), 71–88; *Empire of Religion: Imperialism and Comparative Religion* (Chicago: University of Chicago Press, 2014), 59–89.

4. Daniel Boyarin, *Border Lines: The Partition of Judaeo-Christianity* (Philadelphia: University of Pennsylvania Press, 2004), 14.

5. Jean Comaroff and John L. Comaroff, "On the Founding Fathers, Fieldwork, and Functionalism: A Conversation with Isaac Schapera," *American Ethnologist* 15, no. 3 (1988): 555.

6. Isaac Schapera, "The Present State and Future Development of Ethnographical Research in South Africa," *Bantu Studies* 8, no. 3 (1934): 258.

7. W. M. Eiselen, "Geloofsvorme van Donker Afrika," *Tydskrif vir Wetenskap en Kuns* 3 (1924–25): 84–98.

8. John Lubbock, *The Origin of Civilization and the Primitive Condition of Man*, 5th ed. (1870; London: Longmans, Green, 1889), 205–10.

9. W. M. Eiselen, "Die Seksuele Lewe van die Bantoe," *Tydskrif vir Wetenskap en Kuns* 2 (1923–24): 166, 174.

10. W. M. Eiselen, "Die Aandeel van die Blanke ten Opsigte van die Praktiese Uitvoering van die Beleid van Afsonderlike Ontwikkeling; Kultureel en Maatskaplik," *Journal of Racial Affairs* 16, no. 1 (1965): 6–23; cited in T. Dunbar Moodie, *The Rise of Afrikanerdom* (Berkeley: University of California Press, 1974), 275.

11. W. M. Eiselen, "Die Eintlike Reendans van die Bapedi," *South African Journal of Science* 25 (December 1928): 387–92.

12. W. M. Eiselen, *Stamskole in Suid Afrika: 'n Ondersoek oor die funksie daarvan in die lewe van die Suid-Afrikaanse Stame* (Pretoria: L. J. van Schalk, 1929), 76.

13. W. M. Eiselen, "Christianity and the Religious Life of the Bantu," in *Western Civilization and the Natives of South Africa: Studies in Culture Contact*, ed. Isaac Schapera (London: Routledge, 1934), 66–67.

14. John Sharp, "The Roots and Development of *Volkekunde* in South Africa," *Journal of Southern African Studies* 8, no. 1 (1981): 16–36.

15. David Chidester, "Unity in Diversity: Religion Education and Public Pedagogy in South Africa," *Numen* 55, no. 2 (2008): 272–99.

16. Talal Asad, *Genealogies of Religion: Discipline and Reasons of Power in Christianity and Islam* (Baltimore: Johns Hopkins University Press, 1993), 17.

17. Tomoko Masuzawa, *The Invention of World Religions: Or, How European Universalism Was Preserved in the Language of Pluralism* (Chicago: University of Chicago Press, 2005).

18. Robert Young, *Colonial Desire: Hybridity in Theory, Culture, and Race* (London: Routledge, 1995), 19.

19. David Chidester, "Dreaming in the Contact Zone: Zulu Dreams, Visions, and Religion in Nineteenth-Century South Africa," *Journal of the American Academy of Religion* 76, no. 1 (2008): 27–53.

20. Gustavo Lins Ribeiro, "World Anthropologies: Cosmopolitics for a New Global Scenario in Anthropology," *Critique of Anthropology* 26, no. 4 (2006): 363; see Gustavo Lins Ribeiro and Arturo Escobar, *World Anthropologies: Disciplinary Transformations within Systems of Power* (Oxford: Berg, 2006).

11. SHAMANS

1. Äke Hultkrantz, "A Definition of Shamanism," *Temenos* 9 (1973): 34.

2. David Chidester, "Colonialism," in *Guide to the Study of Religion*, ed. Willi Braun and Russell T. McCutcheon (London: Cassell, 2000), 423–37.

3. Caroline Humphrey, "Shamanic Practices and the State in Northern Asia: Views from the Center and the Periphery," in *Shamanism, History, and the State*, ed. Nicholas Thomas and Caroline Humphrey (Ann Arbor: University of Michigan Press, 1994), 196.

4. Andrei A. Znamenski, *Shamanism and Christianity: Native Encounters with Russian Orthodox Missions in Siberia and Alaska, 1820-1917* (Westport, CT: Greenwood Press, 1999).

5. Roberte Hamayon, "Southern Siberian Religions," in *Encyclopedia of Religion*, ed. Mircea Eliade (New York: Macmillan, 1995), 13:546–53.

6. David Chidester, *Christianity: A Global History* (London: Penguin, 2000), 417–19.

7. Gloria Flaherty, *Shamanism and the Eighteenth Century* (Princeton, NJ: Princeton University Press, 1992), 23.

8. Robert Moffat, *Missionary Labours and Scenes in Southern Africa* (London: John Snow, 1842), 305; David Chidester, *Savage Systems: Colonialism and Comparative Religion in Southern Africa* (Charlottesville: University Press of Virginia, 1996), 192.

9. Michael Taussig, *Shamanism, Colonialism, and the Wild Man: A Study in Terror and Healing* (Chicago: University of Chicago Press, 1987), 143, 376.

10. Martin Sauer, *An Account of a Geographical and Astronomical Expedition to the Northern Parts of Russia* (London: T. Cadell, 1802), 110.

11. Sauer, *Account of a Geographical and Astronomical Expedition*, 308.

12. Giuseppe Acerbi, *Travels through Sweden, Finland, and Lapland, to the North Cape in the Years 1798 and 1799*, 2 vols. (London: Joseph Mawman, 1802), 2:294.

13. Acerbi, *Travels*, 2:311.

14. Flaherty, *Shamanism*, 26; Chidester, *Savage Systems*, 40–41.

15. David Chidester, *Religions of South Africa* (London: Routledge, 1992), 43.

16. Karen E. Fields, *Revival and Rebellion in Colonial Central Africa* (Princeton, NJ: Princeton University Press, 1985), 156.

17. Dominic J. Capeci Jr. and Jack C. Knight, "Reactions to Colonialism: The North American Ghost Dance and the East African Maji-Maji Rebellions," *Historian* 52, no. 4 (1990): 584–601.

18. Chidester, *Religions of South Africa*, 4–5; David Chidester, *Wild Religion: Tracking the Sacred in South Africa* (Berkeley: University of California Press, 2012), 27–28.

19. Taussig, *Shamanism, Colonialism, and the Wild Man*, 99, 236–37.

20. Stephen Hugh-Jones, "Shamans, Prophets, Priests, and Pastors," in *Shamanism, History, and the State*, ed. Nicholas Thomas and Caroline Humphrey (Ann Arbor: University of Michigan Press, 1994), 47–49.

21. Joseph Conrad, *Heart of Darkness* (1899; Harmondsworth: Penguin, 1973), 9.

22. Mircea Eliade, *Shamanism: Archaic Techniques of Ecstasy*, trans. Willard R. Trask (New York: Pantheon, 1964).

23. Daniel C. Noel, *The Soul of Shamanism: Western Fantasies, Imaginal Realities* (New York: Continuum, 1997).

12. MOBILITY

1. Arjun Appadurai, "Disjuncture and Difference in the Global Cultural Economy," in *Modernity at Large: Cultural Dimensions of Globalization* (Minneapolis: University of Minnesota Press, 1996), 27–47; David Chidester, *Authentic Fakes: Religion and American Popular Culture* (Berkeley: University of California Press, 2005), 134.

2. See, for example, Peter F. Beyer, *Religion and Globalization* (London: Sage, 1994); Mark Juergensmeyer, ed., *The Oxford Handbook of Global Religions* (Oxford: Oxford University Press, 2006); Manuel A. Vásquez, "Studying Religion in Motion: A Networks Approach," *Method and Theory in the Study of Religion* 20 (2008): 151–84; Manuel A. Vásquez and Marie F. Marquardt, *Globalizing the Sacred: Religion across the Americas* (New Brunswick, NJ: Rutgers University Press, 2003).

3. Walter H. Capps, "Commentary," in *Science of Religion: Studies in Methodology*, ed. Lauri Honko (The Hague: Mouton, 1979), 185.

4. J. W. Cullum, review of *Hope against Hope: Moltmann to Merton in One Theological Decade*, by Walter Holden Capps, *Journal of the American Academy of Religion* 45, no. 2 (1977): 253–54.

5. Eric J. Sharpe, "The Study of Religion in Historical Perspective," in *The Routledge Companion to the Study of Religion*, ed. John Hinnells (London: Routledge, 2005), 41.

6. C. J. Bleeker, "Commentary," in *Science of Religion: Studies in Methodology*, ed. Lauri Honko (The Hague: Mouton, 1979), 173, 176, 177.

7. John Locke, *An Essay Concerning Human Understanding*, 2 vols., ed. Alexander Campbell Fraser (1690; New York: Dover, 1959), 1:14; Capps, "Commentary," 177.

8. Capps, "Commentary," 178, 179.

9. Capps, "Commentary," 179.

10. Capps, "Commentary," 180.

11. Capps, "Commentary," 181, 182.

12. Walter H. Capps, *Religious Studies: The Making of a Discipline* (Minneapolis: Fortress Press, 1995), xxi–xxii.

13. Capps, "Commentary," 184; *Religious Studies*, xxi.

14. Capps, "Commentary," 185.

15. C. J. Bleeker, "The Phenomenological Method," *Numen* 6, no. 2 (1959): 110.

16. C. J. Bleeker, *The Sacred Bridge: Researches into the Nature and Structure of Religion* (Leiden, Netherlands: E. J. Brill, 1963), 16.

17. Bleeker, "Phenomenological Method," 110; *Sacred Bridge*, 16–24.

18. Walter Benjamin, "The Work of Art in the Age of Mechanical Reproduction," in *Illuminations*, ed. Hannah Arendt, trans. Harry Zohn (1933; New York: Schocken, 1968), 238; David Chidester, *Authentic Fakes: Religion and American Popular* Culture (Berkeley: University of California Press, 2005), 74.

19. Capps, "Commentary," 185.

20. Walter H. Capps, *Hope against Hope: Moltmann to Merton in One Theological Decade* (Philadelphia: Fortress Press, 1976), xi.

21. Robert Jay Lifton, *Boundaries: Psychological Man in Revolution* (New York: Random House, 1970); Norman O. Brown, *Love's Body* (New York: Random House, 1966); James E. Dittes, "When Idols Crumble: The Art and Agony of Disengagement," presidential address, Society for the Scientific Study of Religion, October 1973.

22. Erik H. Erikson, *Young Man Luther: A Study in Psychoanalysis and History* (New York: W. W. Norton, 1958); *Gandhi's Truth: On the Origin of Militant Nonviolence* (New York: W. W. Norton, 1969); Donald Capps and Walter H. Capps, eds., *The Religious Personality* (Belmont, CA: Wadsworth, 1970).

23. Capps, *Hope against Hope*, 40–41; Walter H. Capps, *Time Invades the Cathedral: Tensions in the School of Hope* (Philadelphia: Fortress Press, 1972).

24. Capps, *Hope against Hope*, 53–54.

25. Capps, *Hope against Hope*, 75–76.

26. Capps, *Hope against Hope*, 76, 77, 78.

27. Capps, *Hope against Hope*, 79.

28. Capps, *Hope against Hope*, 81.

29. Jürgen Moltmann, *Religion, Revolution, and the Future*, trans. M. Douglas Meeks (New York: Charles Scribner's Sons, 1969).

30. Walter H. Capps, review of *Religion, Revolution, and the Future,* by Jürgen Moltmann, *Journal of Religion* 51, no. 1 (1971): 69. See Henri Bergson, "Dynamic Religion," in *The Two Sources of Morality and Religion,* trans. R. Ashley Audra and Cloudesley Brereton (New York: Holt, Rinehart, and Winston, 1963), 209–65; Capps, *Time Invades the Cathedral,* 104–10.

31. Capps, *Hope against Hope,* 41, 87, 16.

32. Walter H. Capps, *The Monastic Impulse* (New York: Crossroad, 1983); Walter H. Capps and Wendy Wright, eds., *Silent Fire: An Invitation to Western Mysticism* (San Francisco: Harper and Row, 1978).

33. Walter H. Capps, *The Unfinished War: Vietnam and the American Conscience* (Boston: Beacon Press, 1982); *The New Religious Right: Piety, Patriotism, and Politics* (Columbia: University of South Carolina Press, 1990); Alessandro Duranti, "Narrating the Political Self in a Campaign for U.S. Congress," *Language in Society* 35 (2006): 467–97.

34. Capps, *Hope against Hope,* 87.

13. POPULAR

1. Douglas Brode, *From Walt to Woodstock: How Disney Created the Counterculture* (Austin: University of Texas Press, 2004), xxi.

2. Eric Michael Mazur and Tara K. Koda, "The Happiest Place on Earth: Disney's America and the Commodification of Religion," in *God in the Details: American Religion in Popular Culture,* ed. Eric Michael Mazur and Kate McCarthy, 2nd ed. (New York: Routledge, 2011), 307–21.

3. Edward T. Linenthal, *Sacred Ground: Americans and Their Battlefields* (Urbana: University of Illinois Press, 1991); Erika Doss, *Elvis Culture: Fans, Faith, and Image* (Lawrence: University Press of Kansas, 1999); Mike DiGiovanna, "Sutton Finally Gets Hall Pass," *Los Angeles Times,* January 6, 1998, http://articles.latimes.com/1998/jan/06/sports/sp-5409; Mark Pendergrast, *For God, Country, and Coca-Cola: The Unauthorized History of the World's Most Popular Soft Drink* (New York: Charles Scribner's Sons, 1993), 401; George Ritzer, *The McDonaldization of Society,* 6th ed. (Thousand Oaks, CA: Pine Forge Press, 2011), 9.

4. Charles H. Long, "Popular Religion," in *The Encyclopedia of Religion,* 2nd ed., ed. Lindsay Jones (New York: Macmillan, 2005), 11:7324–33.

5. Grant McCracken, *Culture and Consumption: New Approaches to the Symbolic Character of Consumer Goods and Activities* (Bloomington: Indiana University Press, 1988), 84–88.

6. S. Brent Plate, *Religion and Film: Cinema and the Re-creation of the World* (New York: Columbia University Press, 2017).

7. R. Laurence Moore, *Selling God: American Religion in the Marketplace of Culture* (New York: Oxford University Press, 1994); Leigh Eric Schmidt, *Con-*

sumer Rites: The Buying and Selling of American Holidays (Princeton, NJ: Princeton University Press, 1995); Nicole W. Biggart, *Charismatic Capitalism: Direct Selling Organizations in America* (Chicago: University of Chicago Press, 1989).

8. David Chidester, "The Church of Baseball, the Fetish of Coca-Cola, and the Potlatch of Rock 'n' Roll: Theoretical Models for the Study of Religion in American Popular Culture," *Journal of the American Academy of Religion* 64, no. 4 (1996): 743–65.

9. Eric Benner, "Defending the 'Sport' to the Very End," *Slam! Pro Wrestling*, December 4, 1998, http://slam.canoe.com/SlamWrestlingTheTruth/dec4_benner .html.

10. Kathryn Lofton, *Oprah: The Gospel of an Icon* (Berkeley: University of California Press, 2011).

11. James B. Twitchell, *Adcult USA: The Triumph of Advertising in American Culture* (New York: Columbia University Press, 1995).

12. Dave Marsh, *Louie, Louie* (New York: Hyperion, 1993), 73–74.

13. Alison J. Clarke, *Tupperware: The Promise of Plastic in 1950s America* (Washington, DC: Smithsonian Institution Press, 1999), 41.

14. Clarke, *Tupperware*, 89.

15. Clarke, *Tupperware*, 150.

16. Régis Debray, *Transmitting Culture*, trans. Eric Rauth (New York: Columbia University Press, 2000).

17. Clarke, *Tupperware*, 3.

18. Clarke, *Tupperware*, 136.

19. Clarke, *Tupperware*, 137.

20. Clarke, *Tupperware*, 142.

21. Clarke, *Tupperware*, 157, 165.

22. Arjun Appadurai, *Modernity at Large: Cultural Dimensions of Globalization* (Minneapolis: University of Minnesota Press, 1996), 27–47.

23. Edward Alsworth Ross, *Social Psychology: An Outline and Sourcebook* (1908; New York: Macmillan, 1919), 331, 335.

24. Henri Bergson, *Laughter: An Essay on the Meaning of the Comic*, trans. Claudesley Brereton and Fred Rothwell (New York: Macmillan, 1911), 35.

25. Roland Barthes, *Mythologies* (London: Palladin, 1988), 97.

26. Barthes, *Mythologies*, 99.

14. TOUCHING

1. Mark C. Taylor, *About Religion: Economies of Faith in Virtual Culture* (Chicago: University of Chicago Press, 1999), 1.

2. David Chidester, *Word and Light: Seeing, Hearing, and Religious Discourse* (Urbana: University of Illinois Press, 1992), 2–8.

3. Augustine, *On Free Choice of the Will*, trans. Anna S. Benjamin and L. H. Hackstaff (Indianapolis, IN: Bobbs-Merrill, 1964), 2.14.147.

4. Emmanuel Levinas, "Ethics as First Philosophy," in *The Levinas Reader*, ed. Seán Hand (1984; Oxford: Oxford University Press, 1989), 79.

5. Emmanuel Levinas, "Language and Proximity," in *Collected Philosophical Papers*, trans. Alphonso Lingis (1967; Dordrecht, Netherlands: Martinus Nijhoff, 1987), 118.

6. Walter Benjamin, "The Work of Art in the Age of Mechanical Reproduction," in *Illuminations*, ed. Hannah Arendt, trans. Harry Zohn (1933; New York: Schocken, 1968), 238.

7. Benjamin, "Work of Art," 242.

8. Benjamin, "Work of Art," 224.

9. Edmund S. Morgan, *The Puritan Dilemma: The Story of John Winthrop* (Boston: Little, Brown, 1958), 40; Sacvan Bercovitch, *The Puritan Origins of the American Self* (New Haven, CT: Yale University Press, 1975), 117–19.

10. Increase Mather, *The Times of Men* (Boston, 1675), 7.

11. Michael Wigglesworth, "God's Controversy with New-England," in *The Puritans: A Sourcebook of Their Writings*, 2 vols., ed. Perry Miller and Thomas H. Johnson (1662; New York: Harper and Row, 1963), 2:611.

12. John Winthrop, "A Model of Christian Charity," in *The Puritans: A Sourcebook of Their Writings*, 2 vols., ed. Perry Miller and Thomas H. Johnson (1630; New York: Harper and Row, 1963), 1:195.

13. William Clinton, "Accepting the Democratic Nomination for President," *Congressional Quarterly Weekly Report* (July 18, 1992): 21–30; see Jack R. Van der Slik and Stephen J. Schwark, "Clinton and the New Covenant: Theology Shaping a New Politics or Old Politics in Religious Garb?" *Journal of Church and State* 40 (1998): 873–90.

14. Emile Durkheim, *The Elementary Forms of Religious Life*, trans. Karen E. Fields (1912; New York: Free Press, 1995): 44; Rudolf Otto, *The Idea of the Holy*, trans. John W. Harvey (1917; London: Oxford University Press, 1923): 23–24.

15. Bernard Semmel, *The Methodist Revolution* (New York: Basic Books, 1973), 31; W. W. Sweet, *The American Churches: An Interpretation* (New York: Abingdon-Cokesbury Press, 1945), 46–47.

16. Perry Miller, "From the Covenant to the Revival," in *Religion in American History: Interpretive Essays*, ed. John M. Mulder and John F. Wilson (Englewood Cliffs, NJ: Prentice-Hall, 1978), 146.

17. Horace Bushnell, "Our Obligations to the Dead," in *God's New Israel: Religious Interpretations of American Destiny*, ed. Conrad Cherry (1865; Englewood Cliffs, NJ: Prentice-Hall, 1971), 204.

18. Fire Tribe, www.firetribe.com, accessed April 14, 2004; Wings of Fire, www.firewalking.org, accessed April 14, 2004. See Loring M. Danforth, *Fire-*

walking and Religious Healing: The Anastenaria of Greece and the American Firewalking Movement (Princeton, NJ: Princeton University Press, 1989).

19. Rick Gore, "Cascadia: Living on Fire," *National Geographic* 193, no. 5 (May 1998): 14.

20. Bernard J. Leikind and William J. McCarthy, "An Investigation of Firewalking," in *The Hundredth Monkey and Other Paradigms of the Paranormal*, ed. Kendrick Frazier (Buffalo, NY: Prometheus Books, 1991), 271–77.

21. Gore, "Cascadia," 14; Rick Gore, "Fire Walking: Embrace the Fear," *National Geographic*, www.nationalgeographic.com/2000/physical/firewalk, accessed April 14, 2005.

22. Flag Burning Page, "The Flag Flames Page," www.esquilax.com/flag /flagflames.html, accessed May 4, 2016; Jean Bethke Elshtain, "Citizenship and Armed Civic Virtue: Some Critical Questions on the Commitment to Public Life," in *Community in America: The Challenge of Habits of the Heart*, ed. Charles H. Reynolds and Ralph V. Norman (Berkeley: University of California Press, 1988), 51. See Robert Justin Goldstein, *Saving Old Glory: The History of the American Flag Desecration Controversy* (Boulder, CO: Westview Press, 1996).

23. David Chidester, "'A Big Wind Blew Up during the Night': America as Sacred Space in South Africa," in *American Sacred Space*, ed. David Chidester and Edward T. Linenthal (Bloomington: Indiana University Press, 1995), 275–79.

24. David Chidester, *Wild Religion: Tracking the Sacred in South Africa* (Berkeley: University of California Press, 2012), 45–46.

25. Peter Collier and David Horowitz, *The Fords: An American Epic* (New York: Summit Books, 1987), 52; James J. Flink, *The Automobile Age* (Cambridge, MA: MIT Press, 1988); Joseph J. Corn, *The Winged Gospel: America's Romance with Aviation, 1900–1950* (New York: Oxford University Press, 1983), 30; Douglas Curran, *In Advance of the Landing: Folk Concepts of Outer Space* (New York: Abbeville Press, 1985).

26. Philip Fisher, "Democratic Social Space: Whitman, Melville, and the Promise of American Transparency," in *The New American Studies: Essays from "Representations*," ed. Philip Fisher (Berkeley: University of California Press, 1991), 85–86.

27. Jeff Goodell, "Lost in Space," *Rolling Stone* 809 (April 1, 1999): 57–64, 115; Joseph Firmage, "The Word Is Truth," May 15, 1999, www.firmage.org.

28. Alien Abduction Experience and Research, "What Is an Alien Abduction Experience?" www.abduct.com/experien.php, accessed November 23, 2017. See C. D. B. Bryan, *Close Encounters of the Fourth Kind: A Reporter's Notebook on Alien Abduction, UFOs, and the Conference at M.I.T.* (New York: Arkana, 1996); John E. Mack, *Abduction: Human Encounters with Aliens*, rev. ed. (New York: Ballantine Books, 1995).

29. Official Alien Abduction Test-Site, "Alien Abduction Test," www.alien-abduction-test.com, accessed April 14, 2005.

30. Guide to Economic Reasoning, www.apu.edu/~puerdugo.html, accessed May 15, 1999.

31. Mary Catherine Bateson and Richard Goldsby, *Thinking AIDS: The Social Response to the Biological Threat* (New York: Addison-Wesley, 1988), 30.

32. Jacques Derrida, "Faith and Knowledge," in *Religion*, ed. Jacques Derrida and Gianni Vattimo (Stanford: Stanford University Press, 1998), 36.

33. Marita Sturken, *Tangled Memories: The Vietnam War, the AIDS Epidemic, and the Politics of Remembering* (Berkeley: University of California Press, 1997), 247. See Steve Connor and Sharon Kingman, *The Search for the Virus: The Scientific Discovery of AIDS and the Quest for a Cure* (New York: Penguin, 1988), 2; John M. Dwyer, *The Body at War: The Miracle of the Immune System* (New York: Penguin, 1990), 39.

34. Zach Thomas, *Healing Touch: The Church's Forgotten Language* (Louisville, KY: Westminster/John Knox Press, 1994).

35. Annie E. Proulx, *Accordion Crimes* (London: Fourth Estate, 1996), 338.

36. Proulx, *Accordion Crimes*, 338.

37. Vatican, "Christian Prayer," *Catechism of the Catholic Church*, www.vatican.va/archive/ccc_css/archive/catechism/p4s1c3a2.htm, accessed June 10, 2014.

38. Jean Baudrillard, *Illusion of the End*, trans. Chris Turner (Oxford: Polity Press, 1994), 21–27.

39. Robert Bellah, Richard Madsen, William Sullivan, and Ann Swidler, *Habits of the Heart: Individualism and Commitment in American Life*, updated ed. (1985; Berkeley: University of California Press, 1996).

40. Michel Foucault, *Discipline and Punish: The Birth of the Prison*, trans. Alan Sheridan (New York: Vintage Books, 1979); Martin Jay, "Scopic Regimes of Modernity," in *Vision and Visuality*, ed. Hal Foster (Seattle: Bay Press, 1988), 3–28.

41. Karl Marx, *The Economic and Philosophic Manuscripts of 1844*, ed. D.J. Struik (New York: International Publishers, 1972), 140–41.

42. Sigmund Freud, *Standard Edition of the Complete Psychoanalytic Works of Sigmund Freud*, trans. James Strachey, 24 vols. (London: Hogarth, 1953–74), 17:241.

43. Michel de Certeau, *The Practice of Everyday Life*, trans. Steven Rendall (Berkeley: University of California Press, 1984), 37, 88.

15. OCEANS

1. Cited in Charles H. Long, *Significations: Signs, Symbols, and Images in the Interpretation of Religion* (1986; Aurora, CO: Davies Group, 1999), 92.

2. Cited in Long, *Significations*, 113.

3. Frantz Fanon, *The Wretched of the Earth*, trans. Constance Farrington (London: Penguin, 1967), 41.

4. Charles H. Long, *The Gift of Speech and the Travail of Language* (Cape Town: University of Cape Town, T. B. Davie Academic Freedom Lecture, 1993), 3.

5. Charles H. Long, "What Is Africa to Me? Reflection, Discernment, and Anticipation," *Journal of Africana Religions* 1, no. 1 (2013): 100.

6. Charles H. Long, "Mircea Eliade and the Imagination of Matter," *Journal for Cultural and Religious Theory* 1, no. 2 (2000), www.jcrt.org/archives/01.2 /long.shtml.

7. Patricia Seed, *Ceremonies of Possession in Europe's Conquest of the New World 1492–1640* (Cambridge: Cambridge University Press, 1995), 69.

8. Rolena Adorno, "The Rhetoric of Resistance: The 'Talking' Book of Felipe Guaman Poma," *History of European Ideas* 6, no. 4 (1985): 452.

9. Sabine MacCormack, "*Pachacuti*: Miracles, Punishments, and Last Judgment: Visionary Past and Prophetic Future in Early Colonial Peru," *American Historical Review* 93, no. 4 (1988): 995.

10. Adapted from David Chidester, "Colonialism," in *Guide to the Study of Religion*, ed. Willi Braun and Russell T. McCutcheon (London: Cassell, 2000), 425. See Alcira Dueñas, *Indians and Mestizos in the "Lettered City": Reshaping Justice, Social Hierarchy, and Political Culture in Colonial Peru* (Boulder, CO: University Press of Colorado, 2010); Sabine MacCormack, *Religion in the Andes: Vision and Imagination in Early Colonial Peru* (Princeton, NJ: Princeton University Press, 1991).

11. Charles H. Long, "Cargo Cults as Cultural Historical Phenomena," *Journal of the American Academy of Religion* 42, no. 3 (1974): 403–14; "Indigenous People, Materialities, and Religion: Outline for a New Orientation to Religious Meaning," in *Religion and Global Culture: New Terrain in the Study of Religion and the Work of Charles H. Long*, ed. Jennifer I. M. Reid (New York: Lexington Books, 2003), 172–77; "A Postcolonial Meaning of Religion: Some Reflections from the Indigenous World," in *Beyond Primitivism: Indigenous Religious Traditions and Modernity*, ed. Jacob K. Olupona (New York: Routledge, 2004), 96–97; "Transculturation and Religion," in *Encyclopedia of Religion*, 2nd ed., ed. Lindsay Jones (New York: Macmillan, 2005), 14:9296; "Religion, Discourse, and Hermeneutics: New Approaches in the Study of Religion," in *The Next Step in Studying Religion: A Graduate Student's Guide*, ed. Mathieu E. Courville (New York: Continuum, 2007), 183–91.

12. William Pietz, "The Problem of the Fetish I," *Res: Anthropology and Aesthetics* 9 (Spring 1985): 5–17; "The Problem of the Fetish II: The Origin of the Fetish," *Res: Anthropology and Aesthetics* 13 (Spring 1987): 23–45; "The Problem of the Fetish IIIa: Bosman's Guinea and the Enlightenment Theory of Fetishism," *Res: Anthropology and Aesthetics* 16 (Autumn 1988): 105–24.

13. Long, *Significations*, 129.

14. Long, *Significations*, 133.

15. Kenelm Burridge, *Mambu: A Melanesian Millennium* (London: Methuen, 1960); Peter Lawrence, *Road Belong Cargo: A Study of the Cargo Movement in the Southern Madang District, New Guinea* (Manchester, U.K.: Manchester University Press, 1964); Peter Worsley, *The Trumpet Shall Sound: A Study of "Cargo" Cults in Melanesia*, 2nd ed. (1957; London: MacGibbon and Kee, 1968).

16. Lamont Lindstrom, "Cargo Cult at the Third Millennium," in *Cargo, Cult, and Culture Critique*, ed. Holger Jebens (Honolulu: University of Hawaii Press, 2004), 16; see Lamont Lindstrom, *Cargo Cult: Strange Stories of Desire from Melanesia and Beyond* (Honolulu: University of Hawaii Press, 1993).

17. Nils Bubandt, "Violence and Millenarian Modernity in Eastern Indonesia," in *Cargo, Cult, and Culture Critique*, ed. Holger Jebens (Honolulu: University of Hawaii Press, 2004), 115.

18. Gwyneira Isaac, "Anthropology and Its Embodiments: 19th Century Museum Ethnography and the Re-enactment of Indigenous Knowledges," *Etnofoor* 22, no. 1 (2010): 11–29.

19. Karl-Heinz Kohl, "Mutual Hopes: German Money and the Tree of Wealth in East Flores," in *Cargo, Cult, and Culture Critique*, ed. Holger Jebens (Honolulu: University of Hawaii Press, 2004), 87.

20. Cited in Gregory T. Cushman, *Guano and the Opening of the Pacific World: A Global Ecological History* (Cambridge: Cambridge University Press, 2013), 23.

21. Cushman, *Guano*, 169.

22. Michael Taussig, *The Devil and Commodity Fetishism in South America* (Chapel Hill: University of North Carolina Press, 1980).

23. Alexander J. Duffield, *Peru in the Guano Age* (London: Richard Bentley and Son, 1877), 78.

24. Duffield, *Peru in the Guano Age*, 89–90.

25. Long, "Mircea Eliade and the Imagination of Matter."

26. Duffield, *Peru in the Guano Age*, 121–22.

27. Pietz, "The Problem of the Fetish IIIa," 109; cited in Long, "Indigenous People, Materialities, and Religion," 175.

28. Charles H. Long, "Perspectives for a Study of Afro-American Religion in the United States," *History of Religions* 11, no. 1 (1971): 65; Long, *Significations*, 197.

CONCLUSION

1. David Chidester, *Word and Light: Seeing, Hearing, and Religious Discourse* (Urbana: University of Illinois Press, 1992).

2. On the classification of persons, see David Chidester, *Salvation and Suicide: Jim Jones, the Peoples Temple, and Jonestown*, rev. ed. (1988; Bloomington: Indiana University Press, 2003), 51–78.

3. On orientation in space and time, see Chidester, *Salvation and Suicide*, 79–128.

4. David Chidester, *Savage Systems: Colonialism and Comparative Religion in Southern Africa* (Charlottesville: University Press of Virginia, 1996).

5. David Chidester, *Empire of Religion: Imperialism and Comparative Religion* (Chicago: University of Chicago Press, 2014).

6. David Chidester, *Wild Religion: Tracking the Sacred in South Africa* (Berkeley: University of California Press, 2012); Greg Johnson and Siv Ellen Kraft, eds., *Handbook of Indigenous Religion(s)* (Leiden, Netherlands: Brill, 2017).

7. David Chidester, *Authentic Fakes: Religion and American Popular Culture* (Berkeley: University of California Press, 2005); Kathryn Lofton, *Consuming Religion* (Chicago: University of Chicago Press, 2017).

Index

243

labor: and apartheid, 77, 124, 127; and capitalism, 50, 91; and colonialism, 7, 21, 56,
59, 68, 76, 85, 105–106, 110, 117, 127, 139,
144, 196, 198, 203, 205, 208; of interpretation, x, 4, 36, 47, 96; migrant, 203; of
producing space, 3, 36–37; of producing
time, 3, 47; of ritualization, x, 4, 36, 47,
96; spiritual, 141; and surplus, 36, 91;
symbolic, 90, 100. *See also* slavery
lamas, 141, 168
land, and sea, 40–41, 45, 137, 182, 197–201,
205
Landscapes of the Sacred (Howe), 3–4
Lash, Scott, 92
Latour, Bruno, 112
laughter: as bodily eruption, 68; and caniva-
lesque, 68; and Christian missions,
59–62; collective, 93; and comparative
religion, 21, 59–62, 68–72; and intercultural relations, 58–59; and machines,
62–64, 66, 207; and pain, 70–72; as plastic, 177; theories of, 62
law: and accounting, 14–15, 206; and colonialism, 122; and Hindu temple ritual, 35;
of karma, 54; and *Laws of Manu*, 54; and
legal system, 44; and materiality, 14, 206;
and permanence, 157, 162; and religion,
3–4; of supply and demand, 90
Lawrence, Peter, 201
Laws of Manu, 54
Le Vaillant, François, 59
Leach, Edmund, 34–35, 49, 66
Lefebvre, Henri, 38
Lennon, John, 171
Levinas, Emmanuel, 137, 181
Lévi-Strauss, Claude, 49, 162
Lévy-Bruhl, Lucian, 68–70
Lichtenstein, Henry, 25, 61
Lifton, Robert Jay, 160–161
liminality, 40, 45, 50
Lindstrom, Lamont, 201
Lion King (Disney), 167
Livingstone, David, 60
locative, 43–45, 87
Locke, John, 47–48, 106, 155
logosphere, 87
London Missionary Society, 59, 62, 69
Long, Charles H.: and agriculture, 203–204;
and *arche*, 197; and cargo, 197, 200–201;
and fetish, 197; and materiality, 80; and
oceans, 137, 195–201, 205
"Louie, Louie," 173
Lowe, Lisa, 7

Lubbock, John, 25, 128
Luckmann, Thomas, 9
Luther, Martin, 33, 88

MacGaffey, Wyatt, 40
machines, 62–64, 66, 93, 177, 188, 207
Mackenzie, John, 60
Madagascar, 119
Madness and Civilization (Foucault),
195–195
magic, 3, 25, 30, 35, 95, 117–118, 120, 146, 201
Make Mine Freedom (Sutherland), 97
Makonde, 111
Malagasy, 119
Mambu, 200–201
Mamre, 42
Manchu, 140
Manenberg, 187
Mani, 112
Manichaean, 112, 119, 126
Mannoni, Octave, 117, 119
Mansi, 142
Manu, 54
market: capitalist, 76, 89–91, 95, 97–101, 173;
and competition, 90, 95–98; global, 85; in
hair, 32–34; and invisible forces, 189–190,
192; in relics, 82; religion of, 6, 76, 80, 85,
93–94; and shamans, 9
Mars, 94–96
Marsh, Dave, 173
Martinique, 120
Marx, Karl: and alienation, 91; and fetishism,
29, 84, 101, 201; and history of religions,
81; and senses, 85, 193–194; and social
hieroglyphic, 97–98; and spiritual intercourse, 10; and theft, 102
Mary, 83, 111, 143, 180
Mary Kay Cosmetics, 169
masks, 147
Mason, Perry, 14
material culture: and body, 75, 79; and
exchange, 79; and media, 76; and objects,
75; and senses, 75, 79, 85–86; and technology, 79
*Material Religion: The Journal of Objects,
Art, and Belief*, 81
materialism: colonial, 108; new, 14, 179; old,
14; religious, 79–80; scientific, 4, 23, 28;
spiritual, 85
materiality: and accounting, 14–15, 206; and
conditions, xi, 3, 6, 14, 37, 39, 48, 71–72,
76, 87, 99, 108, 160, 181–182, 184, 193–
194, 206, 209–210; and consequences, xii,